JESUS UNVEILED

SHARON AUBREY

SUTTON, ALASKA

All biblical references are taken from the Authorized King James Version Bible, public domain. The use of quotes from various authors does not necessarily represent an endorsement of their theology; rather, it represents recognition of their conclusion drawn from the Scriptures or a historical source.

Cover Art: Public Domain Pictures: Scribble Heart by Dawn Hudson, publicdomainpictures.net. Edited & redesigned by Sharon Aubrey.

© 2015 Sharon Aubrey
P.O. Box 505
Sutton, AK 99674

All rights reserved. Except as permitted under the U.S. Copyright Act of 1976, no part of this publication may be reproduced, distributed, or transmitted in any form or by any means, or stored in a database or retrieval system, without the prior written permission of the publisher.

Relevant Publishers LLC
P.O. Box 505
Sutton, AK 99674

Visit our website at www.relevantpublishers.com

Printed in the United States of America

Aubrey, Sharon
Jesus Unveiled / Sharon Aubrey – 1st ed. Includes bibliographical references and index.

ISBN: 978-0-9909984-0-2
LCCN: 2015930212

DEDICATION

This book is dedicated to all seekers who hunger and thirst for Truth in God's Word and unity in the Body of Christ and to our Lord Jesus Christ whose amazing love surpasses our understanding.

Contents

Page	
1	Introduction
7	**Chapter 1: Calendars & Dates**
	God's Timing & the Jewish Calendar
	Calculating a Day
	The Jewish Week
	Determining a Month
	Establishing a Calendar Year
	God's High Holy Days
	The Debate Over When to Celebrate
	The Julian & Gregorian Calendars
41	**Chapter 2: Passover**
	Passover Defined
	Torah Mandates & Historical Setting
	Selection of Lamb
	Date of Lamb's Death
	Must Stay Inside Homes
	How to Eat the Lamb
	Spiritual Analogies
	The Abrahamic Lamb
	A Lamb, The Lamb, Your Lamb
	Fault Finding at Home
	Bloodstained Doorposts
	Migdal Eder – The Tower of the Floc
	Timing & Place of Death for the Lam
	Consumption of the Lamb
83	**Chapter 3: Feast of Unleavened Bread**
	Unleavened Bread Defined
	Torah Mandate & Historical Setting
	Spiritual Relevancies

Contents (continued)

92   **Chapter 4: Nisan 17th Significance**
Principle of First Mention – The Ark
Principle of Progressive Mention
Red Sea Crossing
Entering the Promise Land
True Worship Restored
Deliverance from Death
Culmination – The Resurrection

127   **Chapter 5: The Sign of Jonah**
What Constitutes a Day?
How It Impacts the Death Timeline
The "Preparation Day" Controversy

141   **Chapter 6: Feast of First Fruits & Pentecost**
Torah Mandate
Pharisees vs. Sadducees
Spiritual Relevance
Jesus as The First Fruits
Pentecost the Second Fruits Harvested

159   **Chapter 7: The Last Supper Dilemma**
The Last Supper vs. Seder Supper
Nisan 13/14th vs. Nisan 14/15th
The Last Supper Meal

188   **Chapter 8: Passover Week Detail of Events**
Daily Prophetic Details Defined
Charts of Possible Crucifixion Days
Saturday
Sunday
Monday

Contents (continued)

188	Chapter 8: Passover Week Detail of Events (contin
	Thursday
	Friday
	Comprehensive List of Weekly Events
271	Chapter 9: The Conclusion
288	Bibliography
293	Other Reference Materials
296	Index of Illustrations & Charts
298	Topical Index

Introduction

The events surrounding Jesus' crucifixion and resurrection during Passover are the defining moments in human history. Yet, far too few Christians know or understand the intricacies associated with this pivotal point in our history. God tirelessly painted an exquisite portrait of His love and salvation in prophetic promises dispersed throughout the Old Testament, which echo in fulfillment in the New Testament. Like a beautiful Monet painting created entirely of relatively small visible brush strokes, so too is the image created in God's word. One looking from a distance sees the image of scenic water lilies, but this graceful picture wasn't created with only one movement of the brush. Instead, the lilies are an intricate blending of many small, colorful strokes operating in harmony, each building upon the other. The image of Christ is similarly portrayed in the Bible. While one can look only at the New Testament scriptures and behold the broad picture of Christ, His divine personality and purpose had been intricately painted line upon line and precept upon precept (Isaiah 28:9-10) until at last the fulfillment of those prophecies appeared.

Many people are content to simply see the overall image of Monet's water lily pond from a distance, never caring to know the intricacies that make up the image or appreciating the deeper knowledge that lies within the small dots. Similarly many Christians are content to simply know that Jesus died on the cross for their sins and rose from the grave three days later. To them, this is the core of the story, and it is enough. But there are those of us, who instinctively draw closer to the scene, and we see something so magnificent! We perceive the essence of the story is far beyond what rests on the surface or the casual view from a distance. The real beauty of the vision lies in the elaborate details, the intense accuracy, the incredible patience, and love it took to transform each brush stroke into the totality of the picture. These exploring Christians understand Proverbs 25:2 which states, *"It is the glory of God to conceal a thing, but **the glory of kings is to search out a matter**."* In the searching, more knowledge and truth are revealed. Each fresh revelation brings a deeper appreciation for the wondrous love and wisdom of the Word of God. The image, which seemed so basic on the surface, transforms itself and becomes alive and multidimensional, touching the very heart of mankind and providing a glimpse into the Divine.

As we examine the small brush strokes of prophetic verses in the Old and New Testaments, we will be using hermeneutics, which are the recognized principles for studying and interpreting the Bible. These standards enable a clearer understanding of the Word of God within its historical context, spiritual perspective, practical application, symbolism, numerical value, and grammatical framework (definitions & verb tense). The foundation of hermeneutics rests on the Bible being the true word of God, the highest level of authority. It also asserts that whenever possible the Bible should interpret itself. We cannot read Scripture and put our own private interpretation on it (2 Peter 1:20). Whenever possible, Scripture should always be interpreted in context of the surrounding verses. Each section of Scripture must also harmonize with the rest of the Scriptures concerning a particular subject. Any interpretation of one text cannot contradict other Scriptures regarding that specific theme.

The other important concepts in hermeneutics used in this book include the **Principle of First Mention.**[1] The first time God presents a truth in the Bible, that truth never changes throughout the Scriptures. The **Principle of Progressive Mention** continues the original truth mentioned by God in first scripture and provides increasing knowledge on that particular truth until the full revelation is finally revealed. These two principles basically mean when God mentions a truth in Scripture for the first time, He continues that same theme throughout the bible often hidden in various other analogies, prophecies, parables, and words of wisdom. The original theme is expounded upon with each new story providing a deeper level of the same truth. Finally, as one progresses through the Bible, a wider revelation of the same Truth is revealed in its fullness.

Here is an example of how these two principals actually work. In the book of Genesis, we read the story of Abraham being instructed by God to take his son, Isaac, and sacrifice him upon Mount Moriah (Genesis 22:2-19). As Isaac realizes he and his father have all the provisions necessary to worship the Lord except the sacrifice, he questions his father regarding the required sacrificial animal. Abraham responds with, "God Himself will provide a lamb" (Genesis 22:8). After reaching the mountain, Abraham binds Isaac and lays him on the altar. However, before Abraham can kill Isaac, God intervenes sparing Isaac's life. God also provides a ram caught in the thicket by it's horns (Genesis 22:13) as the sacrificial animal. Abraham sacrifices the ram instead of Isaac. This general story provides the Principal of First Mention for the Biblical theme of *the Lamb of God*. This theme of *the Lamb of God* is continued as a Progressive Mention principal throughout the Bible.

While the Abraham/Isaac story alludes to God's only Son being sacrificed. We can't parallel God's command to Abraham to "take your only son..." with anything prior to this account in Genesis to conclude God is going to sacrifice His own son. Only after reading Isaiah 9:6, "unto us a Son is given" and John 3:16, "For God so loved the world that He gave His only begotten Son" does the Principal of First Mention progress into a deeper truth: God is giving His son as a sacrifice. Additionally, verses in Genesis indicating God Himself provided a substitutionary sacrifice of a ram in place of Isaac cannot be completely understood as foreshadowing God sending His son, Jesus as the Lamb of God to be sacrificed as a propitiation for our sins (Romans 3:25) until we progress through the bible (Progressive Mention Principle). Later in the Bible, in the Book of Exodus we see additional requirements (progressive principles) that the sacrificial lamb must be without blemish. This lack of blemishing explains why the original ram was caught in the thorn by its horns. The thorns on its horns did not cause any blemishing to its body. If the ram had been caught in the thorns by its fleece, it would have been damage or bruised and not a sufficient sacrifice. The mentioning of the substitute sacrificial ram being caught in the thorns by the horns was also an illusion to the crown of thorns that would one day encircle the head of Jesus. Once we read the New Testament scriptures that Jesus was the "a lamb without blemish" (1 Peter 1:19), the fullness of God's Son being the spotless lamb sacrificed for us becomes evident. Therefore, all of the Progressive Principals build upon the Principal of First Mention, and with each additional illumination, we comprehend a clearer understanding of the fullness of the Truth God was articulating.

Using these two basic principles, we will travel close to God's canvas and explore the enormous details, accuracy of timing, prophetic verses and their fulfillment in the life of Jesus the Christ that compose the overall portrait of salvation.

Many commentaries found in today's "study" or "reference" bibles regarding the timelines around the events of the crucifixion week are only superficial. One does not glean the historical truth behind the Jewish calendar and Torah principles that deeply affect the accuracy of the Old Testament prophecies, which must have been fulfilled to complete the image of Jesus as the Passover lamb. Therefore, this book will also provide a deeper insight into God's prophetic calendar, the calendars of men, and details that only become apparent upon extensive evaluation which many Christian commentators are unwilling to explore, because such exploration will take them out of the comfort zone of Christian tradition into the truth of God's word. Each Christian must decide for himself/herself the impact of the Truth of God's word upon his/her future and face the impending question, "if you were wrong, would you want to know it?"

Jesus taught in Matthew 15:1-9 and Mark 7:1-7 that people who exalt tradition above the Word of God essentially make the Word of God of no real value in their lives. While not adhering to legalism as followers of Jesus, we must be careful that our lives and what we teach others about God truly lines up with His Word and His Spirit, or else we are in danger of compromising Truth for tradition and missing the depth, wisdom, and understanding God's Word can impart to our lives. It is for this reason, I felt compelled to diligently search the Scriptures regarding the correlation of the events surrounding Passover and the timeline of events in the crucifixion and resurrection of Jesus, researching and comparing Scripture with the traditions, history, and teachings of Judaism and the Christian church. May you be blessed with increased wisdom and understanding of the richness in God's Word that continues to unveil Jesus Christ and His ministry of Grace and love on every page.

CHAPTER 1

CALENDARS & DATES

God's Timing & The Jewish Calendar

It is imperative that we understand time and events the way God has ordained them in order to correctly interpret the events of the Bible and prophetic scriptures still to be fulfilled. The calendar method used by today's societies (the solar calendar) does not calculate time, determine days or months, nor recognize special days based on the original model established by God. The misunderstandings of time calculations and scheduled events have led to many misinterpretations about what we understand from the bible. A warning against the altering of God's timing for events echoes from the Book of Daniel 7:25, where Scripture declares that the Antichrist will "speak against the most High, and shall wear out the saints of the most High, **and think to change times and laws.**" The word for *"times"* is the Hebrew word "zemân" which literally interpreted means "a set time, an appointed occasion, season or time." If the Antichrist will seek to change or alter the times established by God's calendar, Believers today should heed this warning and give serious consideration to the timeline of prophetic events declared by God in His Word, which will help them avoid future deception.

God states in the Book of Genesis that He created the sun, moon, and stars to provide mankind with a way to measure time, determine appointed seasons or festivals, and to discern omens or signals from Him. Additionally, the heavenly lights would also provide physical light to the Earth.

> "And God said, Let there be lights in the firmament of the heaven to divide the day from the night; and let them be for signs, and for seasons, and for days, and years: And let them be for lights in the firmament of the heaven to give light upon the earth: and it was so."
> Genesis 1:14-15

Since God has created the heavenly bodies to serve as a calendar for mankind, we should listen to how He ordered time to better understand the timing of prophetic events He has ordained in Scripture.

Calculating A Day

Throughout the first chapter of Genesis, God decreed a twenty-four (24) hour period of time by recognizing first the evening, then the morning. Each period of evening or morning corresponds to twelve hours. This twenty-four (24) hour period of time created a complete day.

"And God called the light Day, and the darkness he called Night. **And the evening and the morning were the first day."** Genesis 1:5

"And God called the firmament Heaven. **And the evening and the morning were the second day."** Genesis 1:8

"**And the evening and the morning were the third day.**" Genesis 1:13

"**And the evening and the morning were the fourth day.**" Genesis 1:19

"**And the evening and the morning were the fifth day.**" Genesis 1:23

"And God saw every thing that he had made, and, behold, it was very good. **And the evening and the morning were the sixth day.**" Genesis 1:31

The timeline for calculating the days of the week according to God's calendar can clearly be seen from the first day to the sixth day of creation in the book of Genesis, with each "day" beginning in the evening. However, the seventh day of creation provides unique spiritual insight to God's prophetic calendar because the seventh day has no reckoning of physical time recorded in the book of Genesis.

> "$_1$Thus the heavens and the earth were finished, and all the host of them. $_2$And on the seventh day God ended his work which He had made; and He rested on the seventh day from all His work which He had made. $_3$And God blessed the seventh day, and sanctified it: because that in it He had rested from all His work which God created and made."
> Genesis 2:1-3

This lack of a specific accounting from "evening to morning" for the seventh day is not an oversight by the Holy Spirit. God specifically recorded He sanctified that day and rested from all His work. This holy seventh day isn't just a physical day as the calculating in Genesis clearly leaves out. Rather, it is a perpetual spiritual day according to the book of Hebrews where God's Sabbath or God's Rest is a spiritual and physical resting place that mankind can by faith enter into or be excluded from it. A review of the end of the third chapter and the beginning of the fourth chapter of the Book of Hebrews clearly demonstrates the concept that the seventh day of creation, God's Sabbath, is more than just a mere twenty-four (24) hour period of time lasting from evening to evening. It is stated Israel could not enter into God's Sabbath rest because they lacked faith. There is also an exhortation to the Christian to enter into God's Sabbath rest by faith.

"$_1$Let us therefore fear, lest, a promise being left us of entering into His rest, any of you should seem to come short of it. $_2$For unto us was the gospel preached, as well as unto them [Israel]: but the word preached did not profit them, not being mixed with faith in them that heard it. $_3$For we which have believed do enter into rest, as He said, As I have sworn in my wrath, if they shall enter into My rest: although the works were finished from the foundation of the world. $_4$**For He spake in a certain place of the seventh day on this wise, and God did rest the seventh day from all his works.** $_5$**And in this place again, If they shall enter into My rest.** $_6$Seeing therefore it remaineth that some must enter therein, and they to whom it was first preached entered not in because of unbelief: $_7$Again, He limiteth a certain day, saying in David, Today, after so long a time; as it is said, Today if ye will hear His voice, harden not your hearts. $_8$For if Joshua had given them rest, then would he not afterward have spoken of another day. $_9$**There remaineth therefore a rest to the people of God.** $_{10}$**For he that is entered into His rest, he also hath ceased from his own works, as God did from His.** $_{11}$Let us

labour therefore to enter into that rest, lest any man fall after the same example of unbelief."
Hebrews 4:1-11

The bold highlight in the scriptures above emphasize the fact that these verses make reference to the seventh day of creation, God's Sabbath, which is an everlasting day of rest that man can enter into or be excluded from by faith. Therefore, the seventh day of creation's Sabbath represents much more than a physical twenty-four (24) hour day. For if it were merely a physical day, it would have ended when the eighth day began. However, the Holy Spirit in the Book of Hebrews explains the seventh day still remains. It is interesting to note in the Book of Leviticus, God provides insight to the Jewish nation on how to establish the timeline for a Sabbath. The calculation provided is in complete agreement with the first six days of creation, with the day beginning at evening.

"$_{32}$It shall be unto you a sabbath of rest, and ye shall afflict your souls: in the ninth day of the month at even, **from even unto even, shall ye celebrate <u>your sabbath</u>**."
Leviticus 23:32

Interestingly, God uses the words **"your Sabbath"** when delineating the physical timeline of a seventh day of the week, a Sabbath day for mankind. In the book of Exodus chapter 20, God referring to the physical seventh day of the week joins the physical day (24-hour period) with the everlasting spiritual significance of the original Sabbath day of creation. God's entire prophetic calendar has dual references, literal physical days with eternal and spiritual significance. In recognition of God's time pronouncements in Genesis and Leviticus, the nation of Israel has always observed a day to begin at sundown (approximately 6:30 PM) ending at the following sundown.

Hours in a Jewish Day

A Hebrew day is divided into twelve parts between sunset and sunrise (night) and twelve parts between sunrise and sunset (day).

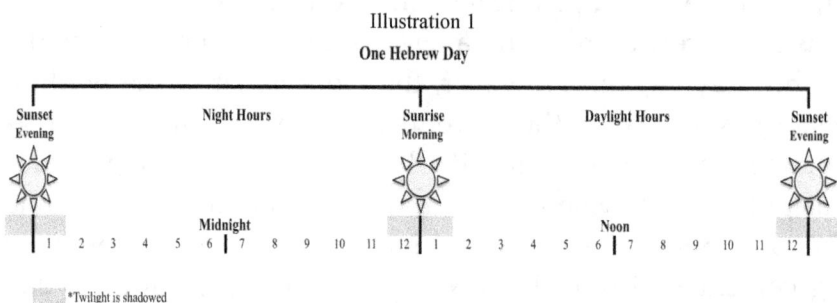

Illustration 1
One Hebrew Day

The only scripture reference for the time of a Hebrew day is found in John 11:9, "Jesus answered, 'Are there not twelve hours in a day?'" The duration of a Hebrew hour varies slightly with the season. In the winter, the 'day hour' is shorter than the 'night hour' in duration; while in the summer, the hours are reversed, and a 'day hour' is longer than a 'night hour.' A Jewish hour is calculated by taking the total time of daylight (from sunrise until sunset) of any particular day and dividing it into twelve equal parts.

For example:
In Jerusalem in the year 2014 on Passover, April 14th, the sunrise will be at 6:12 AM and sunset at 7:07 PM, giving 12 hours and 55 minutes of daylight, or 775 minutes, making the night time total 665 minutes.

775 minutes ÷ 12 hours = 64.58 minutes per daylight hour

665 minutes ÷ 12 hours = 55.42 minutes per nighttime hour

Averaging the twelve-hour sections into one-hour periods, the following table describes the Jewish hour with the corresponding Roman or Gregorian hour of the day.

Chart 1

Jewish	Roman	Gregorian	Jewish	Roman	Gregorian
Night			**Day**		
1st	7th	7 PM	1st	7th	7 AM
2nd	8th	8 PM	2nd	8th	8 AM
3rd	9th	9 PM	3rd	9th	9 AM
4th	10th	10 PM	4th	10th	10 AM
5th	11th	11 PM	5th	11th	11 PM
6th	12th	**Midnight**	6th	12th	**Noon**
7th	1st	1 AM	7th	1st	1 PM
8th	2nd	2 AM	8th	2nd	2 PM
9th	3rd	3 AM	9th	3rd	3 PM
10th	4th	4 AM	10th	4th	4 PM
11th	5th	5 AM	11th	5th	5 PM
12th	6th	6 AM	12th	6th	6 PM

When reading the Bible, it is important to delineate the Jewish hour from the Roman hour. The **third hour** (Hebrew) of the day is referred to in Matthew 20:3-4 and Mark 15:25 would equal 9:00 AM; while in John 19:14, Pilate questioned Jesus at the (Roman) **sixth hour,** which was 6:00AM Roman time. Understanding the differences in calculating time will help a reader better understand the

13

parables and events of the New Testament. It also prevents confusion in the Gospels. Skeptics wrongly assert contradictions in the Gospels occur in the timeline because they have not rightly divided the Word, nor have they applied the correct understanding of distinguishing a Roman hour from a Jewish hour of the day.

The Jewish Week

The Hebrew calendar arranges the days of the week as God originally ordered them in Genesis. It does not add additional terminology or words for each day to have its own name, but instead assigns them by the order they occurred: first day, second day, etc. The only day of the week to have an actual name is the seventh day, the Shabbat (or Sabbath). Shabbat literally means "rest," and it is the day God rested from His work. In the Book of Exodus, God sanctifies this day as a Holy Day of rest for His people (Exodus 20:8-10).

Chart 2

Hebrew Word	English Translation & Equivalent
Yom Rishon	First Day (Sunday)
Yom Sheini	Second Day (Monday)
Yom Shlishi	Third Day (Tuesday)
Yom R'vi'i	Fourth Day (Wednesday)
Yom Chamishi	Fifth Day (Thursday)
Yom Shishi	Sixth Day (Friday)
Yom Shabbat	Sabbath Day (Saturday)

The Jewish Day/Gregorian Day Table below combines God's structure of a day beginning in the evening with the seven "Western" days of the week. A Jewish week would correspond to the following days on our current calendars. This table will help non-Jewish people understand the Sabbath day of rest begins on Friday evening and lasts until Saturday evening.

Jewish days corresponding to Gregorian calendar days:

Chart 3

Jewish Days		Sun	Mon	Tues	Weds	Thurs	Fri	Sat
Morning		1st	2nd	3rd	4th	5th	6th	Shabbat 7th
Evening	1st	2nd	3rd	4th	5th	6th	Shabbat 7th	

Determining a Month

Not only does Scripture provide the calculation for measuring a day, but it also provides guidance for determining a month, which is based on a lunar cycle. Psalms 104:19 declares, "He [God] appointed the moon for seasons: the sun knoweth his going down." The word "seasons" is the Hebrew word "mow'ed" which translated means an appointed place, time, meeting; a sacred season; appointed festival or sign. The first day of the month in the original Jewish calendar began when the first sliver of the Hodesh moon became visible after the new moon (or dark of the moon). The crescent New Moon was called "Hodesh" in Hebrew (meaning "to make new or renew") because it was the first time the moon is seen *anew* after being concealed at the end of the lunar cycle. When the first sliver of the crescent moon became visible in Jerusalem, lookouts reported to the Sanhedrin. The Jewish Sanhedrin were a group of seventy (70) elders from all the tribes originally chosen in the Book of Numbers, chapter 11, to share responsibility with Moses for leading the nation of Israel. After two confirmed witnesses reported sighting of the new moon, the priests would blow the trumpets indicating the counting of the first day of the month had begun. Some Scriptures supporting this pattern are Numbers 10:10 and Psalm 81:3. During the ancient world, new months were always determined by observation. Various lookouts were appointed by the Sanhedrin to watch for the first sighting of the new moon. When a new moon was spotted, the lookouts would travel to inform the Sanhedrin. Upon receiving confirmation from two reliable witnesses of independent sightings, the Sanhedrin would announce the Rosh Chodesh[2] (which means the first of the moon). Messages would be sent from the Sanhedrin to all the people in the Jewish communities proclaiming when the month began. On cloudy nights or nights with bad weather, the identification of the new moon could be delayed.

Establishing A Calendar Year

Tishri meaning "beginning" is the first month of the Jewish Civil Calendar. It is used to calculate the epoch year of time since the beginning of creation. As of the Gregorian year 2014 A.D., the Jewish calendar had a total of 5,774 years. The first day of the first year of the Jewish calendar began on the sixth day of creation according to the Book of Genesis, because this was the date mankind was created. Therefore, viewing time on the Jewish Civil Calendar, the sixth day of creation, Adam's birthday was Tishri 1 of year one. Ever since creation, every year on the Jewish Civil Calendar has been calculated from mankind's birthday. Thus, the civil calendar for the Jewish year 5,775 will begin on Tishri 1, corresponding to the Gregorian calendar date of September 25, 2014. As almost a symbolic or prophetic play on words, it seems Adam was born to fall, because his birthday, Tishri 1, is in the "Fall" (autumn).

Jewish Religious Annual Calendar

Chart 4

Name of Month	Length of Days	Gregorian Equivalent
*Abib / Nisan	30	March – April
Iyar	29	April – May
Sivan	30	May – June
Tammuz	29	June – July
Av	30	July – August
Elul	29	August – September
* Ethanim / Tishri	30	September – October
Heshvan	29 or 30	October – November
Kislev	29 or 30	November – December
Tevet	29	December – January
Shevat	30	January – February
Adar I (leap years)	30	February – March
**Adar II	29	March - April

* Before Babylonian Exile, three months had different names:
   Abib = Nisan (Ex 13:4, 23:15, 34:18; Duet 16:1)
   Zif = Iyar (1 Kings 6:1; 6:37)
   Ethanim = Tishri (1 Kings 8:2)

** In leap years, Adar I is added. In non-leap years, Adar I does not exist and Adar has 29 days and is simply called Adar.

The Jewish nation calculated time according to their ancestors as indicated above; however in the Book of Exodus, God changed the order of months for calculating a calendar year. He ordained the counting of a year to begin with the month of Nisan. This rearrangement of mankind's calendar heralds prophetically a new beginning coming for the world.

> "This month *shall be* unto you the beginning of months: it *shall be* the first month of the year to you." Exodus 12:2

Upon deep reflection of the calendar adjustment by God, one begins to perceive the prophetic announcement of the "Prince of Life" (Acts 3:15) bringing new hope to humanity. No longer will the world's timeline remain on the schedule brought by the fall of Adam. Instead, the new calendar initiated in the "Spring" reflects God's redeeming Grace restoring mankind and bringing rebirth back to the creation after a long, cold season of sin and death. The rebirth necessary to overcome the old agenda can only spring forth from Jesus' New Covenant, sealed by His death and resurrection. Through Jesus, a spiritual rebirth for mankind is achieved.

As a result of God's commandment in the Book of Exodus to rearrange time, Nisan became the first month of the Jewish Religious Calendar. Therefore, the Jews have two calendars:

one calculating time from the beginning of creation, (Tishri 1: the Civil Calendar) and God's new calendar (beginning Nisan 1: the Religious Calendar). Originally in the Bible, Nisan (also spelled Nissan) was called Abib. When examining references in the Old Testament for this month, it is valuable to look for the usage of both names. In the Book of Exodus chapters 13:4, 23:15, 34:18 and in Deuteronomy 16:1, the word Abib is used. However, after the captivity of Israel to Babylon during 586-516 B.C., Abib's name was changed to Nisan, which is noted in both Nehemiah 2:1 and Esther 3:7. The name change of this very significant month is a reflection of the Babylonian influence upon the children of Israel, but it should not impede a bible scholar from correctly interpreting prophetic events in scripture. The Lord ordained Passover to be associated with the spring barley harvest or Feast of First Fruits, which was prophetic of Jesus becoming "the first fruits" from the dead (1 Corinthians 15:20). The month of Nisan can never occur in any other season of the year. Therefore, the commencement of the God's prophetic calendar, portrayed in the Jewish Religious Calendar, began with spring.

The Jewish Religious Calendar is a complicated calendar that while based on moon cycles is not strictly a lunar calendar because it recognizes that a year consists of 12.4 months. The traditional lunar calendar held by many early pagan civilizations was about eleven days shorter than a solar year, which often led to difficulties in resolving time due to moving seasons. However, because the Jewish calendar is a hybrid lunar-solar calendar, it recognizes the counting of seasons to prevent the backward shift that a precise lunar calendar experiences. Therefore, to accommodate the lunar eleven-day annual discrepancy effecting seasons, an entire month was inserted seven times in each nineteen-year cycle to insure the four annual seasons lined up appropriately.

This additional month created a "leap year" every two or three calendar years.

Basically, the original Jewish calendar consisted of twelve to thirteen months depending upon the year. A regular year consisted of twelve months; a leap year consisted of thirteen months. Each month is comprises either 29 or 30 days, totaling 354 days annually in a regular year. A year with 13 months is known as "Shanah Me'uberet," which literally means 'a pregnant year.' During a leap year or Shanah Me'uberet, the insertion of an additional month was necessary to insure Nisan always began in the spring, since the month of Nisan celebrated the spring barley harvest. A 29-day month of Adar was inserted during winter if upon examining the seasonal timeline and the coming new moon the Sanhedrin believed it would be too early for a barley harvest. The inserted month was called Adar I. The regular "Adar" was referred to as Adar II because it came after the additional inserted month. In non-leap years, Adar II was simply called Adar.

In Biblical times during the First and Second Temples, a leap year month was added by observation. The Sanhedrin did not add an additional month far in advance of the upcoming year. Instead, the Sanhedrin relied on observations of current conditions in the environment of Israel. They would evaluate the conditions of the current crop growth status, the behavior of livestock, and weather patterns to determine if the conditions were significantly advanced enough to be considered the season of Spring. If they were not, the Sanhedrin would declare the insertion of Adar into the calendar to allow for another month of growth and warm weather for Pesach (Passover) would occur during the Spring. As Pesach is referred to in the Torah as 'Chag he-Aviv,' literally meaning the Festival of Spring.[2]

Rabbi Nathan Bushwick wrote an article, which supported the Hebrew historical practice of the addition of Adar based on analysis of weather and agricultural conditions combined with calculations for the Spring equinox. If the climate and timing supported Pesach occurring in the Spring, Nisan would follow Adar; however, if it was two early, Adar I (Sheni) would be added to make Nisan occur later in the year.[3] This meant two Adars would occur back to back.

It should be noted that Adar II is considered the "real" Adar and is the one referred to in the book of Esther in which Purim was celebrated. The Jewish calendar based on witnesses observing the moon survived the destruction of the Second Temple and continued until the middle of the fourth century C.E. A series of signal fires on hilltops was used to notify the Jewish world of the new moon. This communication system at best caused significant delays and was made worse when the Samaritans intentionally sabotaged the signals by lighting false fires. Additional problems for communicating the new moon in a timely manner to Jews in the Diaspora occurred. Many days were "lost" between the witnessing of the new moon and the news finally arriving to Jewish communities thousands of miles away. In response to these problems, the Sanhedrin mandated a second holy day for each festival or holy convocation week in the Diaspora.

Like the days of a week, Jewish years also cycle in periods of seven with the number seven being a holy day of rest. Every seventh year was a Sabbatical (Sabbath) year, and the land was required to rest from labor. After seven cycles of seven years, there was a Year of Jubilee observed, which also required the land to rest as well as inhabitants of the land to go free.

"₂Speak unto the children of Israel, and say unto them, When ye come into the land which I give you, then shall the land keep a Sabbath unto the LORD. ₃Six years thou shalt sow thy field, and six years thou shalt prune thy vineyard, and gather in the fruit thereof; ₄But in the seventh year shall be a Sabbath of rest unto the land, a Sabbath for the LORD: thou shalt neither sow thy field, nor prune thy vineyard. ₅That which groweth of its own accord of thy harvest thou shalt not reap, neither gather the grapes of thy vine undressed: for it is a year of rest unto the land."
Leviticus 25:2-5

"₈And thou shalt number seven Sabbaths of years unto thee, seven times seven years; and the space of the seven Sabbaths of years shall be unto thee forty and nine years. ₉Then shalt thou cause the trumpet of the jubilee to sound on the tenth day of the seventh month, in the day of atonement shall ye make the trumpet sound throughout all your land. ₁₀And ye shall hallow the fiftieth year, and proclaim liberty throughout all the land unto all the inhabitants thereof: it shall be a jubilee unto you; and ye shall return every man unto his possession, and ye shall return every man unto his family. ₁₁A jubilee shall that fiftieth year be unto you: ye shall not sow, neither reap that which groweth of itself in it, nor gather the grapes in it of thy vine undressed. ₁₂For it is the jubilee; it shall be holy unto you: ye shall eat the increase thereof out of the field. ₁₃In the year of this jubilee ye shall return every man unto his possession."
Leviticus 25:8-13

The Christian Byzantine Empire in the Fourth Century became extremely hostile to the remaining Jewish community in Israel and eventually banned the proclamation of their calendar through the traditional means of sighting the new moon in Jerusalem. The Byzantine Empire even arrested and jailed envoys conveying the timing of the new moon to Jewish communities. Rabbi Hillel II, who held the office of Prince in the Jewish Sanhedrin between 320 and 385 CE, called a council to adopt an established calendar based on mathematical and astronomical principals used by the Sanhedrin, which could be circulated to communities in the Diaspora. Hillel II was a Pharisee from the House of Hillel. Ga-ma'-il-el in the Bible (Acts 5:24-42, Acts 22:3) is also discussed in Jewish history (called Ga-ma'-il-el the Elder) and was the son of Simeon Ben Hillel and grandson of Hillel the Elder who founded the House or School of Hillel. Rabbi Hillel II came from the House of Hillel. He standardized the Jewish calendar for regular distribution accounting for leap years, length of months, and formally established rules to insure that no two Sabbaths (or holy convocations and a weekly Sabbath) could occur consecutively (back to back) in accordance with practices held by the Pharisees dating to as early as 57 A.D. Hillel II's calendar centered upon new moon calculations that the Sanhedrin had relied upon in lieu of two witnesses or in cases of extremely bad weather.

Hillel II's calendar is still in use today and standardized the Jewish year by making each month a specific length and added months in a cyclic pattern that insured the course of a nineteen-year cycle which realigns the solar calendar with the lunar calendar. In this cycle, Adar I is added during the third, sixth, eighth, eleventh, fourteenth, seventeenth, and nineteenth years during the nineteen year cycle, making it similar to the musical scale of notes on a major scale. For each whole step on the major scale, there are two regular years without Adar I. For each half-step on the musical scale, there is one regular year and one leap year.[4]

With the adoption of this calendar, Jewish communities throughout the world were able for the first time to celebrate in unity the Holy Days without basing the calculations on sighting the actual new moon in Jerusalem. This fixed calendar was essential to helping the Jewish nation survive the persecution and obsession of hostile governments to eliminate their religion, culture, and traditional religious calendar. Many scholars theorize Rabbi Hillel II did not invent an entirely new calendar, but rather he formalized practices of observation and mathematical reckoning held by the Sanhedrin for hundreds of years, dating back to even around the time of the destruction of the Second Temple. Unfortunately, this fixed calendar has inherent errors in the calculation of a year causing it to shift backwards several hours over long periods of time. This backward shift will eventually cause Nisan to drift into winter. It is likely the Sanhedrin will have to insert a correction into the calendar in the future to ensure Nisan continues to appear during spring harvest-time.

God's High Holy Days

Now that we've discussed the calendar established by God with regard to the timing of a day, a week, a month and the annual calendar, a good bible scholar also needs to understand that within the annual calendar God ordained "holy convocations" or days of celebration. These holy days of celebration are similar to the concept of "national holidays." The words "holy convocation" are derived from two different Hebrew words:

Holy: "qadash" (Strong's #6942)[5] meaning "holy" or to be set-apart or to be holy/sanctified for God, and

Convocation: "miqra" (Strong's #4744)[5] meaning rehearsal, assembly, reading or called out.

Together they portray the idea that a specific time has been set apart by God for an assembly of the people before Him or for the people to gather as a holy rehearsal before Him. According to the New Testament, convocations are foreshadowing pictures of the good things to come regarding Jesus the Christ. In the scripture below, the word "holyday" can be translated literally as "a festival" or "feast, holy day." Thus, it refers to the appointed festivals or holy convocations implemented by God in the Old Testament.

> "Let no man therefore judge you in meat, or in drink, or in respect of an holyday, or of the new moon, or of the Sabbath *days*: which are a shadow of things to come; but the body *is* of Christ."
> Colossians 2:16-17

Therefore, when examining the convocations established by God, we are looking at portraits on God's calendar prophetically reflecting Christ, His ministry and reign on Earth. Each holy convocation day on God's prophetic timeline will have a spiritual fulfillment by Jesus, either during His first incarnation or at His second coming, and this spiritual fulfillment will be literally accomplished on the date assigned on God's calendar to that convocation day in scripture. However, it should be noted that the date assigned in scripture may or may not be the date currently celebrated by men on today's calendar, as men have altered God's calendar by their own limiting interpretations of scripture and for their own purposes. One example of this is Hillel II's effect on the Jewish calendar, which prohibited holy convocations from occurring on specific days to eliminate consecutive Sabbath days and fixed the Feast of First Fruits and Pentecost to specific dates.

During holy convocations, Israel is instructed to do no "servile work." While the restriction on work is similar to the Sabbath law forbidding all work, a holy convocation permits specific "work" to be performed such as preparation of meals by cooking, keeping or transferring fire, and carrying of water and other items; all of which are forbidden on a regular weekly Sabbath. Only "work" performed to enhance the pleasure of the festival/ holy convocation day was allowed. If a convocation day occurs on regular Sabbath, all Sabbath regular restrictions are observed.

In the Jewish calendar, these holy convocations (or Annual Sabbaths) are celebrated every year on the date established by God in the Old Testament. Just as a man's birthday is celebrated on the date of the month he was born regardless of the day of the week his birthdate lands, so too is Passover always celebrated on Nisan 14th regardless of the day of the week. In addition to the "Shabbat" or Sabbath (the weekly day of rest), the Bible lists seven holy convocations identified in scripture in Leviticus chapter 23:

1. Nisan 15th, 1st day of Unleavened Bread,
2. Nisan 21st, 7th day of Unleavened Bread,
3. Sivan 6th, Pentecost (50 days from Firstfruits)
4. Tishri 1st, Rosh HaShanah, The Head of the Year (Adam's birthday)
5. Tishri 10th, Yom Kippur, Day of Atonement

6. 15th Tishri, 1st day of the Feast of Tabernacles,

7. 22nd Tishri, 7th day of the Feast of Tabernacles

As these additional holy convocations occurred, a week would contain multiple Sabbaths: an Annual Sabbath (holy convocation) and the weekly Sabbath. Albert Barnes, a Presbyterian commentator wrote the following description regarding the Sabbath:

> "The word 'Sabbath' in the Old Testament is applied not only to the seventh day, but to all the days of holy rest that were observed by the Hebrews, and particularly to the beginning and close of their great festivals."[6]

Sometimes, the Jewish people would experience consecutive Sabbath days in which no servile work could be performed. Historical records are vague regarding the initiation of rules designed specifically to avoid consecutive Sabbaths by the Sanhedrin. Most accounts by historians and the Talmud indicate these rules to avoid consecutive Sabbaths appeared either late during the end of the Second Temple (50 AD) or shortly after its destruction in 70 AD. This is significant, because it is extremely possible that consecutive Sabbaths occurred during Jesus' earthly lifetime. Additionally, there is no specific Torah mandate preventing consecutive Sabbaths. While it is easier for the Jewish nation to avoid consecutive Sabbath days, there is no Biblical justification for the practice of averting consecutive Sabbaths seen in today's Jewish calendar. The effects of this dogmatic practice essentially alters God's established calendar away from its purest form. Thus, the current Jewish calendar is an example of how men under the guise of upholding God's law sometimes reinterpret scripture to meet their own comforts. The end consequence is the exaltation of the traditions of men over God's word, usurping the authority of God in their lives. The results of Hillel's calendar rules become important later when examining the timeline of crucifixion events.

In addition to the seven holy convocations, God also arranged these Holy Days into three pilgrimages. These pilgrimages required all Jewish males to appear before Him in Jerusalem annually. While the first feast begins with Passover, it is titled the Feast of Unleavened Bread and also includes the Feast of First Fruits within its timeline week. The second pilgrimage is named the Feast of Harvest and refers to the second grain harvest or the wheat harvest experienced in the summer. The Jews refer to this holy convocation as Shavuot, but Christians know the name better as Pentecost. The final pilgrimage required for Jewish males is the Feast of Ingathering, which includes the holy convocations for the Feast of Trumpets (Tishri 1), the Day of Atonement, and the Feast of Tabernacles.

Required Annual Pilgrimages

Chart 5

First	Second	Third
Title: Unleavened Bread	**Title:** Feast of Harvest	**Title:** The Ingathering
Holy Convocations: Passover, Unleavened Bread, First Fruits	**Holy Convocations:** Shavuot (Pentecost)	**Holy Convocations:** Trumpets, Day of Atonement, Tabernacles

Each of the three required appearances before the Lord is prophetic of the ministry of Messiah. The first pilgrimage during Passover, Unleavened Bread and First Fruits was fulfilled by Jesus' death and resurrection from the grave, after which He presented before the Lord the First Fruits from the Dead. During second pilgrimage, Jesus before the Father in Heaven sent the Holy Spirit to His believers (Acts 1:9-2:41). The third pilgrimage will correspond to events surrounding the second coming of Christ, Judgment Day, and Jesus' millennial reign on Earth, where He will tabernacle with men for a thousand years.

The Debate Over When to Celebrate

The second century brought with it the rumblings of what would later become a great division in the Church regarding the timing of when to celebrate the Lord's Passover and resurrection. While all the early churches were in agreement of observing the Passover and resurrection of Jesus, they believed differently as to the particular day of when it should be observed. Some Christians celebrated the Jewish Passover of Nisan 14th, the date of the Last Supper in which Christ gave the New Covenant. Other disciples held to honoring the Sunday following the Passover because it was the day of the discovery of Christ's resurrection.

Polycarp, bishop of Smyrna and disciple of John the Apostle, was among the leaders of the churches in Asia minor who kept the tradition of celebrating the Lord's Passover on the night of Nisan 14th which they held was the original date Jesus held the meal the Church commonly refers to as "The Last Supper." As a result of celebrating on the fourteenth, these Christians became known as the Quartadecimans, literally translated "the fourteenthers." There were two primary reasons Nisan 14th was held in such high regard by the Quartadecimans. The first was because of Jesus' death occurred on the fourteenth foreshadowing His prophetic fulfillment of the ultimate Passover lamb. Just as the first Passover lamb was sacrificed on Nisan 14th, so too was Jesus killed on Nisan 14th. The second justification for the Quartadecimans celebrating on Nisan 14 was in recognition that Nisan 14th was the actual anniversary date Jesus established the New Covenant by administering the Eucharist (Holy Communion) at the Last Supper and fulfilled His passion resulting in His crucifixion. This early tradition of celebrating on Nisan 14th was kept by the Apostles and handed down to their disciples for observance. Because of the direct instruction from Jesus and the Apostles, Polycarp defended the Church's right to celebrate on the fourteenth of Nisan.

The remaining churches of Europe and Egypt celebrated Jesus' Passover and resurrection on the first Sunday following the Jewish Passover. They observed this date in recognition of the discovery of Jesus' resurrection occurring on a Sunday morning. In the early church, Christians who celebrated the Sunday following Passover relied exclusively on the Jewish community to determine the correct date of Passover (Nisan 14th). Later, dependence upon the Jewish calendar would prove to be a deterring factor for Christians when the Catholic church formally established which date to celebrate by rejecting every thing Jewish.

Within the Church at Rome, another reason for enforcing a Sunday celebration date resulted from a claim in the year 147 C.E. made by Hermes, who was the brother of the reigning bishop Pope Pius. Hermes stated he "had received instruction from an angel, who commanded that all men should keep the Pasch [Passover] on the Lord's day [Sunday]."[7] Since Passover's date for celebration was ordained by God in the books of Exodus and Leviticus, an angel giving information contrary God's instruction to Moses regarding the timing and celebration of Passover is highly questionable. The apostle Paul wrote in his letter to the Galatians, chapter one verse eight, "But though we, or an angel from heaven, preach any other gospel unto you than that which we have preached unto you, let him be accursed." In verse nine of this same chapter, Paul repeats the warning that instructions from an angel *never* supersede God's already established written word. One cannot help but wonder if the zeal for upholding a Sunday celebration caused the church to embrace Hermes' lie and reinforced the preference of Sunday which later became an issue with the presiding bishop of Rome.

Pope Anicetus, the bishop of Rome from 153–68CE, held the Sunday celebration position as a result of teachings from the Apostles Peter and Paul. Anicetus met with Polycarp at a church council (synod) meeting to discuss the variance in celebration dates of the Lord's Passover. While neither Polycarp nor Anicetus were willing to change the date of celebration within their respective churches, they were in agreement to preserve Christian peace and brotherly love, parting on peaceful terms. Both agreed that "no division in the church"[8] be made over contrary dates to celebrate, and that they should "live in peace and communion with those that differed from them."[7] Thus, the doctrinal differences were minimal. Whether the church upheld the date the institution of the New Covenant was given by Christ in the Upper Room (Nisan 14th) or the date the Covenant was observed to be eternally sealed by Christ's resurrection from the dead (the following Sunday), the celebration of Christ's

New Covenant was being honored. It was documented that Anicetus even allowed Polycarp to hold the Eucharist (communion) in his church after the synod ended[7]. The disciples' mutual conclusion reinforced the Holy Spirit's teaching regarding harmony in the body of Christ and the observance of days (or lack thereof) in the New Testament.

> "One man esteemeth one day above another: another esteemeth every day *alike*. Let every man be fully persuaded in his own mind. He that regardeth the day, regardeth *it* unto the Lord; and he that regardeth not the day, to the Lord he doth not regard *it*."
> Romans 14:5-6

Unfortunately, this harmony would not last. By the late-second century, the debate over which date to celebrate surfaced again. Sadly, instead of the firm commitment to brotherly love and Christian peace modeled by first century Christian leaders and churches, the thundering of an approaching ecclesiastical storm echoed. Roman papal authority superseding biblical and apostolic teachings began to surface when Pope Victor of Rome in 193 CE issued an order against Polycrates, disciple of Polycarp, and all the Quartadeciman churches of Asia for not celebrating the resurrection of Jesus on Sunday. Pope Victor sought to excommunicate all Believers who did not agree to his interpretation of when to celebrate. Immediately, many bishops and brethren came to Polycrates' defense and rebuked Pope Victor. Irenaeus, Bishop of France, sent a rebuke to Victor recalling the previous synod's discussion and outcome of Polycarp's meeting with Anicetus. Irenaeus' appealed for brotherly love to be extended to the Quartadecimans. Pope Victor relented, and the debate was once again pacified.

In his study *The Eucharistic Words of Jesus*, the Lutheran scriptural scholar Joachim Jeremias made a compelling argument that the Quartodecimans preserved the original understanding and character of the Christian Passover celebration. He stated that in Jewish tradition four major themes are associated with Passover,

1. The creation of the earth,

2. The binding of Isaac which is often referred to as the Akedah,

3. The redemption of the nation of Israel from Egypt,

4. The announcement by Elijah of the coming Messiah.[9]

Scripturally, the events of the mystery of Jesus' passion, death and resurrection are obviously associated with Passover. Thus, the earliest Christians of the first century expected the imminent return of Christ to occur during the Passover celebration. Jeremias noted that the Quartodecimans began their Christian Passover celebrations by reading from the Hebrew Scriptures, which are the same twelve readings from the Scriptures read at the Easter Vigil by the Roman Catholic, Eastern Orthodox and Armenian churches. At midnight, if Christ had not reappeared to initiate the great marriage supper banquet, Christians celebrated Holy Communion in anticipation of the final redemption of Christ still to come, the resurrection of the dead and the quickening of the mortal bodies still alive at His return. As this original celebration of the seconding coming fervor began to die down within the first/second century and Christianity became an increasingly Gentile movement, the original eschatological orientation of the Christian Passover celebration was lost. Simultaneously, there was a rise in celebration on the date of the discovery of the Resurrection (Sunday), which later became predominate throughout the church as a whole.

In 325 CE, bishops from Eastern and Western churches met for the Council of Nicaea synod at the demand of Constantine and formally ended the ongoing debate over when to celebrate along with many other issues. The Sunday celebration was declared the winner. Yet ironically, the Church ruled that the Sunday date of celebration should be independent of the Jewish calendar and instead follow the spring equinox. This surprising detachment from the Jewish calendar resulted from an increase in anti-Semitism and a growing hatred of any thing of Jewish origin. By this action, the Christian Church separated itself from God's established time-line in Scripture with regard to the observance of Holy Days on a lunar calendar. No biblical justification can be found for this detachment from God's ordained calendar, which resulted in mankind again creating a tradition that exalted itself above the Word of God.

Eusebius, an early church historian who lived between 263 – 339 CE, wrote the following regarding the Council of Nicaea's justification for the chosen day of Sunday to be independent of the Jewish calendar (**bold emphasis added**):

> "When the question relative to the sacred festival of Easter arose, it was universally thought that it would be convenient that all should keep the feast on one day; for what could be more beautiful and more desirable, than to see this festival, through which we receive the hope of immortality, celebrated by all with one accord, and in the same manner? *It was declared to be particularly unworthy* for this, the holiest of all

festivals, *to follow the custom* [the calculation] *of the Jews, who had soiled their hands with the most fearful of crimes, and whose minds were blinded*. In rejecting their custom, (1) we may transmit to our descendants the legitimate mode of celebrating Easter, which we have observed from the time of the Savior's Passion to the present day [according to the day of the week]. *We [Christians] ought not,* therefore, *to have anything in common with the Jews,* for the Savior has shown us another way; our worship follows a more legitimate and more convenient course (the order of the days of the week); and consequently, in unanimously adopting this mode, *we desire, dearest brethren, to separate ourselves from the detestable company of the Jews, for it is truly shameful for us to hear them boast that without their direction we could not keep this feast.* How can they be in the right, they who, after the death of the Savior, have no longer been led by reason but by wild violence, as their delusion may urge them? They do not possess the truth in this Easter question; for, in their blindness and repugnance to all improvements, they frequently celebrate two Passovers in the same year. We could not imitate those who are openly in error. How, then, could we follow these Jews, who are most certainly blinded by error? For to celebrate the Passover twice in one year is totally inadmissible. *But even if this were not so, it would still be your duty not to tarnish your soul by communications with such wicked people [the Jews].* Besides, consider well, that in such an important matter, and on a subject of such great solemnity, there ought not to be any division. Our Savior has left us only one festal day of our redemption, that is to say, of his holy passion, and he desired [to establish] only one Catholic (universal) Church. Think, then, how unseemly it is, that on the same day some should be fasting whilst others are seated at a banquet; and that after Easter, some should be rejoicing at feasts, whilst others are still observing a strict fast. For this reason, a Divine Providence wills that this custom should be rectified and regulated in a uniform way; and everyone, I hope, will agree upon this point. As, on the one hand, *it is our duty not to have anything in common with the murderers of our Lord."*[10]

The justification for selecting a date for celebration completely devoid of any semblance of Judaism by condemning all things Jewish was laced with noticeable arrogance, promoted a hatred of the nation of Israel, and was against Biblical New Testament scriptures. Throughout the eleventh chapter of The Epistle of Paul the Apostle to the Romans, Paul admonishes Christians not to boast themselves against Israel (verse 18). He instructed the church to understand the mystery of God, which caused the Jewish nation to reject their Messiah in order to bring salvation to the gentiles (verses 22, 25, 30-33). The Apostle Paul further stated that Israel "is beloved for the Father's sake," and shall eventually be saved "for God is able to graft them in again" (verse 23). In addition, the rejection of a Jewish timeline for Passover by the Church also undermined the authority of Scriptures in the Old Testament, where God Himself established the calendar date for Passover.

As the anti-Semitic history of the Church unfolded, Believers today should acquire a new appreciation of the Holy Spirit's counsel given to the early Church, which forewarned of the temptation of Christian pride and resentment against Israel because of its rejection of Jesus. It is heartbreaking to know the Church ignored the cautionary language spoken by the

Holy Spirit through the Apostle Paul and allowed the sin of pride to become the essence behind the Church's justification for moving the celebration of Jesus' Passover away from God's ordained lunar calendar and onto a pagan solar calendar.

Ironically, the quest for unity within the church of Christ by demanding a single specific date to celebrate the Passover & resurrection of Christ has ultimately ended with division yet again between the Orthodox denomination and other mainline Roman Catholic and Protestant denominations. Followers of the Orthodox-Catholic Church have strictly adhered to the tradition of celebrating Easter according to the decision of the Council of Nicaea in 325AD, which was created under the Julian calendar. Roman Catholics and Protestants, however, observe the Pasch (Easter) celebration on a different date as a result of the Gregorian calendar change being instituted in the sixteenth century, which altered the Julian calendar calculation of time. In 1997, the Council of World Churches gathered once again to seek agreement in resolving the date of celebration for Pasch (Easter), but unfortunately, the divide continues. One wonders if harmony on a date of celebration can truly be obtained without the acknowledgement of the Church's rejection of God's preordained calendar and corporate repentance for the anti-Semitic and anti-Christ decision made so long ago.

The Julian & Gregorian Calendars

The Julian calendar was introduced by Julius Caesar in 45 BC and consisted of "a common year of 365 days divided into twelve months with a leap day added to the month of February every four years."[11] It was the first calendar in

Rome to use a leap year; however, due to a counting error, leap years were not observed initially and then occurred every three years instead of four. The Julian calendar error resulted in a shift of one day backwards every 128 years. By the time of Pope Gregory in the sixteenth century, this counting error had resulted in over a ten-day shift, making the spring equinox on March 11th instead of March 21st. This was extremely problematic to the church, which during the twelfth or thirteenth century linked Pasch (Easter) to the vernal equinox by the Zonaras Proviso (a church rule that basically stated that Pasch could not fall before the Jewish calendar date of Nisan 15th).

Therefore, in 1582 Pope Gregory decreed a new calendar would replace the problematic Julian calendar. The new calendar would be strictly solar based, having a regular year of 365 days with a leap year every four years to add an additional day to the calendar. This calendar, which later became known as the Gregorian calendar, would need to allow "for the realignment with the equinox, and a number of days had to be dropped when the change was made."[12] A total of ten days were dropped in October 1582, and new rules were established to keep the calendar on track for leap years. In addition, the Gregorian calendar officially instituted an absolute date for Pasch (Easter) to occur after the vernal equinox. Today, the Gregorian calendar has become the unofficial global standard for telling time.

While one would presume everyone would accept a correction to resolve a counting flaw in the Julian calendar, the contrary happened. A huge division was once again created within Christendom as to the correct date for celebrating Pasch (Easter). The Catholic and Protestant churches adopted the new calendar, but the Eastern Orthodox Church rejected it. Instead they determined to continue with the decision made by the synod at Council of Nicaea in 325AD. The Eastern Orthodox Church's rational for adhering to the original decree was based on their allegiance to the early church fathers' decision, which they believe is independent from how time is reckoned today. Instead of basing the celebration on the vernal equinox, Eastern Orthodox base calculations as outlined by tradition:

> *"Easter Day... is the first Sunday after the Full Moon which happens upon or next after the twenty first of March; and if the Full Moon happens upon a Sunday, Easter Sunday is the Sunday after.... The Eastern Church still observes the rule laid down by the Council of Nicea (A.D. 325) and now disregarded by the Western Church, that the Christian Easter shall never precede or coincide with Jewish Passover, but must always follow it. Easter cannot fall earlier than March 23 or later than April 25. The Eastern Church still uses the Julian Calendar, which since March 1, 1901 has been thirteen days behind the Gregorian calendar."*[13]

CHAPTER 2

PASSOVER

Passover Defined

"Pesach" is the Hebrew word from which the English word "Passover" is derived. Translated literally it confirs the meaning "to pass over, or to cover." In the book, <u>Christ in the Passover, Why This Night is Different</u>, Mr. Rosen noted that "the verb 'pass over' has a deeper meaning here than the idea of stepping or leaping over something to avoid contact. It is not the common Hebrew verb, a-bhar or gabhar, which is frequently used in that sense."[14] Instead, he noted the verb used in the Book of Exodus is "pasha" whose noun counterpart is "pesah," translated Passover. Mr. Rosen commented the Hebrew word for pasha resembled "the Egyptian word pesh, which means 'to spread wings over'"[14] in order to protect. Rosen went further to quote Arthur W. Pink's book <u>Gleanings in Exodus</u>:

> "The word is used... in the sense of Isaiah 31:5: 'As birds flying, so will the Lord of Hosts defend Jerusalem; defending also He will deliver it; and passing over (pasoach, participle of pasach) He will preserve it'. The word has, consequently, the very meaning of the Egyptian term for 'spreading the wings over,' and 'protecting'; and pesach, the Lord's

Passover, means such sheltering and protection as is found under the outstretched wings of the Almighty. Does this not give a new fullness to those words... 'O Jerusalem! Jerusalem! How often would I have gathered thy children together, as a hen does gather her brood under her wings' (Luke 13:34)? This term pesach is applied (1) to the ceremony and (2) to the lamb... the slain lamb, the sheltering behind its blood and the eating of its flesh, constituted the pesach, the protection of God's chosen people beneath the sheltering wings of the Almighty"... It was not merely that the Lord passed by the houses of the Israelites, but that He stood on guard, protecting each blood-sprinkled door![15]"

The word, date, and timeline for celebration of Passover can be highly confusing to many gentiles as the word "Passover" has four individual concepts associated with it that are often used interchangeably and sometimes simultaneously in Scripture and everyday language. The word Passover can be used to indicate the original Passover in Egypt, the lamb sacrifice, a specific date (Nisan 14th), and/or the reference to weeklong celebration, the Feast of Unleavened Bread which begins on Nisan 15th.

> 1. Passover is used to identify the actual lamb sacrifice called the *Pasch*. For centuries in Christianity the word "*Pascha*," the transliteration from the Greek word of the Hebrew pesach, was used to refer to the Resurrection of Christ because He was the Passover Lamb. In most European languages and countries Easter is called by some variant of Pascha.

2. Because the lamb was killed on Nisan 14th, this date is called the Lord's Passover (Leviticus 23:5).

3. As a result of its connection to the lamb's sacrifice, the term "Passover" is biblically associated to two different dates. The first date is outlined above. Since the Jewish day starts at evening, the word "Passover" can also be used to identify Nisan 15th, denoting the holy convocation in which the Passover lamb was eaten.

4. The term "Passover" can refer to either the first event in Exodus or the annual memorial festival celebrating the Exodus event.

5. The word "Passover" is used synonymously with the Feast of Unleavened Bread, a seven-day feast starting on eve of Nisan 15th commemorating the eating of original Passover lamb and events in Egypt (Mark 14:1). Although the Feast of Unleavened Bread can be called by its official title, it is commonly referred to as Passover because eating of the Lamb (the Seder supper) begins the Feasts.

6. Nisan 14th, the Passover date, can be referred to as the preparation day for Passover (John 19:14) or the first day of the Feast of Unleavened Bread (Mark 14:12). Even though Nisan 14th is not part of the official feast period, it is sometimes included because the lamb sacrifice is essential to the other events in the week. Because Nisan 14th precedes the holy convocation/Annual Sabbath day, it is a day to make preparations for the coming holy convocation.

With so many variations in the definition of "Passover," confusion over which context "Passover" is being used in the Bible becomes more understandable. Thankfully, Scripture provides insight to these definitions or aspects of using the word Passover.

Torah Mandate & Historical Setting

The twelfth chapter in the Book of Exodus provides the historical account of the first Jewish Passover and the mandate from God for future generations to commemorate the events that happened that fateful night so long ago in Egypt (Exodus 12:14). During the time of extended slavery in Egypt, God sent Moses to free the nation of Israel; however, Pharaoh stubbornly declined to let Israel go. Pharaoh's refusal resulted in ten plagues as punishment from God upon his nation, the last of which involved Yahweh killing all the first-born children & animals in the land. To save Israel from the final plague of death destroying its people and livestock, Yahweh instituted a sacrifice to exempt His people from death.

Selection of Lamb

God instructed Moses to have each household select a lamb without blemish or spot on ***the tenth of Nisan*** and to take the lamb into their house where it would be cared for four days (Exodus 12:3-6). On the fourteenth of Nisan, the lamb was to be slaughtered in the evening, and its blood sprinkled on the doorpost and lintel (Exodus 13:6-7) of the Jewish house. The sprinkling of the blood on the doorposts would be a sign to God as He passed through the land of Egypt. Upon whoever's house the blood was found, Yahweh would cover them, essentially allowing death to pass over them and exempt them from His judgment upon Egypt. No household covered by the blood would experience death (Exodus 12:12-13). The Israelite households were instructed to stay inside that night, eating on the lamb, as the angel of death went throughout the land of Egypt.

On the fifteenth day of Nisan, "at midnight, the Lord slew all the first-born in the land Egypt, from the first-born of Pharaoh that sat on his throne unto the first-born of the captive that was in the dungeon; and all the first-born of cattle (Exodus 12:29)." Later that night in the early pre-dawn hours of morning, upon the discovery of thousands of Egyptian deaths, including his own son, Pharaoh called for Moses and Aaron and thrust Israel out of his nation, letting them go free. Israel began their departure from the land of Egypt immediately at dawn on Nisan 15th (see Numbers 33:3).

> "$_2$This month shall be unto you the beginning of months: it shall be the first month of the year to you. $_3$Speak ye unto all the congregation of Israel, saying, In the tenth day of this month they shall take to them every man a lamb, according to the house of their fathers, a lamb for an house: $_4$And if the household be too little for the lamb, let him and his neighbor next unto his house take it according to the number of the souls; every man according to his eating shall make your count for the lamb. $_5$Your lamb shall be without blemish, a male of the first year: ye shall take it out from the sheep, or from the goats: $_6$And ye shall keep it up until the fourteenth day of the same month: and the whole assembly of the congregation of Israel shall kill it in the evening. $_7$And they shall take of the blood, and strike it on the two side posts and on the upper

doorpost of the houses, wherein they shall eat it. 8And they shall eat the flesh in that night, roast with fire, and unleavened bread; and with bitter herbs they shall eat it. 9Eat not of it raw, nor sodden at all with water, but roast with fire; his head with his legs, and with the purtenance thereof. 10And ye shall let nothing of it remain until the morning; and that which remaineth of it until the morning ye shall burn with fire. 11And thus shall ye eat it; with your loins girded, your shoes on your feet, and your staff in your hand; and ye shall eat it in haste: it is the LORD's passover. 12For I will pass through the land of Egypt this night, and will smite all the firstborn in the land of Egypt, both man and beast; and against all the gods of Egypt I will execute judgment: I am the LORD. 13And the blood shall be to you for a token upon the houses where ye are: and when I see the blood, I will pass over you, and the plague shall not be upon you to destroy you, when I smite the land of Egypt. 14And this day shall be unto you for a memorial; and ye shall keep it a feast to the LORD throughout your generations; ye shall keep it a feast by an ordinance forever. 15Seven days shall ye eat unleavened bread; even the first day ye shall put away leaven out of your houses: for whosoever eateth leavened bread from the first day until the seventh day, that soul shall be cut off from Israel. 16And in the first day there shall be an holy convocation, and in the seventh day there shall be an holy convocation to you; no manner of work shall be done in them, save that which every man must eat, that only may be done of you. 17And ye shall observe the feast of unleavened bread; for in this selfsame day have I brought your armies out of the land of Egypt: therefore shall ye observe this day in your generations by an ordinance forever. 18In the first

month, on the fourteenth day of the month at even, ye shall eat unleavened bread, until the one and twentieth day of the month at even. ₁₉Seven days shall there be no leaven found in your houses: for whosoever eateth that which is leavened, even that soul shall be cut off from the congregation of Israel, whether he be a stranger, or born in the land. ₂₀Ye shall eat nothing leavened; in all your habitations shall ye eat unleavened bread."
Exodus 12:2-20

Date of Lamb's Death

The Passover described in Exodus 12:6 provides specific instruction for killing the Passover lamb at dusk on Nisan 14th. The word "evening" used in verse six is Hebrew the word "ereb," whose literal translation means "dusk" or "between the evenings." There has been many disagreements within the church as to which evening the Lord meant regarding Nisan 14th, as it has two periods of dusk. The first period occurs at the end of Nisan 13th which begins Nisan 14th; the other time of dusk transpires toward the end of Nisan 14th at the beginning of Nisan 15th.

The reason for disagreement on which evening Passover occurred has resulted from Believers trying to correlate or justify events at Christ's Last Supper. Some Believers maintain the position that scripture teaches Jesus ate a literal Passover meal on the night of Nisan 13th/Nisan 14th. The justification for their position is found in the synoptic gospels (Matthew, Mark, and Luke), which on the surface seem to portray the final meal as a Passover meal, a meal consumed on the night of Nisan 14/15th. Other Believers believe the original Passover occurred on Nisan 13th/Nisan

14th and use the Gospel of John to affirm that Jesus indeed ate the Passover meal on Nisan 13/14th. John records the Last Supper occurred on the actual date the lamb was to be killed, not the night the Pesach lamb was traditionally eaten. The tables below examine the scriptural differences between the two opinions:

Opinion 1: The Passover killed and eaten on the night of Nisan 14th

Chart 6

	Nisan 13th	Nisan 14th	Nisan 15th
Morning		Pharaoh lets Israel go before sunrise	Israel leaves in the morning
Evening	**Nisan 14th** Lamb killed at sunset; roasted & eaten; Angel of Death at midnight	**Nisan 15th** Israel still in Egypt	**Nisan 16th**

If **Opinion 1** is correct and the original Passover in Egypt occurred at the end of Nisan 13th beginning Nisan 14th, then Christ could have eaten the genuine Passover lamb meal with unleavened bread on the night of the fourteenth before He died without any contradictions to scripture regarding this last meal. This position would imply the long held Jewish understanding of scripture and tradition of killing the lamb on the 14th between 3:00 PM and twilight would be wrong. It would also denote that Jesus had not actually been sacrificed at the same time the Jewish Passover lambs were being offered as recorded by Josephus, the Jewish first century historian.

Opinion 2 (the Traditional view): The Passover killed in the day of the 14th (at 3PM) and eaten the night of Nisan 15th

Chart 7

	Nisan 13th	Nisan 14th	Nisan 15th
Morning		Lamb killed 3 PM, before "sunset"	Pharaoh lets Israel go. Israel leaves Egypt immediately
Evening	Nisan 14th	Nisan 15th Lamb roasted & eaten; Angel of Death at midnight	Nisan 16th

If Opinion 2 is correct then the lamb sacrifice occurred on the evening of Nisan 14th close to the beginning of Nisan 15th, and the meal described in the New Testament as Passover meal could not have been a literal Passover meal observing the Exodus. This would denote the Last Supper could have been only a spiritual Passover meal, not a literal Passover memorial meal.

Scripture is extremely detailed in the Old Testament regarding the timeline of events in Egypt which makes discerning which viewpoint is correct much easier. Those holding the position of Opinion 1 to harmonize New Testament scriptures are wrong because they neglect the context of the original Passover Old Testament passages and the surrounding events. During the first Passover in Egypt, the lamb was to be sacrificed and its blood sprinkled directly on the doorposts on Nisan 14th. The lamb was then to be consumed *immediately* that night, with none remaining until morning (see Exodus 12:8, 10). In verse eleven, Israel is instructed to eat the lamb *fully dressed with shoes on their feet*, because they will be leaving *quickly*. Later in verse twelve of the same chapter, the Lord declares that He will pass through the land of Egypt *"this night."* The night the lamb sacrifice was eaten was the same night the Lord passed through the land of Egypt at midnight to kill the first-born. Exodus 12:17 further declared "for *in this selfsame day* have I brought your armies out of the land of Egypt." Scripture further reports in Numbers 33:3 that the Israelites departed Egypt on Nisan 15th. The term "selfsame day" can only refer to Nisan 15th.

In Exodus 12:33, it records, "the Egyptians were urgent upon the people (Israel), that they might send them *out of the land in haste*." Later in verse thirty-nine of the same chapter, Scripture chronicles that "they (Israel) baked unleavened cakes of the dough which they brought forth out of Egypt, for it was not leavened; because they were thrust out of Egypt, and could not tarry." These last two Scriptures provide a very clear impression that little to no time lapsed between the events of killing and eating the lamb and their departure from Egypt. Israel's dough did not even have time to ferment or rise. The only way for the Exodus timeline to accommodate all these facts would be if the lamb sacrifice occurred on the evening of Nisan 14th as it began Nisan 15th.

If the Exodus event timeline began (as Opinion 1 implies) on the night of Nisan 13th/Nisan 14th, Israel would have a period of at least 24 hours between the sacrificing of the lamb and a departure date on the fifteenth of Nisan as recorded in Numbers 33:3. A delay of twenty-four hours would have been ample enough time for the fermentation of bread and preparation of food. Therefore, the concept of Israel having only unleavened bread would not make sense in this scenario. Additionally, it is not possible for Israel to eat the lamb on the night of Nisan 13th/14th and leave on the self-same day of Nisan 15th.

However, if the event timeline began (as Opinion 2 implies) on Nisan 14th/Nisan 15th, then Israel would have killed the lamb before sunset, sprinkled its blood on the doorpost and ate it immediately. They would still have been eating the lamb as the angel of death went out at midnight, causing their immediate departure from Egypt around sunrise the next morning. In this timeline, there would not be enough time for fermentation of bread, and Israel would leave in the self-same day the Lord went out to fight for them in Egypt (Nisan 15th). Thus, the only way for all the Scriptures to be in agreement would require the date for the lamb sacrifice to be on the fourteenth just before the fifteenth of Nisan.

In addition to the sacrifice of the Passover lamb, a Feast of Unleavened Bread for seven days is ordained beginning on Nisan 15th at the eve of Nisan fourteenth beginning the fifteenth. The Lord pronounced the Passover lamb was to be **eaten with unleavened bread**, thus starting the seven-day period of unleavened bread outlined in Exodus 12:8. However, since the lamb was killed before sunset on the fourteenth and eaten that night as dinner, it was actually eaten on the fifteenth. Therefore, the fifteenth of Nisan marks the beginning of the Feast of Unleavened Bread, "seven days though shalt eat unleavened bread" (Exodus 13:6, 23:15, 34:18; Deuteronomy 16:3).

Anatolius of Alexandria who later became the Bishop of Laodicea also describes the timing of the Passover Day and the Feast of Unleavened Bread beginning on Nisan 14th. In trying to describe the Jewish feast days, Anatolius stated:

> "For the Lord ascribes no less praise to the 20th day than to the 14th. For in the book of Leviticus the injunction is expressed thus: 'In the first month, **on the fourteenth day of this month, at even, is the Lord's Passover**. And on the fifteenth day of this month is the feast of unleavened bread unto the Lord. Seven days ye shall eat unleavened bread. This first day shall be to you one most diligently attended and holy. Ye shall do no servile work thereon. And the seventh day shall be to you more diligently attended and holier, ye shall do no servile work thereon... we should keep the solemn festival of Passover on the Lord's day and after the equinox, and yet not beyond the limit of the moon's 20th day."[16]

Additional Scriptures provide further details regarding God's intent of the Passover Feast of Unleavened Bread. The passage in Deuteronomy 16:6 reiterates the sacrifice of the lamb must occur "at the going down of the sun" on the fourteenth. Afterwards, it was roasted and eaten immediately on the fifteenth. The Book of Deuteronomy, chapter sixteen provides a Passover Feast timeline:

> "₁Observe the month of Abib [Nisan], and keep the Passover unto the LORD thy God: for in the month of Abib the LORD thy God brought thee forth out of Egypt by night. ₂Thou shalt therefore sacrifice the Passover unto the LORD thy God, of the flock and the herd, in the place which the LORD shall choose to place his name there. ₃Thou shalt eat no leavened bread with it; seven days shalt thou eat unleavened

bread therewith, even the bread of affliction; for thou camest forth out of the land of Egypt in haste: that thou mayest remember the day when thou camest forth out of the land of Egypt all the days of thy life. ₄And there shall be no leavened bread seen with thee in all thy coast seven days; neither shall there any thing of the flesh, which thou sacrificedst the first day at even, remain all night until the morning."
Deuteronomy 16:1-4

Must Stay Inside Homes

The Torah required the Jewish nation to remain inside their homes during the night of Nisan 14th/15th to eat the Passover lamb. This ordinance was established forever. The following verse from Exodus clearly describes that forbiddance of Jews to leave their homes.

> ₂₂And ye shall take a bunch of hyssop, and dip it in the blood that is in the bason, and strike the lintel and the two side posts with the blood that is in the bason; ***and none of you shall go out at the door of his house until the morning.*** ₂₃For the Lord will pass through to smite the Egyptians; and when he seeth the blood upon the lintel, and on the two side posts, the Lord will pass over the door, and will not suffer the destroyer to come in unto your houses to smite you. ₂₄And ye shall observe this thing for an ordinance to thee and to thy sons for ever."
> Exodus 12:22-24

How to Eat the Lamb

Torah is also very specific about the cooking and eating of the Pesach lamb. No bone of the lamb's body could be broken, and it was to be roasted with fire. It could not be boiled. Furthermore, the lamb must be eaten with unleavened bread and bitter herbs. Additionally, Torah required no part of the lamb may leave the dwelling, and any remaining uneaten lamb was to be burned in the morning by fire. The following scriptures from the Torah outline how to eat the lamb:

> "$_8$And they shall eat the flesh in that night, *roast with fire, and unleavened bread; and with bitter herbs they shall eat it.* $_9$*Eat not of it raw, nor sodden at all with water, but roast with fire*; his head with his legs, and with the purtenance thereof. $_{10}$And ye shall **let** *nothing of it remain until the morning;* and *that which remaineth of it until the morning ye shall burn with fire.* $_{11}$And thus shall ye eat it; with your loins girded, your shoes on your feet, and your staff in your hand; and ye shall eat it in haste: it is the LORD's passover."
> Exodus 12:8-11

> "$_{46}$In one house shall it be eaten; *thou shalt not carry forth ought of the flesh abroad out of the house; neither shall ye break a bone thereof.*"
> Exodus 12:46

> "$_3$*Thou shalt eat no leavened bread with it;* seven days shalt thou eat unleavened bread therewith, even the bread of affliction; for thou camest forth out of the land of Egypt in haste: that thou mayest remember the day when thou camest forth out of the land of Egypt all the days of thy life. $_4$And there shall be no

leavened bread seen with thee in all thy coast seven days; *neither shall there any thing of the flesh, which thou sacrificedst the first day at even, remain all night until the morning."*
Deuteronomy 16:3

Another Torah requirement for Passover was the absence of any leaven in the house on the night of Nisan 15th while eating the lamb. The Hebrew word for 'leaven' is "chametz" or "hametz." Chametz refers to food prepared from five species of grain: barley, wheat, oats, spelt, and rye, which have been combined with water and allowed to rise or ferment. Originally, only barley and wheat grew in the Middle East during Biblical times and were subject to the original Torah Passover requirements. Chametz represents foods that ferment such as yeast breads and is symbolically associated with the sins of pride and self-righteousness, when people are puffed up in their egos against God. The removal of the chametz was a requirement before Nisan 15th. The process of removing leaven began on Nisan 14th and was typically completed by noon. The ban on leavening remained in effect for the entire weeklong celebration of the Feast of Unleavened Bread. The following Torah scriptures outline the forbiddance of chametz in the Jewish household and diet during this festival.

[17]And ye shall observe the feast of unleavened bread; for in this selfsame day have I brought your armies out of the land of Egypt: therefore shall ye observe this day in your generations by an ordinance forever. [18]In the first month, on the fourteenth day of the month at even, ye shall eat unleavened bread, until the one and twentieth day of the month at even. [19]*Seven days shall there be no leaven found in your houses: for whosoever eateth that which is leavened,*

> *even that soul shall be cut off from the congregation of Israel*, whether he be a stranger, or born in the land. ₂₀*Ye shall eat nothing leavened;* in all your habitations shall ye eat unleavened bread."
> Exodus 12:17-20

> "₃Thou **shalt eat no leavened bread** with it; seven days shalt thou eat unleavened bread therewith, even the bread of affliction; for thou camest forth out of the land of Egypt in haste: that thou mayest remember the day when thou camest forth out of the land of Egypt all the days of thy life. ₄And **there shall be no leavened bread seen with thee in all thy coast seven days**; neither shall there any thing of the flesh, which thou sacrificedst the first day at even, remain all night until the morning."
> Deuteronomy 16:3-4

In the Book of Leviticus chapter 23, God appointed seven feasts, which were intended to be times for Israel to meet with God. These feasts were holy days unto the Lord. Details surrounding the timeline of events of the feast are further elaborated on in the Book of Numbers.

> "₁And the LORD spoke to Moses saying, Speak to the children of Israel, and say unto them concerning the feasts of the LORD, which ye shall proclaim to be holy convocations, even these are my feasts. ₂These are the feasts of the Lord, holy convocations, which ye shall proclaim in their seasons. *In the fourteenth of the first month at even is the Lord's Passover…* ₄These are the feasts of the LORD, holy convocations, which ye shall proclaim in their seasons. ₅In *the fourteenth day of the first month at even is the LORD's Passover.* ₆And *on the fifteenth day of the*

same month is the feast of unleavened bread unto the Lord: seven days ye must eat unleavened bread. ₇In the first day ye shall have an holy convocation: ye shall do no servile work therein. But ye shall offer an offering made by fire unto the LORD seven days: in the seventh day is an holy convocation: ye shall do no servile work therein."
Leviticus 23:1-2, 4-7

"₁₆And *in the fourteenth day of the first month is the Passover of the LORD.* ₁₇*And in the fifteenth day of this month is the feast*: seven days shall unleavened bread be eaten. ₁₈In the first day shall be an holy convocation: ye shall do no manner of servile work: ₁₉But ye shall offer a sacrifice made by fire for a burnt offering unto the LORD: two young bullocks, and one ram, and seven lambs of the first year: they shall be unto you without blemish… ₂₅And on the seventh day ye shall have an holy convocation: ye shall do no servile work."
Numbers 28:16-19 & 25

Both the Bible and the Jewish nation use the word "Passover" to simultaneously describe "the Feast of Unleavened Bread" (Exodus 12:15 & 19).[17] This feast period was to have two holy convocations (annual Sabbaths) within the seven-day period, not counting any weekly Sabbath (Leviticus 23:7-8) occurring within that timeframe. The first day (Nisan 15th) and last day (Nisan 21st) of the Feast were annual Sabbaths. The Passover lamb sacrifice date of Nisan 14th was not considered the holy convocation because the Feast actually started later that night, on Nisan 15th coinciding with the original Passover events in Egypt. The timing of the Passover sacrifice date and annual Sabbath for the first day of Passover's Feast of Unleavened Bread is vital to correctly interpreting the timeline of events surrounding Jesus' crucifixion in New Testament scriptures.

Passover was so esteemed by God that any ritually clean Israelite who refused to observe this feast was to be killed (Numbers 9:13). If perchance a person was made ritually unclean by touching a dead body and unable to observe the original Passover date, a second Passover date was given for observance. The alternative date for observance occurs in second month of the year on the fourteenth day (Numbers 9:6-12). The Passover is one of three Feasts in which God required all the males of Israel to appear before Him.

Spiritual Analogies of Passover

The Abrahamic Lamb

In the Introduction of this book, we briefly mentioned the relationship between the first sacrificial lamb mentioned in the bible and Jesus as God's lamb. Since the appearance of first sacrificial lamb in Genesis, the Lamb became a Principal of First Mention, which the scriptures later expounded to foreshadow and reveal God's son, Jesus, as the eternal Lamb sacrifice "who takes away the sins of the world" (John 1:29). In the twenty-second chapter of Book of Genesis, Abraham is instructed by God to take his son, Isaac, and sacrifice him upon Mount Moriah:

> "$_1$And it came to pass after these things, that God did tempt Abraham, and said unto him, Abraham: and he said, Behold, here I am. $_2$And he said, Take now thy son, thine only son Isaac, whom thou lovest, and get thee into the land of Moriah; and offer him there for a

burnt offering upon one of the mountains which I will tell thee of. ₃And Abraham rose up early in the morning, and saddled his ass, and took two of his young men with him, and Isaac his son, and clave the wood for the burnt offering, and rose up, and went unto the place of which God had told him. ₄Then on the third day Abraham lifted up his eyes, and saw the place afar off. ₅And Abraham said unto his young men, Abide ye here with the ass; and I and the lad will go yonder and worship, and come again to you. ₆And Abraham took the wood of the burnt offering, and laid it upon Isaac his son; and he took the fire in his hand, and a knife; and they went both of them together. ₇And Isaac spake unto Abraham his father, and said, My father: and he said, Here am I, my son. And he said, Behold the fire and the wood: but where is the lamb for a burnt offering? ₈And Abraham said, My son, God will provide himself a lamb for a burnt offering: so they went both of them together. ₉And they came to the place which God had told him of; and Abraham built an altar there, and laid the wood in order, and bound Isaac his son, and laid him on the altar upon the wood. ₁₀And Abraham stretched forth his hand, and took the knife to slay his son. ₁₁And the angel of the Lord called unto him out of heaven, and said, Abraham, Abraham: and he said, Here am I. ₁₂And he said, Lay not thine hand upon the lad, neither do thou any thing unto him: for now I know that thou fearest God, seeing thou hast not withheld thy son, thine only son from me. ₁₃And Abraham lifted up his eyes, and looked, and behold behind him a ram caught in a thicket by his horns: and Abraham went and took the ram, and offered him up for a burnt offering in the stead of his son. ₁₄And Abraham called the name of that place Jehovahjireh: as it is said

to this day, In the mount of the Lord it shall be seen. ₁₅And the angel of the Lord called unto Abraham out of heaven the second time, ₁₆And said, By myself have I sworn, saith the Lord, for because thou hast done this thing, and hast not withheld thy son, thine only son: ₁₇That in blessing I will bless thee, and in multiplying I will multiply thy seed as the stars of the heaven, and as the sand which is upon the sea shore; and thy seed shall possess the gate of his enemies; ₁₈And in thy seed shall all the nations of the earth be blessed; because thou hast obeyed my voice. ₁₉So Abraham returned unto his young men, and they rose up and went together to Beersheba; and Abraham dwelt at Beersheba."
Genesis 22:1-19

Several spiritual aspects are revealed in this story of the first sacrificial lamb including:

1. Take "thine only son… whom thou lovest" to sacrifice (verse 2)
2. The son carried the wood for his own sacrifice on his back (verse 6)
3. God will provide Himself a lamb as an offering (verse 8)
4. The Father laying his son on the altar, the son willingly lays there (verse 9)
5. The ram is revealed, caught by his horns (verse 13) in a thicket
6. The substitutionary sacrifice of the ram, allowing Isaac to live (verses 12-13)
7. God's covenant will based on His own merit (verse 16)

8. The eternal blessing follow faith (verses 17 and 18)

These spiritual facets are elaborated further in the first Passover story when details surrounding the selection of the lamb and its powerful blood are provided. Parallels from the Passover Lamb Story to the Abrahamic Lamb include:

1. Take "your lamb" – a personal connection to the lamb (Ex 12:5). Just as Abraham must offer his beloved son, the one with whom he had the deepest relationship, so too must the Jewish nation select a lamb with a personal connection to themselves.

2. God provided the way for Israel to escape death thru a sacrificial lamb (Ex 12:12-13). In a similar manner God provided for Isaac as sacrificial substitute that allowed him to escape death through a ram.

3. The whole assembly was responsible for killing the lamb (Ex 12:6)

4. The selected lamb was to be without blemish (Ex 12:5). The ram caught in the thicket by his thorns would not his fleece harmed. Therefore it remained unblemished. The Passover lamb must also be a perfect substitution without blemish upon its body.

5. The lamb's death was a substitution for the death required in the land of Egypt, allowing the Angel to pass over their homes by its blood (Ex 12:13)

6. Blessings followed the faith action of killing the lamb and anointing the doorposts with blood (Ex 12:13, 12:35-36). Blessing followed the action of faith Abraham performed in offering his only son in verses 17 and 18. God offered not only the blessing of Isaac's physical safety but also the eternal promise of protection and blessing to Abraham's offspring.

While there were spiritual aspects associate with the Principle of First Mention in the Abrahamic Lamb and in the Principle of Progressive Mention of the Exodus Passover lamb, there are additional prophetic fulfillments physically and spiritually in the crucifixion and resurrection of Jesus Christ.

As Abraham was told to take Isaac, his only son whom he loved for a sacrifice, New Testament Scriptures report Jesus was God's only begotten & beloved Son (John 3:16 & Mark 1:11). Jesus was the Lamb of God (John 1:29) given as a sacrifice for the world (John 3:16).

Jesus carried His cross up the mountain of Calvary upon which He would later be sacrificed. This action is portrayed in the image of Isaac carrying the wood up the mountain for his own sacrifice.

God offered Jesus as a His lamb (John 1:29), whose blood would be shed for the sins of the world. The Book of Hebrews 9:22 reaffirmed the Old Testament principle that without the shedding of blood there can be no forgiveness of sin. 1 John 1:7 explained Jesus' blood purified Believers from their sins, a concept repeated in Matthew 26:28 and Ephesians 1:7.

The Passover lamb was an offering of blood to escape the wrath of God that was to be poured out upon the sins of Egypt. Similarly, Jesus was an offering for sin (Romans 8:3) so that those who would believe in Him would not experience the wrath of God on their sin.

Just as the Abrahamic lamb was caught in the thicket by its horns so that its body would not have any blemish and the

Passover lamb was ordered to have no blemish in its body, Jesus was without sin (1 Peter 1:19). Jesus' lack of blemish is on a deeper spiritual level than the fleshy aspect of His body. There can be no denying Jesus' body had multiple blemishes from the scourging He endured to bring Believers physical healing; however that physical 'blemish' upon His body inflicted by men did not disqualify His spiritual perfection. No man in his flesh can see God; therefore God was not looking upon the outward body of Jesus but upon His inner man for spiritual blemish. Finding none, Jesus was the perfect sacrifice.

The horns on a ram are obviously at the top of its head. The ram in the thicket on the mountain by its horns was a symbolic portrait of the real Lamb of God who would one day wear a crown of thorns upon His head. While there is no association of thorns to the Passover lamb, the Abrahamic lamb does mention this detail for a clear prophetic picture of God's lamb at the top of the mountain of Golgotha.

One parallel regarding the death of the Abrahamic and Passover lambs that clearly relates to Christ is that the entire nation of the Jews was responsible for the death of the lamb. Abraham being the patriarch symbolized the entire Jewish nation yet to come when he offered the lamb on Mount Moriah. The Passover lamb also represented a national event for which all Jews were required to participate or experience death. Similarly, the entire nation of Israel was figuratively responsible for Jesus' death (Matt 27:24-25 & John 19:6). Together, they selected Jesus as the Passover on Nisan 10th and shouted for His crucifixion on Nisan 14th. However, Jesus stated no man could take His life; He laid it down (John 10:18). Unlike the animal lambs that had no choice in their selection as sacrificial lambs, Jesus embraced His personality as Passover lamb knowing He was the only one capable of taking away the sins of the world. Therefore, Jesus' willingly accepted the identity as Passover Lamb for the nation of Israel and all those who would by faith believe like Abraham.

As the Abrahamic ram in the thicket served as a substitute sacrifice in lieu of Isaac, Jesus was the propitiation or substitute sacrifice for humanity (2 Corinthians 5:21, 1 John 2:2, 1 John 4:10). Similarly, as the Passover lamb was a death substitute representative whose blood was spread upon the lintel and doorposts. Upon seeing death from the lamb's blood, the Angel of Death passed over the houses of Israel in the land of Egypt. Therefore, the Passover lamb's death served as a substitute for the first born of the house whose blood it covered.

In the story of the Abrahamic lamb, God was responsible for providing the sacrificial animal that spared Isaac although Abraham still had to slaughter the lamb and put it on the altar. Similarly, God was responsible for establishing the ordination that allowed Israel to escape the Angle of Death but the Israelites had to slaughter the lamb and place its blood on the doorposts. The initiation of the New Covenant was based on the death of Christ who was crucified by the hands of men. However, that is where the similarities end between these three types of lambs as the New Covenant in Jesus is based on His Actions, not any of a man's own works (Ephesians 2:8-9, Titus 3:5-6).

Faith was the ultimate catalyst for the lamb events mentioned in the Book of Genesis, Exodus, and the gospels. Blessings flowed to those who by faith believed God and followed His commandment to offer a sacrificial lamb. Blessings still flow to those who by faith receive Jesus as Savior (Romans 4:3-8, 8:17) and keep the command of God,

"For this is the work of God, that you believe in Him who He hath sent" (John 6:29).

A Lamb, The Lamb, Your Lamb

The literal physical salvation of Israel exempting them from the plague of death while Egypt experienced destruction has a spiritual inference as well. The first Passover in Egypt foreshadowed Yaweh's salvation for anyone who accepted His lamb and was covered by its blood sacrifice. God's shed blood would provide an escape the curse of sin and death. Just as God instructed Moses to have each household select a lamb without blemish or spot, correspondingly the Lamb of God needed to be without imperfection. While the natural lamb was to be free from physical flaws, the Lamb of God must be free from spiritual flaws (or sin) in order to be accepted as a perfect spiritual sacrifice for any sinner's substitution.

On the tenth of Nisan, Israel was to take a lamb into their house where it would be cared for four days (Exodus 12:3-6). During this time, the lamb was inspected for flaws and loved within the home. One can only imagine the attachment that occurred between household members, especially the children, and the young lamb sleeping in their home. After a period of four days, it would be hard to stay emotionally disconnected from any affection for the lamb. A personal relationship between the people and the lamb would have deepened the impact of its death upon their hearts and minds. Knowing that killing an innocent, perfect lamb was the only method to escape imminent death must have been emotionally disturbing to the Jewish family, making very tangible the consequences of sin and the cost of their redemption from death.

The language in Scripture even portrays a developing emotional relationship between the Jews and the sacrificial lamb. The Bible begins describing the Passover lamb with the article "a" denoting some random lamb. "They shall take to them every man *'a lamb'* according to the house of their fathers, *'a lamb'* for a house" (Exodus 12:3). There is no attachment or delineation made to personally identify any specific lamb at the beginning of the Book of Exodus. The Passover lamb has no distinctive connection to the people for whom it will be sacrificed. However, by the next verse (verse 4), the article before the word "lamb" changes to the word "the." Now, the lamb is no longer some random lamb. "The lamb" is a specific lamb, which can be individually identified from all other lambs. As the scriptures expound a little further in verse four and repeated again in verse five, the chosen Passover lamb is referred to in the most personal manner. It is now identified as "your lamb." The lamb in question is no longer just any lamb, nor is it only the lamb that can be independently identified; it has become deeply personal. It has become "your lamb."

Similarly, a spiritual element of a deepening personal connection must be made with the Lamb of God. All creation has been endowed with the knowledge that *"a God"* exists (Romans 1:19-20). However, this generic concept or knowledge of *"a God"* must transcend into the experience or encounter with *"the Living God."* This individual encounter with *"the God"* enables one to specifically identify the attributes of the real God, delineating Him from all other imitations. At this point, like with the natural lamb, the essential foundations of a personal relationship with *the God* have been laid. Now one must move beyond acknowledgement of *"a God,"* above the ability to simply identify *"the God,"* and transition into the extremely personal position being *"your God."* A Believer transcends the final phase from knowledge of *the God* to a personal relationship with God through a personal encounter of God based on His truth. When one encounters God at this level, there can be no denial of the sinful nature of self or the exceeding goodness and mercy of God. A person is left simply to accept the Grace of God by faith and believe God is his/her Savior (Psalm 38:22, 78:35, 95:1; Isaiah 12:2, 43:11; Matthew 1:21; 1 Timothy 2:3; Titus 2:13; Jude 25). God becomes *"your God."* The perfect Lamb of God is God Himself in human form, and in order for His blood to cover any man there must first exist a personal relationship with the Lamb of God. Therefore, just as the Israelite household was deeply and personally impacted by their relationship to their innocent lamb and its death, Believers are forever changed by their relationship with the amazingly beautiful and innocent Lamb of God and His corresponding horrific cost for their redemption. However, unlike the natural lamb, God's Lamb has been resurrected to eternal life, evermore intertwined in the hearts and lives of Believers.

Fault Finding at Home

In the first Exodus story, as mentioned above, the Pesach lamb was to be taken into the house on the tenth of Nisan and remain inside until the fourteenth of Nisan. The purpose of the lamb staying in the house was to identify the sacrificial lamb with the residents of home and to provide the occupants a period of time to detect any flaws in the lamb that would disqualify it from being a perfect sacrifice. Both of these aspects have spiritual parallels for the life of Christ. As the Lamb of God, Jesus was received by the nation of Israel upon His triumphal entry into Jerusalem on Nisan 10th. The Jewish nation openly embraced Jesus as their Messiah, shouting in Mark 11:9, "Hosanna; Blessed is he that cometh in the name of the Lord." Upon arriving in Jerusalem, Jesus entered into Israel's spiritual house, "And Jesus entered into Jerusalem, and into the temple" (Mark 11:11). Biblical scholars recognize the Temple as the 'spiritual house' for the Jews. Jesus himself stated this fact directly, "Behold your house [Temple] is left unto you desolate" (Matthew 23:38 & Luke 13:35). After arriving inside the Temple, the Scriptures record the children of Israel cried out to Jesus, "Hosanna to the Son of David" (Matthew 21:15). Again this is indicative of the Jewish nation receiving Jesus formally into their house. This action also clearly identifies Jesus with the nation of Israel as their sacrificial lamb.

Not only does the Temple serve as Israel's spiritual house, it also functions as Jesus' Father's house. In Luke 2:49, the King James Version of the Bible is weak in its translation of the Greek. The Greek interlinear wording actually has Jesus responding to His mother's question with the following, "And He said to them, why [is it] that you were seeking me? Know you not that in *the house of my Father* it behooves me to be?" Not only does Jesus refer to the Temple as His father's house as a child, but also calls it His Father's house as an adult.

> "$_{16}$And said unto them that sold doves, Take these things hence; make not *my Father's house* an house of merchandise."
> John 2:16

Therefore, the Jewish Temple had a dual meaning, serving both as the spiritual house of the Jews and the House of God, Jesus' father. Because the lamb was required to remain in the house for inspection, we see Christ appearing daily at the Temple from Nisan 10th to Nisan 14th. It is important to understand that the scriptures record God found no fault or blemish in His Son. On the mount of transfiguration, the Father declares of Jesus the following, "This is my beloved Son, hear Him" (Mark 9:7, Luke 9:35, 2 Peter 1:17). Israel's Sanhedrin also found no fault in Christ when they challenged His knowledge of Scripture. It is recorded that after the Sadducees were silenced by Jesus, the Pharisees tried to ensnare Him with words, but He confounded them all, and afterwards "no man was able to answer him a word, neither durst any man from that day forth ask him any more questions" (Matthew 22:46).

On the morning of Nisan 14th, when Jesus went before the High Priest of Israel for examination by witnesses, no two witnesses could agree on any evil or Torah violation for which Jesus could have been pronounced guilty (Matthew 26:59-60, Mark 14:55-56). The only charge leveled against Him by the High Priest was based on Jesus' confession of being the Son of God. If Jesus had not been the Son of God, He would have violated the Torah being guilty of blasphemy and deserving of death. However, since Jesus was the true Son of God, His statement was not a spiritual blemish or a violation of the Torah. Therefore, Jesus after being presented to His own house was found without blemish and could become the perfect spiritual sacrifice.

Bloodstained Doorposts

The Passover lamb was to be sacrificed on Nisan 14th, and its blood smeared on the doorpost and lintel (Exodus 13:6-7). Blood by its very nature is a liquid. Covering the lintel and doorposts of a dwelling in ancient Egypt with blood would have eventually resulted in the blood dripping down onto the ground on threshold, in front of the door, creating a blood-based seal all the way around the entrance.

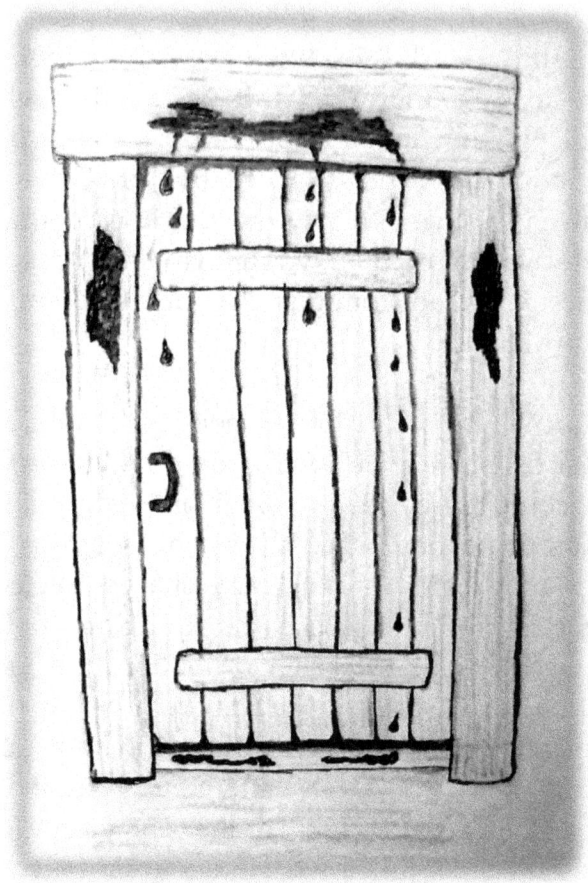

Illustration 2

Upon sealing their doors, the Israelites had to pass thru the bloody entrance of their homes to find refuge from the coming plague of death upon the land of Egypt. This literal, physical event provides a vivid, symbolic imagery enabling Believers to better comprehend Jesus's statements comparing Himself to a door. Jesus said, "I am the door of the sheep" (John 10:7), and "I am the door: by me if any man enter in, he shall be saved, and shall go in and out and find pasture" (John 10:9). The symbolic door to eternal life spoken of by Jesus in the New Testament parallels the physical door to life the Israelites in Egypt entered through to find refuge from the last plague of death. Christ isn't just a door; He is a door sealed by sacrificial blood, His very own blood. It is only by passing thru the blood-sealed door of Jesus that one may find eternal rest in the Kingdom of God and be saved from the second death. Those who take refuge under the blood of Jesus are protected from condemnation. The New Covenant He gave was sealed with His blood.

> "$_{27}$And he took the cup, and gave thanks, and gave it to them, saying, Drink ye all of it; $_{28}$For this is my blood of the new testament, which is shed for many for the remission of sins."
> Matthew 26:27-28

> "$_{23}$And he took the cup, and when he had given thanks, he gave it to them: and they all drank of it. $_{24}$And he said unto them, This is my blood of the new testament, which is shed for many."
> Mark 14:23-24

The concept of a divinely protected home from the enemy of death is reflected just one generation later. In the story of the battle of Jericho, Rahab (the harlot) and her family were protected from death by a scarlet thread placed in the window of her home (Joshua 2:12-21). Unlike the rest of people in Jericho who died, everyone inside Rahab's home was delivered because of her public profession of faith in Israel's God (Joshua 6:22-25), which was demonstrated by the red cord. Interestingly Rahab's scarlet thread served the same purpose as the blood on the doorposts and lintel during the time of the Exodus. When the walls of Jericho fell down, Rahab's house stood firm, even though it was on the wall. Death passed over Rahab's house not only from the attacking Israelites but also from the supernatural destruction of the walls. Just as a generation earlier in Egypt witnessed divine protection form the crimson blood on the doorposts which identified Israel with God's protection, Rahab's scarlet thread allowed her home to be divinely passed over. Rahab's faithfulness also resulted in her own blood intertwining into the lineage of Jesus Christ.

> "… $_{24}$to Jesus the mediator of the new covenant, and to the blood of sprinkling, that speaketh better things than that of Abel"
> Hebrews 12:24

Matthew Henry, a famous bible commentator noted in his notes on Exodus chapter 12 that the Passover lamb's blood was to be sprinkled on the lintel as an act of the person applying the "merits" of the lamb's sacrifice to their own lives. He compared the Israelite's action to Believers who must by faith apply the promises of God in Christ to their lives, openly professing their faith in Jesus for the world to see. Believers will always be protected from death by the blood of Jesus, because His blood covers them spiritually and can be seen by the Holy Spirit of God at all times.

Migdal Eder – The Tower of the Flock

Pastor Joseph Prince preached a Christmas sermon (Sermon #290) regarding the Tower of the Flock or "Migdal Eder" in Hebrew. In this sermon, Pastor Prince noted Jewish scholar Alfred Edersheim's book <u>The Life and Times of Jesus Messiah</u> had significant insight regarding the place of birth for Jesus Christ. Because mangers were prevalent in the First Century, Edersheim concluded Migdal Eder was the reason no directions were given by the angels to the shepherds in Bethlehem regarding which manger the Christ would be lying in when they told the shepherds to go and see the Christ child. While Christmas is a completely different season from Passover, Migdal Eder has an important influence on the Passover story.

During Biblical times, there existed two different Bethlehems. One was Bethlehem Zebulum, which was located about six miles northwest of Nazareth. The other was Bethlehem Ephratah located south of Jerusalem.

> "$_{10}$And the third lot came up *for the children of Zebulun* according to their families: and the border of their inheritance was unto Sarid: $_{11}$And their border went up toward the sea, and Maralah, and reached to Dabbasheth, and reached to the river that is before Jokneam; $_{12}$And turned from Sarid eastward toward the sunrising unto the border of Chislothtabor, and then goeth out to Daberath, and goeth up to Japhia, $_{13}$And from thence passeth on along on the east to Gittahhepher, to Ittahkazin, and goeth out to Remmonmethoar to Neah; $_{14}$And the border compasseth it on the north side to Hannathon: and the outgoings thereof are in the valley of Jiphthahel: $_{15}$And Kattath, and Nahallal, and Shimron, and Idalah, and *Bethlehem*: twelve cities with their villages."
> Joshua 19:10-15

While two cities baring the name Bethlehem existed in Israel, within the Old Testament there was no discrepancy among the Jewish scholars that Messiah would be born in Bethlehem Ephratah:

"₂But thou, Bethlehem Ephratah, though thou be little among the thousands of Judah, yet out of thee shall he come forth unto me that is to be ruler in Israel; whose goings forth have been from of old, from everlasting."
Micah 5: 2

Though Zebulum would have been closer to Joseph and Mary's current dwelling, the prophet Micah declared the Messiah would be born in Bethlehem Ephratah, located south of Jerusalem, which was approximately eighty (80) miles south of Nazareth. Therefore, Joseph and Mary traveled a great distance to fulfill this prophecy. Bethlehem Ephratah was the place where Rachel died and was entombed in Genesis 35:19-20. It was also the setting for the story of Ruth, which portrays the theme of Kinsman Redeemer. Bethlehem was the place of birth for King David and where Samuel anointed him king over Israel (see 1 Samuel 16:4-13). In the remainder of this section, we will refer only to the Bethlehem of Ephratah.

Bethlehem was located a mere six miles south of Jerusalem. As such, this small rural village was an important site for raising sacrificial animals for the Temple in Jerusalem. Alfred Edersheim noted in his book that Mishnic passages (Jewish Oral Traditions and Torah understandings written in 200 AD) provided the following understanding about Migdal Eder located in Bethlehem:

> "That the Messiah was to be born in Bethlehem, was a settled conviction.
>
> Equally so was the belief, that He was to be revealed from *Migdal Eder*, 'the tower of the flock.' This ***Migdal Eder* was *not* the watchtower for the ordinary**

flocks, which pastured on the barren sheepground beyond Bethlehem, but lay close to the town, on the road to Jerusalem.

A passage in the Mishnah leads to the conclusion, *that the flocks, which pastured there, were destined for Temple-sacrifices, and, accordingly, that the shepherds, who watched over them, were not ordinary shepherds.*

The latter were under the ban of Rabbinism, on account of their necessary isolation from religious ordinances, and their manner of life, which rendered strict legal observance unlikely, if not absolutely impossible."[18]

Edersheim's conclusion from Jewish literature was that Messiah would not only be born in Bethlehem but would be revealed at a specific watchtower responsible for overseeing all the Temple's sacrificial sheep. The name of this precise tower was "Migdal Eder" interpreted in English as the Tower of the Flocks. It was Edersheim's scholarly opinion that the shepherds to whom the angels appeared to herald the news of Jesus' birth did not require specific instruction as to which manger among the hundreds in Bethlehem the Savior lay, because the shepherds would have understood about the importance of Migdal Eder. The prophet Micah also mentioned this tower. Connecting the two prophecies in the Book of Micah regarding the birth of the Messiah would indicate Jesus should not only be born in Bethlehem, but specifically in the Tower of the Flock or Migdal Eder.

"And thou, *O tower of the flock*, the strong hold of the daughter of Zion, *unto thee shall it come*, even

the first dominion; *the kingdom shall come to the daughter of Jerusalem."*
Micah 4:8

The spiritual application derived from this verse sheds new insight on Jesus as the Passover lamb to be born in "the tower of the flock." Since this particular place in Bethlehem was responsible for tending all the sacrificial sheep offered at the Temple in Jerusalem, Jesus being laid in Migdel Eder's manger pointed directly to His position and identity as the perfect sacrificial Lamb of God.

Place & Timing of the Death

Deuteronomy 16:5 ascribed a specific condition regarding the location of the place of death the Passover lamb should occur. The lamb could not be killed inside the gates of any city God would give the Israelites in the Promise Land. Thus to fulfill this commandment, Jesus was crucified outside the gates of Jerusalem.

> "₅Thou mayest not sacrifice the passover within any of thy gates, which the LORD thy God giveth thee"
> Deuteronomy 16:5

According to Hebrews 13:12, "Jesus also, that *he* might sanctify the people with his own blood, *suffered without the gate.*" This scripture confirms that Golgotha was located outside of the main city gates of Jerusalem. By being crucified outside the city, Jesus fulfilled the Torah location for the place of death of the Passover lamb.

In addition to the location regarding the place of death for the Passover lamb to be killed (outside the city gates), Jesus literally fulfilled the Scriptural references regarding the timing of the death of the Passover lamb. The Passover lamb was to be killed in the evening, which according to Jewish interpretation is during the evening sacrifice at 3:00 PM and before the sunset on Nisan 14th.

> "₆And ye shall keep it up until the fourteenth day of the same month: and the whole assembly of the congregation of Israel shall kill it in the evening."
> Exodus 12:6

The Jewish Encyclopedia also specifically recounts the time for the Passover sacrificial lamb to be killed after 3:00 PM and before sunset.

> "The sacrificial animal, which was either a lamb or kid, was necessarily a male, one year old, and without blemish. Each family or society offered one victim together, which did not require the "semikah" (laying on of hands), although it was obligatory to determine who were to take part in the sacrifice that the killing might take place with the proper intentions. Only those who were circumcised and clean before the Law might participate; and they were forbidden to have leavened food in their possession during the act of killing the paschal lamb. The animal was slain on the eve of the Passover, on the afternoon of the 14th of Nisan, after the Tamid sacrifice had been killed, *i.e.*, at three o'clock, or, in case the eve of the Passover fell on Friday, at two."[19]

Similarly, Josephus, the famous Jewish historian, documented the day and time of the traditional slaughter of the Passover lamb stating the evening sacrifice was at the ninth hour (3:00 PM) until the 11th hour (5:00 PM).

"Any one may hence learn how very great piety we exercise towards God and the observance of his laws, since the priests were not at all hindered from their sacred ministrations by their fear during the siege, but did still twice each day, in the morning and about the **ninth hour [3:00 PM]**, offer their sacrifices on the altar."[20]

"Cestius, desiring to inform Nero, who was inclined to condemn the nation, of the power of the city, requested the high priests to take a count, if possible, of the entire population. So these high priests did so upon the arrival of their feast which is called the Passover. On this day they slay their sacrifices *from the ninth hour [3:00 PM] until the eleventh [5:00 PM]*, with a company [*phatria*] of not less than ten belonging to every sacrifice -- for it is not lawful for them to have the feast singly by themselves -- and many of us are twenty in a company."[21]

The Gospel of Mark clearly identifies the timeline surrounding Jesus' death from crucifixion after 3:00 PM. This death after 3:00 PM places the timing of Messiah's death within the exact timing of the Passover lambs were being sacrificed by the Levitical priesthood for Israel.

"[33]And when *the sixth hour* [12:00 pm] was come, there was darkness over the whole land until *the ninth hour* [3:00 PM]. [34]And *at the ninth hour* [3:00 PM] Jesus cried with a loud voice, saying, E'lo-i, E'lo-i, la'ma sa-bach'tha-ni? which is, being interpreted, My God, my God, why hast thou forsaken me? [35]And some of them that stood by, when they heard it, said,

> Behold, he calleth Elias. ₃₆And one ran and filled a sponge full of vinegar, and put it on a reed, and gave him to drink, saying, Let alone; let us see whether Elias will come to take him down. ₃₇And Jesus cried with a loud voice, and gave up the ghost."
> Mark 15:33-37

Thus, every aspect surrounding Jesus' death with regard to the date, location, and time of day fulfilled the Torah requirements for the Passover lamb's sacrifice. Not only was Jesus the perfect lamb, without spot or blemish spiritually (1 Peter 1:19), but He died on the correct date of Nisan 14th after 3:00 PM during the same hour the Levitical priests were slaughtering the lambs outside the city gates. "For indeed Christ, our Passover, was sacrificed for us" (1 Corinthians 5:7).

Consumption of the Lamb

Many of the Torah mandates given in the Book of Exodus have prophetic symbology associated with the literal consumption of the Passover lamb. The first allusion to prophecy is in regard to the cooking of the lamb, which had to be roasted with fire.

> "₈And they shall eat the flesh in that night, ***roast with fire, and unleavened bread; and with bitter herbs they shall eat it.*** ₉***Eat not of it raw, nor sodden at all with water, but roast with fire***; his head with his legs, and with the purtenance thereof. ₁₀And ye shall **let *nothing of it remain until the morning;*** and ***that which remaineth of it until the morning ye shall burn with fire***. ₁₁And thus shall ye eat it; with your loins girded,

> your shoes on your feet, and your staff in your hand; and ye shall eat it in haste: it is the LORD's passover."
> Exodus 12:8-11

The roasting of the lamb with fire corresponded to the suffering Christ would endure in taking the fiery wrath of God upon Himself in place of sinners. For God declares "in flaming fire" vengeance will be taken on those who know not God (2 Thessalonians 1:8). By His sacrificial death, Jesus took away the flaming wrath of God from mankind.

> "$_9$Much more then, being now justified by his blood, *we shall be saved from wrath* through him."
> Romans 5:9

Jesus' death appeased and satisfied the righteous demands of God against sin (Romans 3:24-26). God was perfectly satisfied with the death of Christ. As a propitiatory sacrifice, Jesus' death made provision for sins to be forgiven and put away, not just for a single year but forever:

> "$_{25}$Nor yet that he should offer himself often, as the high priest entereth into the holy place every year with blood of others; $_{26}$For then must he often have suffered since the foundation of the world: but now once in the end of the world hath he appeared to put away sin by the sacrifice of himself. $_{27}$And as it is appointed unto men once to die, but after this the judgment: $_{28}$So Christ was once offered to bear the sins of many; and unto them that look for him shall he appear the second time without sin unto salvation."
> Hebrews 9:25-28

It is also interesting to note the Passover sacrificial lamb was never too small. There was a chance the household could be too little as outlined in Exodus 12:4; in such cases, households were encouraged to join together to share one lamb. The Passover lamb however was never too small, not even for the largest of households. This analogy beautifully portrays Jesus, as sacrificial lamb, who would be bigger than all the sins of the world combined. His sacrifice was so perfect and so enormous that it covered every sinner and every sin from the past, present and future. The Passover lamb was the only sacrifice ever large enough to cover the wrath of God permanently. It is also the only sacrifice which men were encouraged by God to share with each other to escape death.

Additionally in verse eleven of Exodus chapter twelve, the Israelites are commanded to eat the lamb "in haste" because "it is the LORD's [Yahweh's] Passover." The awareness of the need for haste in the Exodus account echoes a sense of urgency the world needs to understand. A day has been appointed for all men to appear before the Throne of God to give account for their lives, "because He hath appointed a day, in the which He will judge the world in righteousness by that man [Jesus]" (Acts 17:31).

Only those who have by faith partaken of the LORD's Passover lamb (Jesus) will be spared from the second death, "Blessed and holy is he that hath part in the first resurrection: on such the second death hath no power" (Revelations 20:6). Today is the day of salvation declares God repeatedly in the scriptures. There is no promise of tomorrow given to any man.

> "Boast not thyself of tomorrow; for thou knowest not what a day may bring forth."
> Proverbs 27:1

"₁₄Whereas ye know not what shall be on the morrow. For what is your life? It is even a vapor, that appeareth for a little time, then vanisheth away."
James 4:14

Believers feeding on the Lamb of God are offered protection from eternal death today. Every man is only one heartbeat away from physical death. Therefore, the urgent call goes forth, calling all sinners to repentance; "behold, **now** is the accepted time; behold, **now** is the day of salvation" (2 Corinthians 6:2). Today the world is urged to partake of God's lamb and be spared eternal death, which will befall all those not covered by His blood.

CHAPTER 3

FEAST OF UNLEAVENED BREAD

Unleavened Bread Defined

The Feast of Unleavened Bread is a weeklong celebration of the deliverance of the children of Israel from bondage in Egypt. It begins on the night of Nisan 15th and extends until Nisan 21st. During this week, there are two holy convocation days: the first day (Nisan 15th) and the last day (Nisan 21st) of the week. In addition to being called the Feast of Unleavened Bread, both the Bible and the Jewish nation use the term "Passover" to refer to "the Feast of Unleavened Bread" celebration because it was during this night (Nisan 15th) that the Lord passed-over the houses of Israel when the Angel of Death went forth to slay the firstborn in the land of Egypt (Exodus 12:15 & 19).

Torah Mandate & Historical Setting

The twelfth chapter in the Book of Exodus provides the historical account of the first Passover and the mandate from God for future Jewish generations to commemorate the events that happened that fateful night so long ago in Egypt (Exodus 12:14). During the first Passover, the nation of Israel was awaiting deliverance, which was to arrive quickly after the last plague occurred. The last plague would be the death of all the first born in Egypt, from man to beast. Upon the discovery of thousands of deaths in the land of Egypt, including Pharaoh's own son, Pharaoh thrust Israel out of Egypt. The nation of Israel left quickly, and as a result, they did not have time for their bread to rise before baking. Thus, the Lord told them to eat their Passover lamb with unleavened bread.

> *",Thou shalt eat no leavened bread with it [the Passover lamb]; seven days shalt thou eat unleavened bread therewith, even the bread of affliction; for thou camest forth out of the land of Egypt in haste: that thou mayest remember the day when thou camest forth out of the land of Egypt all the days of thy life. And there shall be no leavened bread seen with thee in all thy coast seven days;* neither shall there any thing of the flesh, which thou sacrificedst the first day at even, remain all night until the morning."
> Deuteronomy 16:3

In addition to the Torah requirement to consume the Passover lamb with unleavened bread, Israel was not to eat leavened bread for the entire seven day time period following Nisan 14th. This time of unleavened bread was to memorialize the journey of the nation of Israel's flight from slavery in Egypt. Israel left Egypt on the morning of Nisan 15th. They crossed the Red Sea on the morning of the seventeenth. Exodus 15:22 records after crossing the Red Sea, Israel traveled three more days in the wilderness without water. On the sixth day of their wondering, Israel came to Mar'ah, where God supernaturally provided fresh water from bitter waters. The Scriptures report Israel then moved from Mar'ah to camp at E'lim, where there were twelve wells of water and numerous palm trees. Thus, the time period of travel from their slave dwellings in Egypt to the camp at E'lim was seven days. It was at E'lim Israel finally obtained rest and could prepare leaven bread. Unleavened bread is called the bread of affliction (Deuteronomy 16:3) because Israel suffered great affliction in slavery in Egypt and also on their journey from Egypt, which lasted seven days.

In addition to the absence of leavened bread during mealtime, Torah Law required the removal of all leaven from the house. The Hebrew word for 'leaven' is *"chametz."* Originally, chametz referred to barley or wheat combined with water and allowed to rise or ferment.

> "₃Thou *shalt eat no leavened bread* with it; *seven days shalt thou eat unleavened bread* therewith, even the bread of affliction; for thou camest forth out of the land of Egypt in haste: that thou mayest remember the day when thou camest forth out of the land of Egypt all the days of thy life. ₄And *there shall be no leavened bread seen with thee in all thy coast seven days*; neither shall there any thing of the flesh, which thou sacrificest the first day at even, remain all night until the morning."
> Deuteronomy 16:3-4

> ₁₇And ye shall observe *the feast of unleavened bread*; for in this selfsame day have I brought your armies out of the land of Egypt: therefore shall ye observe this day in your generations by an ordinance forever. ₁₈In the first month, on the fourteenth day of the month at even, ye shall eat unleavened bread, until the one and twentieth day of the month at even. ₁₉*Seven days shall there be no leaven found in your houses: for whosoever eateth that which is leavened, even that soul shall be cut off from the congregation*

of Israel, whether he be a stranger, or born in the land. $_{20}$*Ye shall eat nothing leavened;* in all your habitations shall ye eat unleavened bread."
Exodus 12:17-20

The Feast of Unleavened Bread is one of the seven feasts appointed by God in the twenty-third chapter of the Book of Leviticus and in the twenty eighth chapter of the Book of Numbers, in which all of Israel must appear before Him (Deuteronomy 16:16). These feast days were intended to be holy days for Israel to meet with God.

"$_1$And the LORD spoke to Moses saying, Speak to the children of Israel, and say unto them concerning the feasts of the LORD, which ye shall proclaim to be holy convocations, even these are my feasts. $_2$These are the feasts of the Lord, holy convocations, which ye shall proclaim in their seasons. In the fourteenth of the first month at even is the Lord's Passover... $_4$These are the feasts of the LORD, holy convocations, which ye shall proclaim in their seasons. $_5$In the fourteenth day of the first month at even is the LORD's Passover. $_6$And on the fifteenth day of the same month is the feast of unleavened bread unto the Lord: seven days ye must eat unleavened bread. $_7$In the first day ye shall have an holy convocation: ye shall do no servile work therein. But ye shall offer an offering made by fire unto the LORD seven days: in the seventh day is an holy convocation: ye shall do no servile work therein."
Leviticus 23:1-2, 4-7

"$_{16}$And in the fourteenth day of the first month is the Passover of the LORD. $_{17}$And in the fifteenth day of this month is the feast: seven days shall unleavened

bread be eaten. ₁₈In the first day shall be an holy convocation: ye shall do no manner of servile work: ₁₉But ye shall offer a sacrifice made by fire for a burnt offering unto the LORD: two young bullocks, and one ram, and seven lambs of the first year: they shall be unto you without blemish… ₂₅And on the seventh day ye shall have an holy convocation: ye shall do no servile work."
Numbers 28:16-19 & 25

Spiritual Relevance:

Unleavened Bread

Unleavened bread can spiritually represent the Mosaic Law in general because it was during the first Feast of Unleavened Bread that Israel received a covenant with God. The Holy Spirit speaking in the Book of Hebrews states that the first covenant (commonly referred to as the Mosaic Law) was made with Israel not at Mt. Sinai as is traditionally held, but rather the first covenant was made in the day that God took them out of the land of Egypt, on Nisan 15th.

> "₇For if that ***first covenant*** had been faultless, then should no place have been sought for the second. ₈For finding fault with them, he saith, Behold, the days come, saith the Lord, when I will make a new covenant with the house of Israel and with the house of Judah: ₉***Not according to the [first] covenant that I made with their fathers <u>in the day when I took them by the hand to lead them out of the land of Egypt</u>***; because they continued not in my covenant, and I regarded them not, saith the Lord.
> Hebrews 8:7-9

The Hebraic word for unleavened bread is the Strong's #4682, *matstsah*. The definition of matstsah comes from the Hebrew root word *matsats* (Strong's #4711), in the sense of greedily devouring for sweetness, and means *"milk,"* or *"to suck milk."*[22] Thus, the root of "unleavened bread" means milk. The New Testament Scriptures refer to a difference between the milk and the strong meat of the Word of God, obviously giving preeminence to the strong meat.

> "[12]For when for the time you ought to be teachers, ye have need that one teach you again which be the *first principles of the oracles of God*; and are become such as have *need of milk*, and not of strong meat. [13]For *every one that useth milk is <u>unskillful in the word of righteousness</u>: for he is a babe*. [14]But *strong meat belongeth to them that are of full age*, even those who by reason of use have their senses exercised to discern both good and evil".
> Hebrews 5:12-14

Scripture teaches that unto the Jews was committed *"the oracles of God"* (Romans 3:2). The "first principles" of God literally means: the basic elements or something orderly arranged from the beginning or in an order of rank. Thus, "first principles of the oracles of God" can only refer to the Mosaic Law, the first covenant given by God to the Jews. Those operating under a "milk mentality" are intertwined in the Mosaic Law. Anyone using "milk" is stated to be *unskillfull* (Strong's #552). Literally defined, unskillful means *"ignorant"* or *"inexperienced."* Scripture states milk drinkers are ignorant of the Word of Righteousness, the Logos, which is Jesus Christ. It is no wonder that Jews who reject Jesus are ignorant and inexperience with Him. Those entrenched in the law, like the Pharisees and Sadducees of

Christ's day have a difficult time relating to Messiah. Thus, the milk or unleavened bread of the Word (the Mosaic Law) is the most basic level of instruction given to mankind by God.

Leavening

Chametz, representative of fermented dough, has been symbolically associated with the sins of pride and self-righteousness. Jewish tradition teaches the cleansing of chametz from the homes is a symbolic search for sin within a man's life or heart in order to remove it, to be clean before God. It is often the sin of pride or self-righteousness that puffs-up a man and causes him to rebel against God. Chametz is considered to be any corrupting influence, associated with hidden uncleanness that manipulates purer elements over time. As such, it is searched out diligently for removal. On the night of Nisan 14th, the head of the Jewish household performs a search for chametz. Any chametz found is to be destroyed the following morning (on Nisan 14th) before the sixth hour of the day (11:00 AM) usually by fire.

It is no coincidence that Judas Iscariot is revealed to be the traitor, the corrupted influence within the house of Jesus the Christ, on the night of Nisan 14th. Jesus, the head of His spiritual household, is the one who exposes Judas as the sin among His righteous disciples.

> "$_{10}$Jesus saith to him [Peter], he that is washed needeth not save to wash his feet, but is clean every whit: *and ye are clean, but not all.* $_{11}$*For he knew who should*

> *betray him; therefore said he, Ye are not all clean."*
> John 13:10-11

> "₂₄The Son of man goeth as it is written of him: but woe unto that man by whom the Son of man is betrayed! it had been good for that man if he had not been born. ₂₅Then Judas, which betrayed him, answered and said, Master, is it I? He said unto him, Thou hast said."
> Matthew 26:24-25

Nor is it coincidental that Judas Iscariot destroys himself before the death of Jesus. Judas' death even corresponds with the timing of the destruction of the chametz, which must occur before noon. For Judas upon seeing Jesus condemned by Pilate at approximately 9:00 AM returned the thirty (30) pieces of silver to the Priests as penitence. Upon rejection from the priests, he cast the silver upon the temple floor and immediately went out and hanged himself. Thus, Judas was destroyed before the crucifixion of Christ in accordance with prophetic scriptures regarding the removal of chametz from the house.

> "₃Then Judas, which had betrayed him, when he saw that he was condemned, repented himself, and brought again the thirty pieces of silver to the chief priests and elders, ₄Saying, I have sinned in that I have betrayed the innocent blood. And they said, What is that to us? see thou to that. ₅And he cast down the pieces of silver in the temple, and departed, and went and hanged himself."
> Matthew 27:3-5

Judas is removed from the spiritual House of Jesus and called the "son of perdition" (John 17:12), which means son of eternal damnation. Thus, the house [church] of Jesus was spiritually cleansed from all defects along the timeline set forth in scripture. The source of an anti-Christ influence among the disciples was removed on Nisan 14th before noon. While a comparison can be made somewhat regarding the Head of Household in Jewish tradition seeking out the chametz and destroying it, the analogy does not completely transpose to Jesus. Although Jesus uncovered or exposed the false apostle (representing spiritual chametz), He was not willing to destroy Judas. Jesus' forgiveness and mercy extended even to Judas' sins. However, in Judas' own ignorance of the Son of God's teachings of Grace and truth, Judas tried to earn his own righteous redemption by destroying himself. Such a sad fate awaits all those who trust in their own works to save them.

CHAPTER 4

BIBLICAL RELEVANCE OF NISAN 17

Principle of First Mention

Noah's Ark Finds Rest

As discussed earlier, God often uses the Principle of First Mention to introduce a theme, which He later expounds upon in other parables, each one reinforcing or building upon the last, revealing a deeper truth. The ultimate result of all themes is to unveil the revelation of Jesus as the Christ. The themes associated with the seventeenth of Nisan are salvation, deliverance, redemption, and new beginnings. There are several important events connected with the date Nisan 17th in the Bible. The First Principle of Mention states Noah's Ark rested on Mount Ararat on Nisan 17th.

> "₄And the ark rested in the seventh month, on the seventeenth day of the month, upon the mountains of Ararat."
> Genesis 8:4

If you remember from the previous calendar study in Chapter 1, the Jewish nation has two ways of calculating time: the Religious Calendar and the Civil Calendar. While some people have stated Noah's Ark rested in the month of Tishri (the seventh month on the religious calendar), they are in error because the calendar authorizing Tishri as the seventh month did not come into existence until after the Passover in the Book of Exodus. From the beginning, Jews calculated time from the 6th day of creation, which they called Tishri 1. Therefore, the first month of the original calendar was Tishri, not Nisan. This method of calculating of time remains prevalent in Jewish society today as their civil calendar. On the civil calendar, the seventh month would be Nisan. Therefore, because Noah's flood occurred in Genesis before the Passover in Exodus transformation of calculating time hundreds of years later, the verse in Genesis can only refer to the original calendar timeline (or civil calendar). Therefore, the seventeenth day of the seventh month would refer to Nisan 17th.

Noah's Ark resting upon Mount Ararat is a symbolic portrait of the complete redemption of Noah, his family, and the world's animals within the ark from the wrath of God, which has now found rest. After the wrath of God subsided, the resting of the ark represented new beginnings. The first day the Ark found rest upon dry land foreshadowed the first land on which Noah and his family would step out and begin a new life.

In fact, the Hebrew word for the mountain "Ararat" literally means, "the curse reversed."[23] The symbology of the wording regarding Mt. Ararat itself is prophetic of the date Nisan 17th being the date the curse upon mankind would be completely reversed. While no one should ever underestimate the death of Jesus Christ on the cross, it was His resurrection that declared conclusively that the curse of sin and death had indeed been broken and reversed. The curse of death upon the children of Adam no longer reigns supreme. For those who are in Christ Jesus, death is swallowed up in victory (Isaiah 25:8, 1 Corinthians 15:54). Hence, the first mention of Nisan 17th was the day Noah's Ark rested on the mountain where the "curse reversed" painted a vivid illustration of Jesus's resurrection timeline in future events. Jesus would "reverse the curse" on a mountain called Calvary by his death and resurrection from the grave on the day signaling redemption and new beginnings, Nisan 17th.

Principle of Progressive Mention

The Red Sea Crossing - Book of Exodus

The Nisan 17th themes of deliverance and new beginnings originally displayed in the Book of Genesis during the story of Noah's Ark are further developed in the Passover and exodus story. Numbers 33:3 declares that the children of Israel were released from Egyptian bondage and began their journey to freedom on Nisan 15th.

> "₃And they departed from Rameses in the first month, on the fifteenth day of the first month; on the morrow after the passover the children of Israel went out with an high hand in the sight of all the Egyptians."
> Numbers 33:3

Additionally, we know that Israel left immediately after Pharaoh released them. The timeline for Pharaoh's release occurred sometime after midnight but before the dawn, as scripture reports in verse 31 that Pharaoh called for Moses and Aaron by night.

> "₂₉And it came to pass, that *at midnight the Lord smote all the firstborn* in the land of Egypt, from the firstborn of Pharaoh that sat on his throne unto the firstborn of the captive that was in the dungeon; and all the firstborn of cattle. ₃₀And Pharaoh rose up in the night, he, and all his servants, and all the Egyptians; and there was a great cry in Egypt; for there was not a house where there was not one dead. ₃₁And *he [Pharaoh] called for Moses and Aaron by night, and said, Rise up, and get you forth from among my people, both ye and the children of Israel; and go, serve the Lord, as ye have said.* ₃₂*Also take your flocks and your herds, as ye have said, and be gone*; and bless me also. ₃₃And *the Egyptians were urgent upon the people, that they might send them out of the land in haste*; for they said, We be all dead men."
> Exodus 12:29-33

> "₃₉And they baked unleavened cakes of the dough which they brought forth out of Egypt, for it was not leavened; because *they were thrust out of Egypt, and could not tarry*, neither had they prepared for themselves any victual."
> Exodus 12:39

Therefore upon receiving the edict to vacate Egypt by Pharaoh, Israel went out in haste early in the morning of Nisan 15th. The Exodus story is very detailed regarding the route Israel traveled and the duration of their journey.

> "₁₇And it came to pass, when Pharaoh had let the people go, that God led them not through the way of

> the land of the Philistines, although that was near; for God said, Lest peradventure the people repent when they see war, and they return to Egypt: ₁₈But God led the people about, through the way of the wilderness of the Red sea: and the children of Israel went up harnessed out of the land of Egypt. ₁₉And Moses took the bones of Joseph with him: for he had straitly sworn the children of Israel, saying, God will surely visit you; and ye shall carry up my bones away hence with you. ₂₀**And they took their journey from Succoth, and encamped in E'-tham, in the edge of the wilderness.** ₂₁And the Lord went before them by day in a pillar of a cloud, to lead them the way; and by night in a pillar of fire, to give them light; to go by day and night: ₂₂He took not away the pillar of the cloud by day, nor the pillar of fire by night, from before the people."
> Exodus 13:17-22

After leaving Egypt, Israel traveled toward E'tham. Later that evening which began Nisan 16th, Israel camped in E'-tham for the night. Scripture continued to clarify that God led the children the next day toward Pi-ha-hi'-roth near Ba'al-ze'-phon. This day of travel would begin the following morning on Nisan 16th. God also spoke directly to Moses to inform him that He was going to harden Pharaoh's heart to come after Israel.

> "₁And the Lord spake unto Moses, saying, ₂Speak unto the children of Israel, *that they turn and encamp before Pi-ha-hi'-roth, between Mig'-dol and the sea, over against Ba'-al-ze'-phon*: before it shall ye encamp by the sea. ₃For Pharaoh will say of the children of Israel, They are entangled in the land, the wilderness hath shut them in. ₄And I will harden

Pharaoh's heart, that he shall follow after them; and I will be honoured upon Pharaoh, and upon all his host; that the Egyptians may know that I am the Lord. And they did so."
Exodus 14:1-4

As the children of Israel traveled toward Pi-ha-hi'-roth to camp for the second night, Pharaoh's heart was changed toward them, and he ordered his army to pursue after them, to destroy them. The army of Pharaoh left Egypt to pursue Israel on Nisan 16th during the day while Israel was journeying to Pi-ha-hiroth. By late afternoon (still Nisan 16th) towards the evening of Nisan 17th, Pharaoh's army had almost caught up with Israel. The people panicked, but Moses reassured them God would fight for them.

"$_8$And the Lord hardened the heart of Pharaoh king of Egypt, and he pursued after the children of Israel: and the children of Israel went out with an high hand. $_9$But **the Egyptians pursued after them**, all the horses and chariots of Pharaoh, and his horsemen, and his army, and **overtook them encamping by the sea**, beside Pihahiroth, before Baalzephon. $_{10}$And when Pharaoh drew nigh, the children of Israel lifted up their eyes, and, behold, the Egyptians marched after them; and they were sore afraid: and the children of Israel cried out unto the Lord. $_{11}$And they said unto Moses, Because there were no graves in Egypt, hast thou taken us away to die in the wilderness? wherefore hast thou dealt thus with us, to carry us forth out of Egypt? $_{12}$Is not this the word that we did tell thee in Egypt, saying, Let us alone, that we may serve the Egyptians? For it had been better for us to serve the Egyptians, than that we should die in the wilderness. $_{13}$And Moses said unto the people, Fear ye not, stand

still, and see the salvation of the Lord, which he will shew to you to day: for the Egyptians whom ye have seen to day, ye shall see them again no more for ever. [14]The Lord shall fight for you, and ye shall hold your peace."
Exodus 14:8-14

As Pharaoh's army approaches, the angel of the Lord is described as a pillar of the cloud, indicating this event began during the daylight hours. Exodus 13:21-22 describes the difference between the pillar of the cloud and pillar of fire. The cloud was for daytime travel, and the pillar of fire was to give light at night. In Exodus 14:19, the pillar of a cloud went from before the camp of Israel to behind them, standing between Pharaoh's army and the children of Israel. This *"pillar of a cloud"* is later described to give light unto Israel but darkness unto Pharaoh in Exodus 14:20 as it stood between the two camps all night. Therefore, we see the timeline depicted by the angelic pillar of cloud and fire indicates Pharaoh's army originally approached during the day and was held off later that night by darkness; that night was Nisan 17th. To Israel the pillar gave light, but to the Egyptians only darkness abided.

"[15]And the Lord said unto Moses, Wherefore criest thou unto me? speak unto the children of Israel, that they go forward: [16]But lift thou up thy rod, and stretch out thine hand over the sea, and divide it: and the children of Israel shall go on dry ground through the midst of the sea. [17]And I, behold, I will harden the hearts of the Egyptians, and they shall follow them: and I will get me honour upon Pharaoh, and upon all his host, upon his chariots, and upon his horsemen. [18]And the Egyptians shall know that I am the Lord, when I have gotten me honour upon Pharaoh, upon

> his chariots, and upon his horsemen. ₁₉And *the angel of God, which went before the camp of Israel, removed and went behind them; and the pillar of the cloud went from before their face, and stood behind them*: ₂₀*And it came between the camp of the Egyptians and the camp of Israel; and it was a cloud and darkness to them, but it gave light by night to these: so that the one came not near the other <u>all the night</u>.*"
> Exodus 14:15-20

That night on Nisan 17th Moses stretched out his hand over the Red Sea and the Lord caused a night wind to blow, causing the sea floor to dry. Sometime that night between sunset and dawn, Israel crossed over the sea. The words *"all that night"* in Exodus 14:21 of the King James Version of the bible are translated from one Hebrew word, "layil," which literally means "night." Therefore, the wind was not blowing all night long; instead the correct translation should be a "night wind" blew and dried the land. Understanding the original Hebrew words for the English translation of the Bible regarding the Exodus story clarifies how the next verses regarding the children of Israel crossing the Red Sea, being followed by Pharaoh's army, and the Lord watching the events at "the morning watch" all coincide without any conflict.

> "₂₁And Moses stretched out his hand over the sea; and the Lord caused the sea to go back by *a strong east wind all that night*, and made the sea dry land, and the waters were divided. ₂₂*And the children of Israel went into the midst of the sea upon the dry ground*: and the waters were a wall unto them on their right hand, and on their left. ₂₃*And the Egyptians pursued, and went in after them to the midst of the sea,* even

all Pharaoh's horses, his chariots, and his horsemen. ₂₄And it came to pass, that *in the morning watch* the Lord looked unto the host of the Egyptians *through the pillar of fire and of the cloud,* and troubled the host of the Egyptians, ₂₅And took off their chariot wheels, that they drave them heavily: so that the Egyptians said, Let us flee from the face of Israel; for the Lord fighteth for them against the Egyptians. ₂₆And the Lord said unto Moses, Stretch out thine hand over the sea, that the waters may come again upon the Egyptians, upon their chariots, and upon their horsemen. ₂₇*And Moses stretched forth his hand over the sea, and the sea returned to his strength when the morning appeared;* and the Egyptians fled against it; and the Lord overthrew the Egyptians in the midst of the sea. ₂₈And the waters returned, and covered the chariots, and the horsemen, and all the host of Pharaoh that came into the sea after them; there remained not so much as one of them. ₂₉But the children of Israel walked upon dry land in the midst of the sea; and the waters were a wall unto them on their right hand, and on their left. ₃₀Thus the Lord saved Israel that day out of the hand of the Egyptians; and Israel saw the Egyptians dead upon the sea shore."
Exodus 14:21-30

According to _Smith's Bible Dictionary_, the Jews divided the night into three periods of time for military watches. Each watch would represent four hours of time. The morning watch corresponded to the hours between 2:00 AM until sunrise.[24] Therefore, the Exodus story records precisely the timeline the Egyptians were in the Red Sea attempting to cross on dry land pursuing after the Israelites, who had already crossed over. The Lord looked from Heaven in verse 24 during "the morning watch" and saw Pharaoh's army pursuing Israel. From Smith's definition, we conclude Pharaoh's Red Sea crossing occurred between 2 AM and sunrise. God then instructs Moses to wave his hand over the waters to close the opening in the sea, thus drowning Pharaoh's army. In verse 27, Moses "stretched forth his hand over the sea, and the sea returned to his strength <u>*when the morning appeared*</u>." The English words for the phrase "when the morning" again consist of only one Hebrew word, "boqer," which properly means "dawn." The Hebrew word for "appeared" is "panah" which means, "dawning" or "to appear." Thus, Moses stretched forth his hand on the morning of Nisan 17th as daybreak was just occurring, and Pharaoh's army perished forever with rising of the sun.

Israel is redeemed completely on Nisan 17th after crossing through the Red Sea, reinforcing the first Principle of Mention of redemption, deliverance and new beginnings. In this Progressive Mention Principle, Pharaoh's army is utterly destroyed on Nisan 17th after attempting to cross the sea to annihilate Israel. Similarly, the power of Satan's army forever perished with the resurrection of the Son of God from the dead. For the first time in over 400 years, Israel experienced complete freedom and would never again return to Egyptian slavery. Likewise, Believers are delivered from the slavery to sin by faith in Jesus, never again to return to bondage of the enemy (Hebrews 2:15 and Romans 8:15). Therefore, Nisan 17th symbolizes salvation of God for His children, His supernatural deliverance from their enemies, providing a new beginning for the nation of Israel.

Entering the Promise Land - Joshua

The Book of Joshua begins with the children of Israel preparing to enter Canaan, the Promise Land. In chapter three, Israel miraculously crosses the Jordan River during the time of spring flooding because God is with them and divides the river. Upon entering the Promise Land, all the males of Israel are circumcised and given a period of time for healing while camping at Gil'-gal. At Gil'-gal, Israel keeps the Passover for the third time mentioned in Scripture. The first mention of the observance of Passover was in Egypt (Exodus chapter 12). The second record of Israel keeping the Passover is in Numbers chapter 9 verses 1-5. The Book of Joshua is the third account:

> "$_{10}$And the children of Israel encamped in Gil'-gal, and kept the Passover on the fourteenth day of the month at even in the plains of Jericho. $_{11}$And they did eat of the old grain of the land on the morrow after the Passover, unleavened cakes, and parched grain in the selfsame day. $_{12}$And the man'-na ceased on the morrow after they had eaten of the old grain of the land; neither had the children of Israel man'-na any more; but they did eat of the fruit of the land of Canaan that year."
> Joshua 5:10-12

Scripture provides not only the third mention of Passover, but the specific timeline for the disappearance of the Heavenly manna, indicating the manna stopped on the morning of the 16th of Nisan. The significance of the date the manna ceased highlights the day in which the children of God first ate from the new grain of the Promise Land. In order to properly divide the timeline to prove exactly which day the manna ceased, we must examine every aspect of the

Scriptures. It is also important to remember Israel ate manna continually from the time it was first given until the day it stopped: "And the children of Israel did eat man'-na forty years" (Exodus 16:35). The only exception in the daily giving of manna by God was for His Sabbath:

> "25And Moses said, Eat that today; for today is a Sabbath unto the Lord: today ye shall not find it [manna] in the field. 26Six days ye shall gather it [manna]; but on the seventh day, the Sabbath, in it there shall be none."
> Exodus 16:25-26

The timeline for events of the third Passover began in Joshua chapter five verse ten, which explained that Israel kept the Passover on Nisan 14th. The phrase "kept the Passover" does not signify that Israel ate the Passover lamb on the night of the fourteenth; rather it denotes Israel killed the Passover lamb in accordance with Mosaic Law on the fourteenth of Nisan in the evening. Israel would have received manna on that morning. The Passover lamb was killed in the evening of the fourteenth and consumed later that night on Nisan 15th in accordance with Mosaic Law. Scripture notes in verse eleven that Israel ate unleavened bread prepared from old grain of the land of Canaan on the date for the Feast of Unleavened Bread. The Israelites probably found old grain in storehouses when they entered the land of Canaan several days earlier.

Chapter five, verse eleven also clearly identifies that Israel ate old grain as unleavened bread on **the day** after the Passover, which is Nisan 15th. The reason for the absence of manna on Nisan 15th is not obvious at first until one remembers the Lord does not send manna on His Sabbath days. Nisan 15th is a High Sabbath, or Annual Feast Day

Sabbath. While it is not the weekly Sabbath, it is the Sabbath of the Lord. Therefore, Israel would not have found manna to eat in the morning of the fifteenth and would have been forced to continue to eat the old grain of the land as unleavened bread for their breakfast, since it was forbidden to eat any of the new grain until after the Feast of First Fruits had been presented to the Lord.

> "[10]Speak unto the children of Israel, and say unto them, When ye be come into the land which I give unto you, and shall reap the harvest thereof, then ye shall bring a sheaf of the first fruits of your harvest unto the priest: [11]And he shall wave the sheaf before the Lord, to be accepted for you on the morrow after the Sabbath the priest shall wave it... [14]And ye shall eat neither bread, nor parched grain, nor green ears, until the self-same day that ye have brought an offering unto your God: it shall be a statute for ever throughout your generations in all your dwellings." Leviticus 23:10-14

Examining events from strictly a Pharisaical viewpoint, the earliest day the Feast of First Fruits could occur was on Nisan 16th. However, in Joshua 5:12, scripture states on the day after Israel had eaten old grain from the land, the manna ceased. That means the day after Nisan 15th, which is Nisan 16, the manna stopped. Taking a literal interpretation of the scriptures, if manna did not fall on Nisan 16th, then the last day manna would have been given to Israel would have been Nisan 14th. However, the Scripture affirms Nisan 15th to be a Sabbath day (holy convocation), and on Nisan 15th the children of Israel ate old grain as their unleavened bread (Joshua 5:11). Since we know from Joshua 5:12 manna ceased on the day after the fifteenth of Nisan, the last day for manna to have been given must have occurred on Nisan

16th. Therefore, the children of Israel kept the Feast of First Fruits and ate the fresh grain of the land beginning on Nisan 17th, because there was no more manna given by God (verse 12). The chart below provides an outline of biblical events in the Book of Joshua, chapter five.

Chart 8

	Nisan 14 Passover	Nisan 15 Annual Sabbath	Nisan 16	Nisan 17
Morning	Manna Given	No Manna Given Exodus 16:25	Last Day Manna Given (v. 12)	Eat First Fruits of the Promise Land
	Passover lamb killed in evening (v.10)	Eat old grain of the land (v.11)		
	Nisan 15 Annual Sabbath	Nisan 16	Nisan 17	
Evening	Passover lamb eaten with unleavened bread (v. 11)			

The spiritual relevance of the children of Israel eating from the new grain of the Promise Land on Nisan 17 cannot be understated and parallels directly to Jesus' resurrection on Nisan 17. For Jesus institutes a New Covenant with mankind that is based upon His death and resurrection:

> "[16]For where a testament [covenant] is, there must also of necessity be the death of the testator. [17]For a

testament is of force after men are dead: otherwise it is of no strength at all while the testator liveth."
Hebrews 9:16-17

"₂₅Who was delivered for our offences, and was raised for our justification."
Romans 4:25

"₁₇And if Christ be not raised, your faith is in vain; ye are yet in your sins"
1 Corinthians 15:17

Jesus' resurrection on Nisan 17th firmly established the New Covenant of God, which He gave on Nisan 14th to His disciples. Jesus continually referred to Himself as the Bread of Life (John 6:35), upon who if a man feeds will gain eternal life (John 6:51). In the sixth chapter in the Book of John, Jesus had a debate with the Pharisees and explained to them that neither they nor their fathers ever ate of the True Bread from Heaven. While the Pharisees and Sadducees misunderstood the manna sent by God to Israel during their forty years of wandering as the bread of Heaven, Jesus declares that He is the Bread of Heaven, the true bread of God sent down to the world (John 6:32). The fullness of entering into the blessings of Promise Land for Israel occurred on Nisan 17th when they were finally able to eat of good fruit of the land. The ability to enter into the blessings of the New Covenant of God also began with the resurrection of Jesus on Nisan 17th. As a result of Jesus' resurrection, the New Covenant is confirmed and men can now eat from the spiritual Promise Land the true Bread of Heaven.

Restoration of True Worship – 2 Chronicles

During the time of the divided kingdoms of Israel and Judah, many evil kings arose in the land. Successions of evil kings reigned from generation to generation. During their reign, idolatry replaced the true worship of Yahweh God. Even the glorious temple built by Solomon was vandalized and over run with idols. King Ahaz who reigned before Hezekiah was so evil that he robbed the treasury of the House of the Lord of all its gold and silver as a bribe to the King of Assyria to help protect Judah from an invading army. King Ahaz also removed the brazen altar, the laver, and destroyed many of the articles in the Lord's Temple, worshipping false idols instead. As a result all of inhabitants of Judah were tainted and many followed after his folly. Eventually, King Ahaz dismissed the Levites and closed the Temple doors permanently, setting up idols to worship instead (2 Kings chapter 16). The Levitical priesthood became unclean when they stopped ministering before the Lord.

After King Ahaz, his son Hezekiah became King over Judah. The twenty-ninth chapter of the Book of 2 Chronicles outlines events during the reign of King Hezekiah. King Hezekiah immediately began to repair the damage his father performed in the land, specifically with regard to the treatment of God and the Temple, God's house. In the first year of his reign, Hezekiah opened the doors of the Temple and repaired them (2 Chronicles 29:3). He also gathered the Levites and instructed them to sanctify themselves and the House of God (verses 4-17) so true worship could be restored to the Land of Israel. You will note from the Scripture below that these events take place in the first month, which is Nisan.

"₁₅And they gathered their brethren, and sanctified themselves, and came, according to the commandment of the king, by the words of the LORD, to cleanse the house of the LORD. ₁₆And the priests went into the inner part of the house of the LORD, to cleanse it, and brought out all the uncleanness that they found in the temple of the LORD into the court of the house of the LORD. And the Levites took it, to carry it out abroad into the brook Ki'-dron. ₁₇Now they began *on the first day of the first month* to sanctify, and on the eighth day of the month came they to the porch of the LORD: so they sanctified the house of the LORD in eight days; and *in the sixteenth day of the first month they made an end.*"
2 Chronicles 29:15-17

The sanctification of the priests and the cleansing of the Temple took a total of sixteen days. On Nisan 16th, the Levites finally finished the cleansing and repairs necessary for Temple worship to resume the next day. The priests reported to King Hezekiah (in verse eighteen) that they had cleansed the entire House of God, restoring the vessels for worship and the altar for burnt offerings. On Nisan 17th, King Hezekiah rose early, gathered Israel, and resumed temple worship, beginning with the sin offerings, which made atonement for all of Israel.

"₂₀Then Hez-e-ki'-ah the king rose early, and gathered the rules of the city, and went up to the house of the LORD."

It is no coincidence true worship and adoration of God is restored on Nisan 17th in the Book of 2 Chronicles. Jesus in the New Testament tells a woman that, "the time is coming and now is when the true worshippers shall worship the Father in spirit and in truth: for the Father seeketh such to worship him" (John 4:23). Jesus alone was capable of restoring true worship between God and man. He is the high priest from the order of Melchizedek. As a high priest, He was both sin offering and mediator between God and man (1 Timothy 2:5). Upon entering into the heavens, Jesus not only made atonement for our sins as the sacrifice, but also tore the veil between God and man, paving the way for true worship of the Father. Jesus' priesthood continues forever, and He lives eternally to make intercession for Believers.

> "$_{24}$But this man [Jesus], because he continueth ever, hath an unchangeable priesthood. $_{25}$Wherefore he [Jesus] is able to also save them [Believers] to the utmost that come unto God by him, seeing he ever liveth to make intercession for them. $_{26}$For such a high priest became us [was needed for us], who is holy, harmless, undefiled, separate from sinners, and made higher than the heavens;"
> Hebrews 7:24-26

Deliverance from Death - The Book of Esther

The Principle of First Mention and Progressive Mention themes of salvation and redemption on Nisan 17th continue again in the Book of Esther when Israel is spared annihilation on this date. In the story, Ha'man, the enemy of Israel, serves as a type of antichrist. On the thirteenth day of Nisan, Ha'man issues a decree to annihilate all the Jews in the kingdom of Persia.

"₈And Ha'man said unto King Ahasuerus, There is a certain people scattered abroad and dispersed among the people in all the provinces of thy kingdom; and their laws are diverse from all people; neither keep they the king's laws: therefore it is not for the king's profit to suffer them. ₉If it please the king, **let it be written that they [Israelites] may be destroyed:** and I will pay ten thousand talents of silver to the hands of those that have the charge of the business, to bring it into the king's treasuries. ₁₀And the king took his ring from his hand, and gave it unto **Ha'man** the son of Hammedatha the Agagite, *the Jews' enemy*. ₁₁And the king said unto Ha'man, The silver is given to thee, the people also, to do with them as it seemeth good to thee. ₁₂Then were the king's scribes called *on the thirteenth day of the first month*, and there was written according to all that Ha'man had commanded unto the king's lieutenants, and to the governors that were over every province, and to the rulers of every people of every province according to the writing thereof, and to every people after their language; in the name of King Ahasuerus was it written, and sealed with the king's ring."
Esther 3:8-12

In response to Ha'man's decree, Queen Esther declares a three-day fast in preparation to approach the king to defend her people. Since approaching the king without being summoned is a violation of Persian law, Esther knows the probability of her death is high.

"₁₆Go, gather together all the Jews that are present in Shushan, and fast ye for me, and *neither eat nor drink three days, night or day*: I also and my maidens will

> fast likewise; *and so will I go in unto the king*, which is not according to the law: and if I perish, I perish."
> Esther 4:16

On Nisan 16th, Esther risked her life and sought King Ahasuerus. The king spared her life and asked her what she desired. Queen Esther basically replied, "If it pleases the king, may the king and Ha'man *come this day* to the banquet that I have prepared" (see Esther 5:4). At the banquet on Nisan 16th, the king questioned Esther again as to her desire, and she invited the king and Ha'man to a second banquet the following day. On the 17th of Nisan during the second banquet, Queen Esther pleaded the case for the salvation of her people, Israel.

> "₁So the king and Ha'man came to banquet with Esther the queen. ₂And the king said again unto Esther *on the second day* at the banquet of wine, What is thy petition, queen Esther? and it shall be granted thee: and what is thy request? and it shall be performed, even to the half of the kingdom. ₃Then Esther the queen answered and said, If I have found favour in thy sight, O king, and if it please the king, let my life be given me at my petition, and my people at my request: ₄For we are sold, I and my people, to be destroyed, to be slain, and to perish. But if we had been sold for bondmen and bondwomen, I had held my tongue, although the enemy could not countervail the king's damage. ₅Then the king Ahasuerus answered and said unto Esther the queen, Who is he, and where is he, that durst presume in his heart to do so? ₆And Esther said, The adversary and enemy is this wicked Ha'man. Then Ha'man was afraid before the king and the queen. ₇And the king arising from the banquet of wine in his wrath went into the palace

garden: and Ha'man stood up to make request for his life to Esther the queen; for he saw that there was evil determined against him by the king. ₈Then the king returned out of the palace garden into the place of the banquet of wine; and Ha'man was fallen upon the bed whereon Esther was. Then said the king, Will he force the queen also before me in the house? As the word went out of king's mouth, they covered Ha'man's face. ₉And Harbonah, one of the chamberlains, said before the king, Behold also, the gallows fifty cubits high, which Ha'man had made for Mor'de-ca-i, who had spoken good for the king, standeth in the house of Ha'man. Then the king said, Hang him thereon. ₁₀*So they hanged Ha'man* on the gallows that he had prepared for Mor'de-ca-i. Then was the king's wrath pacified."
Esther 7:1-10

As a result of Esther's plea, Ha'man was killed and salvation was granted unto the Jews on the seventeenth of Nisan.

"₁₁Wherein *the king granted the Jews which were in every city to gather themselves together, and to stand for their life, to destroy, to slay and to cause to perish, all the power of the people and province that would assault them, both little ones and women, and to take the spoil of them for a prey.*"
Esther 8:11

"₁Now in the twelfth month, that is, the month Adar, on the thirteenth day of the same, when the king's commandment and his decree drew near to be put in execution, *in the day that the enemies of the Jews hoped to have power over them, (though it was turned to the contrary,* that the Jews had rule over

them that hated them;) ₂The Jews gathered themselves together in their cities throughout all the provinces of the king Ahasuerus, to lay hand on such as sought their hurt: and no man could withstand them; for the fear of them fell upon all people. ₃And all the rulers of the provinces, and the lieutenants, and the deputies, and officers of the king, helped the Jews; because the fear of Mor'de-ca-i fell upon them. ₄For Mor'de-ca-i was great in the king's house, and his fame went out throughout all the provinces: for this man Mor'de-ca-i waxed greater and greater. ₅Thus **the Jews smote all their enemies** with the stroke of the sword, and slaughter, and destruction, and did what they would unto those that hated them."
Esther 9:1-5

The salvation of the nation of Israel began on Nisan 17th with the king giving "the Jews' enemy unto Esther the queen," who had interceded for her people, and killing Ha'man. King Ahasuerus also removed the ring off of Ha'man's hand (representing the king's authority) and gave it to Mordecai. The transfer of authority from their enemy to the children of God is extremely symbolic of the transfer of power from Satan who had the keys of hell and death to the hand of Jesus Christ, who shares His authority with His followers. Because King Ahasuerus' original law (issued under Ha'man) for the destruction of the Jews could not be reversed, additional letters were written and sent throughout the kingdom authorizing the Jews to assemble and defend themselves on the future date originally designed for their destruction by Ha'man.

Persian law did not allow for any change to be made to the original decree of the king. It was believed the king was perfect, and therefore, his decrees were not subject to change. If perchance change was truly required, the king must issue another decree that did not legally contradict the first decree to allow for a loophole. King Ahasuerus' first decree for death was symbolic of God's laws, which are perfect and holy and cannot be reversed by man. God's law condemns sin, requires the death of sinners, and cannot be reversed. King Ahasuerus understood Persian law and knew his first decree declaring death of the Jews at Ha'man's request could not be rescinded. Therefore, only another decree of equal perfection and justice could allow them (the Jews) a chance at life. This is why additional letters were sent throughout the land. Similarly, God's punishment for sin being death cannot be rescinded. Only another decree, equal in perfection and justice, can be extended to give mankind an escape loophole from death. Therefore, God issues another decree in which anyone fulfilling His perfect law may become a substitute for another sinner. Now the penalty of sin being death is legally fulfilled and laid upon the only person capable of completing the requirement. Ironically, God Himself was the only one capable of completing His new decree. Therefore, He stepped into time in the form of a human body as Jesus the Christ and completed the law, becoming the substitutional sacrifice that allowed the true sinners (mankind) to be released.

In Esther 9:3 on the day in Adar (the first decree's execution date), we read the king's governors and army rose up to defend the Jewish people. Thus, the plot by the enemy to annihilate the Jewish nation instead resulted in total destruction for the enemies of the Jews. Similarly God's Host (or army) of Angels will defend and minister to the heirs of salvation (Believers) according to Psalms 91 and Hebrew 1:14.

> "₃And all the rulers of the provinces, and the lieutenants, and the deputies, and officers of the king, helped the Jews; because the fear of Mor'de-ca-i fell upon them."
> Esther 9:3

For all practical purposes, the redemption of the Jews occurred on Nisan 17th, when King Ahasuerus' heart towards the Jewish nation is changed upon the revelation that Queen Esther is a Jew. However, the complete deliverance from physical destruction finally culminates in the month of Adar, when the king's army rises up to defend the Jews on the appointed date. This theme of salvation, beginning on Nisan 17th yet seemingly delayed for a period of time until Adar, portrays again the finished work and ministry of Jesus Christ currently in progress.

Jesus rose from the grave on Nisan 17th and immediately deliverance from sin and death was granted to all who would believe in Him. Believers are spiritually and mentally free at this moment, and yet a period of time remains before the fulfillment of the last enemy of death will be destroyed. Just as a period of time existed between Nisan 17th to Adar 13th indicative of the delay between the king's decree releasing the children of God from death and the final date of deliverance, so too it is for Believers today who have been freed legally from the enemy but still await the final deliverance of their physical bodies.

> "₂₁For since by man came death, by man also the resurrection of the dead. ₂₂For as in Adam all die, even so in Christ shall all be made alive. ₂₃**But every man in his own order: <u>Christ the first fruits</u>; <u>afterwards</u> they that are Christ's at His coming**... ₂₅For He must reign, till He hath put all enemies under His feet. ₂₆**The last**

enemy that shall be destroyed is death. ₂₇For he [God] hath put all things under his [Jesus] feet..."
1 Corinthians 15:21-27

"₂₃And not only they, but ourselves also which have the first fruits of the Spirit, even we ourselves groan within ourselves *waiting for* the adoption, *the redemption of our body.*"
Romans 8:23

"₄₉And as we have borne the image of the earthy, we shall also bear the image of the heavenly. ₅₀Now this I say brethren, that flesh and blood cannot inherit the kingdom of God; neither doth corruption inherit incorruption. ₅₁Behold, I show you a mystery; We shall not all die, but we shall all be changed, ₅₂In a moment, in the twinkling of an eye, at the last trump: for the trumpet shall sound, and the dead shall be raised incorruptible, and we shall be changed. ₅₃*For this corruption must put on incorruption, and this mortal put on immortality.* ₅₄So when this corruptible shall have put on incorruption, and this mortal shall have put on immortality, then shall be brought to pass the saying that is written, **Death is swallowed up in victory.**"
1 Corinthians 15:49-54

"₁₂That we should be to the praise of his glory, who first trusted in Christ. ₁₃In whom ye also trusted, after that ye heard the word of truth, the gospel of your salvation: in whom also after that ye believed, *ye were sealed with that Holy Spirit* of promise, ₁₄Which is the earnest of our inheritance *until the redemption* of the purchased possession, unto the praise of his glory."
Ephesians 1:12-14

As Scripture teaches, Jesus' sacrifice and resurrection from the dead as the first fruits accomplished all the spiritual, physical, and legal requirements of God's law. Everything is under His feet, even death. Believers in Christ also have the promise of the Holy Spirit indwelling them; however, there remains a period of time for the Believer between Nisan 17th (the day of Jesus' resurrection) and the day the physical body is finally redeemed from decay and death.

Culmination – The Resurrection

It is no surprise that the Principle of First Mention and the repeated Principle of Progressive Mention themes of redemption, deliverance, salvation, and new beginnings would culminate in the resurrection of Jesus the Messiah on Nisan 17th. Anatolius the Bishop of Laodicea during the third century (269-283 A.D.) was quoted referring to the timing of the resurrection of Jesus being on the Nisan 17th.

> "For, although they lay it down as a thing unlawful, that the beginning of the Paschal festival would be extended so far as to the moon's twentieth; yet they cannot deny that it ought to be extended to the sixteenth and seventeenth, which coincide with the day on which the Lord rose from the dead."[25]

The Passover Lamb must be killed on Nisan 14th (in the evening) before Nisan 15th. Therefore, we know that Jesus died on Nisan 14th. The following day was a High Sabbath/annual Feast Day Sabbath, Nisan 15th. Jesus was in the grave three days and three nights rising on Nisan 17th, the third day.

The presumption of Jesus rising on the sixteenth of Nisan is based primarily upon the false premise that this is the date for the Feast of First Fruits, ordained by the current Jewish calendar. However, in Jesus' crucifixion week, the date of Nisan 17th corresponded to Feast of First Fruits as recognized by the Sadducees. As ruling class for the Temple during the time of Christ, the Sadducee interpretation of Feast timelines would trump any Pharisaical interpretation of scriptures which would place the Feast of First Fruits on Nisan 16th. Therefore, the Pharisee commandment of Nisan 16th for the date of Feast of First Fruits (as indicated in the current Jewish calendar) would not have any relevance during the time of Christ.

Additionally, if Christ rose on Nisan 16th, there is no mathematical means of acquiring three days, let alone the three days and three nights foretold by Jesus in Matthew 12:40. Knowing Jesus died sometime shortly after 3:00 PM on Nisan 14th, a calculation of the timing He would be dead if He rose on the 16th before or during sunrise would be less than thirty-nine (39) hours. Obviously, thirty-nine (39) hours in nowhere near three days of death.

The following charts comparing Traditional Christian Theology with Realistic Biblical interpretation will be based on a general Jewish timeline for Nisan with the daytime starting with sunrise approximately at 6:30 AM and the night starting at approximately 6:30 PM.

Traditional Christian Theology:

Chart 9

Day	Nisan 14	Nisan 15	Nisan 16
	Jesus dies after 3PM		Jesus alive before sunrise
Night	Nisan 15	Nisan 16	Nisan 17

In the Traditional Theory, Jesus died on Nisan 14th and rose on Nisan 16th. Many Believers holding this theory argue it spans three different days: Friday, Saturday and Sunday or Nisan 14th, 15th, and 16th. Adding all the periods of death together, the maximum amount of time Christ could be in the grave was thirty-nine hours (39) at maximum, or thirty-six hours (36) if calculated from entombment. Never has thirty-six or thirty-nine hours been considered three days. It isn't even two full days of time, let alone the three days and three nights as Christ prophesized in Matthew 12:40. Additionally, there is no Principle of First Mention in the Bible for Nisan 16th either being associated with salvation, redemption, or new beginnings. Neither is there any Principle of Progressive Mention to reinforce Nisan 16th as a significant date for Israel in the Old Testament.

3:00 PM Nisan 14th to 3:00 PM Nisan 15th = 24 hours

3:00 PM Nisan 15th to 6:00 AM Nisan 16th = <u>15 hours</u>

Total   39 hours

If one based the timeline from the time Jesus was in the physical grave, a Friday crucifixion would have been approximately three hours shorter in duration, or thirty-six (36) hours for death. Thirty-six hours is not even close to a three-day timeline.

Realistic Biblical Interpretation:

Chart 10

	Nisan 14	Nisan 15	Nisan 16	Nisan 17
Day	Jesus dies after 3PM			Jesus alive before sunrise
Night	Nisan 15	Nisan 16	Nisan 17	

In a more accurate review of Biblical scriptures, taking into account the ruling Temple practices governed by the Sadducees, Jesus would die on Nisan 14th and rise on Nisan 17th. This timeline would produce approximately sixty-three (63) hours of death, which is beyond two days or forty-eight (48) hours. Sixty-three (63) hours would also qualify literally for Jesus rising on the third day. It would also cover a period of three nights (Nisan 15th, Nisan 16th, Nisan 17th) and three days (daylight hours) (Nisan 14th, Nisan 15th, Nisan 16th). The day portion of Nisan 17th would not qualify to be counted as "daylight" hours because Jesus rose from the grave before the sunrise. Thus, for the period of Nisan 17th only the nighttime hours could be counted. A Nisan 14th crucifixion with a Nisan 17th resurrection fulfills all Biblical prophesies regarding the time for death, and it also fulfills the Sadducee requirement for Feast of First Fruits. Moreover, this time span is the only Biblical interpretation that correlates all New Testament scripture timelines without conflict or compromise.

3:00 PM Nisan 14th to 3:00 PM Nisan 15th = 24 hours
3:00 PM Nisan 15th to 3:00 PM Nisan 16th = 24 hours
3:00 PM Nisan 16th to 6:00 AM Nisan 17th = <u>15 hours</u>
Total   63 hours

In addition to the timeline regarding hours or days Jesus Christ was deceased, the Principle of First Mention and the continued Progressive Mention Principle themes associated with Nisan 17th support this date as the date Jesus rose from the dead. There are no events in scripture that correlate Nisan 16th to any salvation, deliverance, or redemption of Israel. A thorough review of all the symbology associated in the Bible for the date of Nisan 17th follows:

- The Curse Reversed – Mt. Ararat, the ark finds rests, (Genesis)

- Deliverance from Bondage – total deliverance from Egyptian slavery after passing through the Red Sea, (Exodus)

- First day fresh food/grain is eaten from the Promise Land, (Joshua)

- Restoration of True Worship, (2 Chronicles)

- Deliverance from Death, (Esther)

- The Resurrection of Jesus Christ from the Dead (all the Gospels)

Interestingly enough, several of these events are described as occurring predawn hours or around sunrise (Exodus, 2

Chronicles, even in Joshua the children ate breakfast from the new grain of the land). This early morning timeline on Nisan 17th also corresponds to the discovery of the resurrection of Jesus Christ by Mary Magdalene and the other women.

As in Genesis on Nisan 17th, Jesus reversed the curse of sin for Believers by becoming our sin-substitution sacrifice. As the sin sacrifice, He also delivered Believers from the bondage of sin and its penalty of death.

> "$_{34}$Jesus answered them, Verily, verily, I say unto you, **Whosoever committeth sin is the servant [slave] of sin.**"
> John 8:34

> "$_{14}$Forasmuch then as the children are partakers of flesh and blood, he also himself took part of the same; that through death he might destroy him that had the power of death, that is the devil; $_{15}$**And deliver them who through fear of death were all their lifetime subject to bondage.**"
> Hebrews 2:14-15

> "$_{15}$For **ye have not received the spirit of bondage again to fear**; but ye have received the Spirit of adoption, whereby we cry, Abba, Father."
> Romans 8:15

It is no wonder that Jesus is the mountain symbolically portrayed in Daniel's vision that fills the whole Earth. For like the ark that found Mt. Ararat to rest upon in days of the wrath of God when the flood waters covered the Earth, so too can Believers find rest upon the mountain of Jesus Christ. This mountain is available to the whole Earth, as indicative of Daniel's vision, *"became a great mountain, and filled the whole earth."* Jesus is the mountain where Believers from every nation come to find rest from the curse of sin and death currently flooding the Earth. For Jesus is the Mountain of God where the curse is reversed, "upon this rock I will build my church; and the gates of hell shall not prevail against it" (Matthew 16:18).

> "₃₄Thou sawest till that *a stone was cut out without hands*, which smote the image upon his feet *that were* of iron and clay, and brake them to pieces. ₃₅Then was the iron, the clay, the brass, the silver, and the gold, broken to pieces together, and became like the chaff of the summer threshing floors; and the wind carried them away, that no place was found for them: *and the stone* that smote the image *became a great mountain, and filled the whole earth*….₄₄And in the days of these kings shall *the God of heaven set up a kingdom, which shall never be destroyed: and the kingdom shall not be left to other people, but it shall break in pieces and consume all these kingdoms, and it shall stand for ever."*
> Daniel 2:34-35 and 2:44

Through Jesus, Believers also now have new bread to eat from the true Promised Land. For the Bread of Life has come down from Heaven and whosoever partakes of this bread has eternal life (John 6:32-33, 6:35). By accepting Christ, Believers enter into His rest, the ultimate Promise Land (Hebrews 4:9-10), and there they feed continually on the good fruit of the land.

Jesus also restored the Holy Temple of God for True Worship with the Father. The penalty resulting for Adam consuming fruit from the Tree of the Knowledge of Good and Evil was a spiritual separation from God. Jesus' death and resurrection brought the opportunity once again for reconciliation with God. Through Jesus, mankind is again indwelt by the living Holy Spirit of God. Believers are the true Temple of God, in which His Holy Spirit dwells. Mankind can finally worship in Spirit and truth as we did before the Fall of Adam.

> "$_{18}$And all things *are* of **God, who hath reconciled us to himself by Jesus Christ**, and hath given to us the ministry of reconciliation"
> 2 Corinthians 5:18

> "$_{23}$But the hour cometh, and now is, when the *true worshippers shall worship the Father in spirit and in truth*: for the Father seeketh such to worship him. $_{24}$God is a Spirit: and they that worship him must worship him in spirit and in truth."
> John 4:23-24

> "$_{6}$And because ye are sons, **God hath sent forth the Spirit of his Son into your hearts**, crying, Abba, Father."
> Galatians 4:6

> "$_{16}$Know ye not that *ye are the temple of God*, and *that the Spirit of God dwelleth in you*?"
> 1 Corinthians 3:16

There is no longer a need for a physical man on the Earth to stand between God and men as an intermediary as in the days of old when the Levitical High Priest stood as a barrier between God and Israel. For Jesus, High Priest of the Melchizedek Order, stands forever more in Heaven to make intercession for the Saints (Hebrews 7:24-25). Mankind now has direct access to the Throne of God because of the blood of Jesus Christ, and nothing separates Believers from God.

> "$_{16}$Let us ***therefore come boldly unto the throne of grace***, that we may obtain mercy, and find grace to help in time of need."
> Hebrews 4:16

> "$_{38}$For I am persuaded, that neither death, nor life, nor angels, nor principalities, nor powers, nor things present, nor things to come, $_{39}$Nor height, nor depth, nor any other creature, shall be able to separate us from the love of God, which is in Christ Jesus our Lord."
> Romans 8:38-89

Overcoming death by death, Jesus has delivered all those who believe in Him from death. The date of His resurrection from the dead sealed forever the Believer's victory over death.

> "$_{57}$But thanks *be* to God, which giveth us the victory through our Lord Jesus Christ."
> 1 Corinthians 15:57

> "$_{14}$And God hath both raised up the Lord, and will also raise up us by his own power."
> 1 Corinthians 6:14

> "$_{25}$Jesus said unto her, I am the resurrection, and the life: he that believeth in me, though he were dead, yet shall he live:"
> John 11:25

In the story of Esther, Nisan 17th was the date the children of God were released from the death sentence against them, yet there remained a period of time between the decree of release and the culmination of the physical deliverance. Similarly, Believers today have been released from the penalty of sin by the resurrection of Jesus on Nisan 17th, yet there remains a period of time between then and the second coming of Christ before the physical deliverance of their mortal bodies from death. Death is the last enemy to be put under Jesus' feet. At the time of His second coming, death will be swallowed up in victory.

> "[26] The last enemy *that* shall be destroyed *is* death."
> 1 Corinthians 15:26

> "[51] Behold, I show you a mystery; We shall not all sleep [die], but we shall all be changed, [52] In a moment, in the twinkling of an eye, at the last trump: for the trumpet shall sound, and ***the dead shall be raised incorruptible, and we shall be changed.*** [53] For this corruptible must put on incorruption, and this mortal must put on immortality. [54] So when this corruptible shall have put on incorruption, and this mortal shall have put on immortality, then shall be brought to pass the saying that is written, **Death is swallowed up in victory.**"
> 1 Corinthians 15:51-54

Thus, the continued theme of salvation, deliverance, and redemption associated with Nisan 17th concluded with the resurrection of the Messiah. Jesus rising from the dead on Nisan 17th not only completed the illustration of redemption throughout the Old Testament, but also fulfilled the Biblical prophecy of Him rising from the dead on the third day. Simultaneously, Jesus' self-prophecy given in Matthew 12:40 is also accomplished with Him being dead three days and three nights.

Chapter 5

THE SIGN OF JONAH

The Sign of Jonah

Jesus gave only one sign of His Messiahship to the rulers of Israel. He said He would be dead three day and three nights. Jesus compared the timeline of His death with events from Jonah in the Old Testament.

> "$_{38}$Then some of the scribes and Pharisees answered, saying, 'Teacher, we want to see a sign from You.' But He answered and said to them, 'An evil and adulterous generation seeks after a sign, and no sign will be given to it except the sign of the prophet Jonah. For as Jonah was three days and three nights in the belly of the great fish, *so will the Son of Man be three days and three nights in the heart of the earth.*'" Matthew 12:38-40

Many scholars have tried to split theological hairs in the definitions of the words "on" and "after" three days. Unfortunately, such use of the original Greek terminology does not provide any further clarification to the timeline, as many of the parallel verses for Jesus' resurrection use different prepositions with the same meanings: on the third day, after three days, in three days, and until the third day.

The chart below correlates some scriptures referring to Christ rising on the third day.

Chart 11

Mark	Matthew	Luke
After three days Mk 8:31	On the third day Mt 16:21	On the third day Lk 9:22
After three days Mk 9:31	On the third day Mt 17:23	No reference
After three days Mk 10:34	On the third day Mt 20:19	On the third day Lk 18:33

As one can see, the use of "on the third day" and "after three days" are interchangeable in these parallel verses.

What Constitutes a Day?

The general belief among "Christians" is that Christ's prophecy in Matthew 12:40 meant **parts** of three Gregorian days: part of Friday, all of Saturday, and part of Sunday. But this theory is inconsistent with a Jewish Messiah who would have spoken Hebrew to His Jewish disciples and the nation of Israel. Jesus would not have been referring to the Gregorian or Roman for calculating time. Instead, He would have used God's calendar, the Jewish calendar of His day.

One of the most important guidelines of biblical interpretation is to allow the Bible to interpret itself whenever possible. The Bible often explains its symbols and defines its terminology within other passages. The only biblical reference to counting the period of time for a day is revealed by Jesus in John 11:9.

> "Jesus answered, Are there not twelve hours in the day? If any man walk in the day, he stumbleth not, because he seeth the light of this world."
> John 11:9

Using a literal interpretation of twelve hours for daylight and twelve hours for night, many Sabbath worshippers hold the conviction that Jesus had to be literally in the grave for seventy-two hours in order to be dead three days and three nights. The basis for their interpretation is Matthew 12:40 and John 11:9. Additionally, they interpret the meaning of being "in the heart of the earth" to be based from the timeline of Jesus' physical body was in the grave and not at the time He died. The difference between the time of death and the time placed in the grave is somewhere between 2 ½ to 3 ½ hours.

Other Christians have interpreted the phrase "in the belly of the earth" from a spiritual viewpoint, because the soul immediately leaves the body upon death and was sent to a holding place (known as Hades, which scripture reveals to be in the center of the earth). These Christians calculate the three days and three nights timeline from the moment of Jesus' death, just after 3:00 PM on the cross.

While Believers may hold to a viewpoint of a literal seventy-two hour interpretation for death, the possibility of an exact seventy-two hour timeline is inconsistent with other biblical examples calculating time. There are references in Scripture that denote a period of three days and three nights can refer to a timeline that calculates a portion of the day instead of an entire twenty-four hour period of time. Similar scriptural examples are listed below.

Exodus 19:10-11; 16

"₁₀And the LORD said unto Moses, Go unto the people, and sanctify them today and tomorrow, and let them wash their clothes, ₁₁And be ready against the third day: for the third day the LORD will come down in the sight of all the people upon mount Sinai... ₁₆And it came to pass on the third day in the morning..."

Time Period:
More than 48 hours, but less than 72 hours.

Day 1: Moses received the message and brought it to the people right after they had camped, which seems to imply the meeting between God and Moses occurred in the evening of day 1, which gives a time for at least part of the night (approximately six (6) to eight (8) hours) and the next day of twelve (12) hours in this first day. Total approximate time for the day one is anywhere from sixteen (16) to twenty (20) hours of preparation time.

Day 2: A 24-hour period from the beginning of this day to the beginning of the third day (evening to evening)

Day 3: twelve (12) to fourteen (14) hours pass from sunset in the evening to the morning when Israel meets God. At dawn a thick cloud appeared and the voice of a trumpet went out. Moses gathered all the people and brought them to the mountain to meet with God. God later appears in verse 18 & 20. This gathering could have taken a couple of hours to get all the people to the mountain, but the call to meet goes forth at dawn.

Thus the total time for all three days is approximately fifty-two (52) to fifty-eight (58) hours; a period of time more than two days; occurring on the third day but less than a literal seventy-two (72) hour period of time.

1 Samuel 30:12-13

"₁₂And they gave him a piece of a cake of figs, and two clusters of raisins: and when he had eaten, his spirit came again to him: for he had eaten no bread, nor drunk any water, *three days and three nights.* ₁₃And David said unto him, To whom belongest thou? and whence art thou? And he said, I am a young man of Egypt, servant to an Amalekite; and my master left me, because *three days agone* I fell sick"

Time Period:
More than 48 hours, but less than 72 hours.

Notice the reference of three days and three nights in verse 12. Contrast that with verse 13, "three days ago." In the beginning of Chapter 30, verse 1, Scripture states David arrived in Ziklag **on the third day** since the Amalekites had invaded. The distance from Ziklag to Be'sor is approximately four miles. There David's men found an Egyptian slave referenced in the above scriptures. Because the Egyptian reported not eating for three day or nights does not mean that his lack of food occurred entirely during the time he was left behind. He may not have eaten a meal or two while he was still with his master. Yet it is clear from scripture that three days ago his master left him behind. Taking into the account David enters on day 3 of the attack, cries for a unspecified period of time, then inquires of the Lord and begins his pursuit of four miles before coming upon the Egyptian, at minimum more than forty-eight (48) hours has likely occurred since the time the Egyptian was left by his master. It is also likely that exactly seventy-two (72) hours has not passed in this story yet. One thing is certain, the event is happening on the third day. More than forty-eight (48) hours, but less than seventy-two (72) hours have passed.

Esther 4:16 & 5:1
"₁₆Go, gather together all the Jews that are present in Shushan, and fast ye for me, and neither eat nor drink three days, night or day: I also and my maidens will fast likewise; and so will I go in unto the king, which is not according to the law: and if I perish, I perish.
₅Now it came to pass *on the third day,* that Esther put on her royal apparel, and stood in the inner court of the king's house, over against the king's house: and the king sat upon his royal throne in the royal house, over against the gate of the house."

Time Period:
More than 48 hours, but less than 72 hours.

Nisan 13th – Decree issued and Esther's fast begins, probably morning or afternoon (maybe six to eight hours).
Nisan 14th – Entire day, twenty-four (24) hours of time
Nisan 15th – Entire day, twenty-four (24) hours of time

Nisan 16th – Esther appears before the king, perhaps twelve (12) or fourteen (14) hours of time since sunset on Nisan 15th.

Total Time: 24 + 24 + 12 + 6 = 66 hours minimum, possibly 70 hours maximum

Ester's fast starts sometime during Nisan 13th and she appears before the king on Nisan 16th approximately three days later. Verse 4:16 states she asked the nation of Israel to fast three days, night or day. And Esther appears before the king on the third day, verse 5:1. Thus, Esther's three-day timeline was not a literal seventy-two 72 hours.

Jonah 1:17

[17]Now the Lord had prepared a great fish to swallow up Jonah. And Jonah was in the belly of the fish three days and three nights.

Timeline is unspecified in its length; most likely more than 48 hours but less than 72 hours. No evidence for a literal 72-hour period of time.

Matthew 27:63-64

"[63]Saying, Sir, we remember that that deceiver said, while he was yet alive, **After three days** I will rise again. [64]Command therefore that the sepulcher be made sure *until the third day*, lest his disciples come by night, and steal him away, and say unto the people, He is risen from the dead: so the last error shall be worse than the first."

Time Period:
More than 48 hours, but less than 72 hours.
Refer to the phrasing after three days and until the third day. Thus three days was not a literal 72 hours.

Acts 10:3-30

Starting Day 1 at 3:00 PM, Cornelius received a message. Total time on Day 1 equals three hours to sunset. The next day (Day 2) at 12:00 PM Peter had a vision and shortly thereafter Cornelius' servants arrived in Joppa. Counting from sunset on Day 1 to sunset on Day 2 is twenty-four (24) hours. The following day (Day 3) Peter traveled to Cornelius' house. From sunset on Day e to sunset on Day 3 is another twenty-four (24) hours. On Day 4, Peter arrived at Cornelius' house before 3:00 PM. Therefore, from sunset on Day 3 to 3:00PM of Day 4 is nineteen (19) hours.

Day 1 = 3 hours

Day 2 = 24 hours

Day 3 = 24 hours

Day 4 = 21 hours

Time Period: Not a literal 96 hours.

The total time spanning over all four days would equal approximately seventy-two (hours). Cornelius stated "four days ago" in verse 30. Thus, four days was not a literal ninety-six (96) hour timeline but the seventy-two (72) hour period actually spanning four Roman days since two of those days recorded in Scripture were only portions of days.

As seen in similar Scriptures calculating time, never has "three days" or on "the third day" referred to a literal interpretation requiring a period of seventy-two hours to transpire before the person said "three days" or "on the third day." Neither has any Biblical timeline under two days, or forty-eight hours, been called three days. Therefore, the logical conclusion when comparing New Testament passages to other Bible passages of time for Christ "rising on the third day" is that the period of Jesus' death must be more than forty-eight hours but may be less than a precise seventy-two hours.

How It Impacts the Death Timeline

Using the above Biblical calculations of time, it is illogical for Sabbath Day worshipers to reinforce a theory of the crucifixion of Jesus on a Wednesday, because of a requirement for Jesus to rise from the grave exactly seventy-two hours later. In such a seventy-two hour legalistic position, Jesus would actually be officially dead over seventy-two hours, being dead at least seventy-five hours (since he died at 3:00 PM). Ironically, these scholars completely dismiss the additional time of death on the cross, disqualifying it as not being in the grave or "in the heart of the earth." However, if Scriptures stated Jesus would be dead and rise the third day, it would be impossible to fulfill that requirement and be dead for seventy-five hours, which would technically be rising on the fourth day. Twisting scripture to arrive at a seventy-two hour precise requirement just to satisfy the desire of a resurrection on the Sabbath is not in agreement with the Spirit of the Scriptures. It also must discount all the other scriptures supporting the timeline of the resurrection just before dawn on Sunday.

Such a presupposition would stretch the scriptures to an unreasonable interpretation that is not in agreement with other Biblical passages identifying a timeline for an early morning resurrection.

Correspondingly, the custom commonly held by tradition in the Church that Jesus was crucified on Friday would also be disqualified by the above Biblical timeline comparison examples, as the timeline for a Friday crucifixion is at most thirty-nine hours. There is no Biblical example of a thirty-nine hour period of time qualifying for the description of "three days and three nights" or "on the third day." If the timeline were counted from the entombment alone, the maximum hours of death would be thirty-six (36) hours.

3:00 PM Nisan 14th to 3:00 PM Nisan 15th = 24 hours

3:00 PM Nisan 15th to 6:00 AM Nisan 16th = 15 hours

Total   39 hours

Therefore, the only crucifixion date in agreement with previous Biblical examples for rising on "the third day" while also providing for a three-day, three-night timeline is a Thursday.

3:00 PM Nisan 14th to 3:00 PM Nisan 15th = 24 hours

3:00 PM Nisan 15th to 3:00 PM Nisan 16th = 24 hours

3:00 PM Nisan 16th to 6:00 AM Nisan 17th = 15 hours

Total   63 hours

While sixty-three (63) hours is unquestionably longer than two days, the sixty-third hour would actually occur on the third day. Additionally, a review of the Jewish calendar would demonstrate that a Thursday afternoon crucifixion would provide a literal timeline spanning three daylight periods and three nighttime periods. Thus, a Thursday crucifixion is the only weekday that fulfills literally three days and three nights of death while simultaneously fulfilling a rising on the third day requirement.

The "Preparation Day" Controversy

It is interesting to note that the term 'preparation day' usually refers to the Friday before the weekly Sabbath, but it can also refer to the day before any holy convocation Sabbath. The translation of the word "preparation" means to make ready and does not specifically refer to only Fridays as many Christian scholars and commentators have led the Church to believe. Although Friday is the most common usage of a "preparation day," it is not the only meaning. The duplicity in terminology for preparation day has been the cornerstone of many an argument as to whether or not the Scriptures surrounding Jesus' crucifixion actually meant Friday, or if they meant the preparation day for the annual Sabbath on Nisan 15th, which was Passover (Nisan 14th).

Believers who hold to a Wednesday or Thursday crucifixion often view the translation of the preparation day as solely being the day before the holy convocation Sabbath and not just the weekly Sabbath. Scripture specifically clarifies the preparation day in which Christ was crucified as the Preparation Day for the High Sabbath of Nisan 15th:

> "[31]Therefore, because it was **the Preparation Day**, that the bodies should not remain on the cross on the Sabbath (**for that Sabbath was a high day**) besought Pilate that their legs might be broken, and that they might be taken away."
> John 19:31

Since the Bible clarifies that this particular preparation day was the day for the High Sabbath, Believers should hold the position that this particular preparation day is indeed Nisan 14th, possibly but not necessarily a Friday. In addition the Gospel of John in chapter thirteen witnesses to the events of the Last Supper as being "before the Feast of the Passover" (John 13:1). On this night, the Apostle John recorded the events and opinions of the disciples regarding Jesus encouraging Judas to leave after dinner:

> "₂₉And some of them thought, because Judas had the bag, that Jesus had said unto him, buy those things that we have need of *against [before] the feast;* or that he should give something to the poor."
> John 13:29

Since the disciples knew Jesus would not break Sabbath law, it would be unreasonable for them to presume Jesus was sending Judas to purchase items on a Sabbath day. Subsequently because Scripture records the disciples believed Jesus sent Judas to purchase items *before* the Feast, the logical conclusion becomes the Last Supper transpired on Passover, Nisan 14th, referred to as first day of unleavened bread in Matthew 26:17; Mark 14:12-16; and Luke 22:7-13 because of its association with the Feast. Again, these scriptures support events of the crucifixion transpired on Nisan 14th, which was the day before the annual Sabbath feast day or holy convocation day observed on Nisan 15th.

Some biblical commentators have stated the position that a "High Sabbath" (as referred do in John 19:31) can only refer to a holy convocation day that falls concurrently on a weekly Sabbath. There is no biblical or historical evidence during the Second Temple for the supposition that a High Sabbath must be a day in which two Sabbaths overlapped. Therefore, trying to determine the crucifixion date based solely upon the terminology of the words "preparation day" is not possible. The preparation day for the Feast of Unleavened Bread in the First Century could literally be on any Gregorian day of the week but would always be on the fourteenth day of Nisan in the Jewish calendar. As mentioned earlier in Chapter 1 of this book, during the lifetime of Jesus the Jewish calendar was based upon viewing of the new moon, not on the current Jewish calendar with fixed dates from Hillel II. Thus, there were no restrictions on which day of the week the Feast of Unleavened Bread could occur. During the Second Temple, it was possible to experience consecutive Sabbaths if the Annual Sabbath came directly before the weekly Sabbath in the same week.

Thankfully, the Lord provided more than just "the preparation day" for the high day Sabbath as guidance for understanding the timeline of events.

> "$_{28}$Then led they Jesus from Caiaphas unto the hall of judgment: and it was early; and they themselves went not into the judgment hall, **lest they should be defiled: but that they might eat the Passover.**"
> John 18:28

> "$_{39}$But ye have a custom, that I should release unto you one ***at the Passover:*** will ye therefore that I release unto you the King of the Jews?"
> John 18:39

"₁₄And it was *the preparation for the Passover*, and about the sixth hour: and he saith unto the Jews, Behold your King!"
John 19:14

"₁₇Now the *first day of the feast of unleavened bread* the disciples came to Jesus, saying unto him, Where wilt thou that we prepare for thee to eat the Passover?"
Matthew 26:17

"₁After *two days was the feast of the Passover, and of Unleavened Bread:* and the chief priests and the scribes sought how they might take Him by craft and put Him to death."
Mark 14:1

"₁₂And *the first day of unleavened bread*, when they killed the Passover, his disciples said unto him, Where wilt thou that we go and prepare that thou mayest east the Passover?"
Mark 14:12

"₇Then came *the day of unleavened bread when the Passover must be killed.*"
Luke 22:7

All the scriptures combined clearly demonstrate the terminology for "the preparation day" meant the day of preparation for the Feast of Unleavened Bread on Nisan 15th (which was Passover, Nisan 14th) and not the weekly day of preparation for the weekly Sabbath of Friday.

CHAPTER 6

FEAST OF FIRST FRUITS & PENTECOST

Torah Mandate

The Feast of First Fruits is a celebration of the reaping of the first grain of the Promised Land, the barley harvest. It occurs within the seven-day Feast of Unleavened Bread. Called Yom HaBrikkurim in Hebrew, this festival is not considered a holy convocation day. Although Feast of First Fruits is not Sabbath day, it has one important restriction associated with it. Chiefly no Jewish person could eat of the new grain of the land until the High Priest had formally offered the sheaf to the Lord. The "sheaf" is also translated "omer" which is a dry unit of measuring grain approximately equal to 3.64 liters. The barley stocks growing the field were selected and cut. Then the grain was worked out of the stocks and collected in containers. Later this grain would be ground into fine flour and presented to the Lord. Unlike animal sacrifices, the omer or sheaf was not burned or consumed upon the fiery altar. Instead the priests would present a holy vessel with the fresh grain or freshly ground flour to God. They would literally lift up the vessel and wave it before the Lord. Afterward, the wave offering would become property of the Levitical priests and their families because God had stated He would be their inheritance.

"₂₀And the Lord spake unto Aaron, Thou shalt have no inheritance in their land, neither shalt thou have any part among them: *I am thy part and thine inheritance* among the children of Israel."
Numbers 18:20

"₉Wherefore Levi hath no part nor inheritance with his brethren; *the Lord is his inheritance*, according as the Lord thy God promised him."
Deuteronomy 10:9

"₈And the Lord spake unto Aaron, *Behold, I also have given thee* the charge of mine heave offerings of all the hallowed things of the children of Israel; unto thee have I given them by reason of the anointing, and to thy sons, by an ordinance for ever.... ₁₁And *this is thine; the heave offering of their gift, with all the wave offerings of the children of Israel:* I have given them unto thee, and to thy sons and to thy daughters with thee, by a statute for ever: every one that is clean in thy house shall eat of it. ₁₂*All the best of the oil, and all the best of the wine, and of the wheat, the firstfruits of them which they shall offer unto the Lord, them have I given thee.* ₁₃*And whatsoever is first ripe in the land, which they shall bring unto the Lord, shall be thine;* every one that is clean in thine house shall eat of it. ₁₄*Every thing devoted in Israel shall be thine.*"
Numbers 18:8-12

The Feast of First Fruits was a momentous celebration honoring God as the provider of the harvest. It acknowledged that the daily bread each family had to eat was directly from the His hand. As King of the harvest, no one could eat of the new harvest until it was dedicated to

God. The people were forced to eat from their stored, old grain until after the wave-offering was presented.

> "₁₀Speak unto the children of Israel, and say unto them, When ye be come into the land which I give unto you, and shall reap the harvest thereof, ***then ye shall bring a sheaf of the first fruits of your harvest unto the priest:*** ₁₁***And he shall wave the sheaf before the Lord***, to be accepted for you on the morrow after the Sabbath the priest shall wave it… ₁₄***And ye shall eat neither bread, nor parched grain, nor green ears, until the self-same day that ye have brought an offering unto your God:*** it shall be a statute for ever throughout your generations in all your dwellings."
> Leviticus 23:10-14

> "₁And it shall be, when thou art come in unto the land which the Lord thy God giveth thee for an inheritance, and possessest it, and dwellest therein; ₂***That thou shalt take of the first of all the fruit of the earth, which thou shalt bring of thy land that the Lord thy God giveth thee, and shalt put it in a basket, and shalt go unto the place which the Lord thy God*** shall choose to place his name there. ₃And thou shalt go unto the priest that shall be in those days, and say unto him, I profess this day unto the Lord thy God, that I am come unto the country which the Lord sware unto our fathers for to give us. ₄And the priest shall take the basket out of thine hand, and set it down before the altar of the Lord thy God… ₈And the Lord brought us forth out of Egypt with a mighty hand, and with an outstretched arm, and with great terribleness, and with signs, and with wonders: ₉And he hath brought us into this place, and hath given us this land, even a land that floweth with milk and

honey. ₁₀*And now, behold, I have brought the firstfruits of the land, which thou, O Lord, hast given me.* And thou shalt set it before the Lord thy God, and worship before the Lord thy God"
Deuteronomy 26:1-10

The Feast of First Fruits highlighted the preeminence of God, as Yahweh decreed the firstfruits of the land belonged to Him. The theme of bringing to God the first fruits is repeated several times in the Old Testament and includes not only the first grain of the harvest, but also the firstborn of both livestock and men (Exodus 22:29, 23:19, 34:26; and Deuteronomy 18:4, 26:2). The wave-sheaf offering was presented to the Lord in the Temple during the morning sacrifices, as a thanksgiving offering and honored God as the giver of all things. The Feast of First Fruits' wave-sheaf offering was an act of worship and harvest dedication to God. The wave-sheaf was selected on the morning of Nisan 14th, the Passover. The next day on the Feast of Unleavened bread, the sheaf was cut from the field and the grain formally prepared for the offering. On Yom HaBikkurim, the third day, the priest would wave the sheaf before the Lord.[26]

The day of the Feast of First Fruits' wave-sheaf offering has not been celebrated since the destruction of the Second Temple. However, its connotation to the symbology and timeline surrounding the resurrection of Jesus has not diminished. Neither has its prophetic declaration that Jesus would be "the first fruits" of the dead (1 Corinthians 15:20).

Pentecost

The Feast of the Harvest, called Shavuot by the Jews, is more commonly known as Pentecost to Christians. While the Feast of First Fruits commemorates the beginning of the barley harvest, Shavuot celebrated the summer wheat harvest. It is directly connected to the timeline of the Feast of First Fruits, because its timing is 50 days from the "omer."

> "$_{15}$And you shall count for yourselves from the day after the Sabbath, from the day that you brought the sheaf of the wave offering: seven Sabbaths shall be completed. $_{16}$**Count fifty days to the day** after the seventh Sabbath; then you shall offer a new grain offering to the LORD."
> Leviticus 23:15-16

Shavuot is also known as the Feast of Weeks because it is seven weeks from the Feast of First Fruits. Pentecost, derived from the Greek root word "pente," literally interpreted means five. Thus, Pentecost is the fiftieth day from the Feast of First Fruits. Before the destruction of the Second Temple, which altered Jewish practices from a Temple-based style of worship to a Talmudic practice, Shavuot was calculated fifty (50) days after the Sunday following the Feast of Unleavened Bread. Thus, Pentecost was observed on a Sunday during Sadducee control of the Temple. With the rise of Talmudic principles and the establishment of Hillel II's mathematical calendar, Shavuot is now an immovable date on Sivan 6th, regardless of the day of the week it occurs.

The Old Testament records that very first Pentecost observation took place at the foot of Mount Sinai. In the Book of Exodus, chapter 31, God presented the Law (the Ten

Commandments) to Moses engraved on tablets with the finger of God. In the very next verse, beginning chapter 32, the children of Israel immediately violated God's law and 3,000 people died.

> "₂₈And the children of Levi did according to the word of Moses: and there fell of the people that day about three thousand men."
> Exodus. 32:28

The New Testament book of Acts of the Apostles records that on the day of Pentecost that 3,000 people were saved and filled with the Holy Spirit. It is no surprise that the numerical value of five, which correlates to "pente," is associated with the image of Grace in the Bible. The Grace of God poured out on the day of Pentecost and filled the Believers.

> "₁And when the day of Pentecost was fully come, they [the disciples of Jesus] were all with one accord in one place. ₂And suddenly there came a sound from heaven as of a rushing mighty wind, and it filled all the house where they were sitting. ₃And there appeared unto them cloven tongues like as of fire, and it sat upon each of them. ₄And they were all filled with the Holy Ghost, and began to speak with other tongues, as the Spirit gave them utterance. ₅And there were dwelling at Jerusalem Jews, devout men, out of every nation under heaven… ₃₈Then Peter said unto them, Repent, and be baptized every one of you in the name of Jesus Christ for the remission of sins, and ye shall receive the gift of the Holy Ghost. ₃₉For the promise is unto you, and to your children, and to all that are afar off, even as many as the Lord our God shall call. ₄₀And with many other words did he testify

and exhort, saying, Save yourselves from this untoward generation. ₄₁Then they that gladly received his word were baptized: and the same day there were added unto them about three thousand souls. ₄₂And they continued steadfastly in the apostles' doctrine and fellowship, and in breaking of bread, and in prayers.
Acts 2:1-5 and 38-42

Pharisees versus Sadducees

In order to correctly interpret the timeline of events surrounding the Passover and crucifixion of Jesus Christ, a good bible scholar must understand the difference between a Pharisee and a Sadducee with regard to calculating the date for the Feast of First Fruits. Understanding the different scriptural interpretation each sect maintained will help readers better understand their influence upon the Jewish Religious Calendar. While New Testament Scriptures teach a variance between the Pharisees and the Sadducees regarding the resurrection of the dead, this was not their only difference when interpreting the Scripture. The interpretation of Leviticus 23:11-15 also varied between these two groups.

> "₁₁And he shall wave the sheaf before the Lord, to be accepted for you: ***on the morrow after the sabbath*** the priest shall wave it. ₁₂And ye shall offer that day when ye wave the sheaf an he lamb without blemish of the first year for a burnt offering unto the Lord. ₁₃And the meat offering thereof shall be two tenth deals of fine flour mingled with oil, an offering made by fire unto the Lord for a sweet savour: and the drink offering thereof shall be of wine, the fourth part of an hin.

> ₁₄And ye shall eat neither bread, nor parched corn, nor green ears, until the selfsame day that ye have brought an offering unto your God: it shall be a statute forever throughout your generations in all your dwellings. ₁₅And *ye shall count unto you from the morrow after the sabbath, from the day that ye brought the sheaf of the wave offering; seven sabbaths shall be complete."*
> Leviticus 23:11-15

Specifically, the interpretation of the phrase **"on the morrow after the Sabbath"** divided these two sects. The Sadducess understood the meaning of the day after the Sabbath to refer to the day after the weekly Sabbath. Since the weekly Sabbath occurs from Friday night to Saturday night, the following day would be Saturday night to Sunday.

Chart 12

Sun	Mon	Tues	Wed
1st day	2nd day	3rd day	4th day
Yom Rishon	Yom Sheini	Yom Shlishi	Yom R'vi'i
Feast of First Fruits			

Thurs	Fri	Sat	
5th day	6th day	**Sabbath Day**	
Yom Chamishi	Yom Shishi	**Yom Shabbat**	

By interpreting the Sabbath in Leviticus 23:11 to mean the weekly Sabbath, Sadducees always observe the Feast of First Fruits on a Sunday. By reckoning of the Feast of First Fruits to be on a Sunday, the counting of the omer for Shavuot (Pentecost) also always occurred on a Sunday.

In the Septuagint, the translation of the two Hebraic words from which the phrase "on the morrow after the Sabbath" is rendered in Leviticus chapter 23, the Greek word "protos" meaning "first" is used. This is indicative of the first day of the week, or the Sunday following the weekly Sabbath, thus supporting the Sadducee viewpoint.

> "Thus, the *Septuagint* suggests that the Sunday First Fruits and Pentecost was observed throughout the centuries before the First Coming of the Messiah…
>
> "the rabbis who compiled the Talmud after the destruction of the Temple, had a very different interpretation of the term Sabbath in this passage: The Sages' view was that this *shabbat* is the generic for day of rest, referring to the first day of Pessah. Accordingly, the count begins the second day of Pessah rather the night before and Shavuot always falls on Sivan 6…
>
> "The testimony of the *Septuagint* is important because it represents the thinking of Jewish authorities long before the first coming of Christ and the development of the Talmudic positions on controversial matters.[27]"

The Pharisees have a different interpretation of the phrase on "morrow after the Sabbath" in Leviticus. Pharisees believe the Sabbath of reference in the statement is the High Sabbath or holy convocation, (Nisan 15th) the Feast of Unleavened Bread. By Pharisaical interpretation, the Feast of First Fruits is always observed on Nisan 16th. Thus the counting of the omer and subsequent date for Pentecost varies based on the date occurrence of Nisan 16th within the week.

Chart 13

Day Nisan 13	Day Nisan 14	Day Nisan 15	Day Nisan 16
	Passover	Feast of Unleavened Bread	Feast of First Fruits
Night Nisan 14	Night Nisan 15	Night Nisan 16	Night Nisan 17
Passover	Feast of Unleavened Bread	Feast of First Fruits	

Understanding the difference in interpretation of which Sabbath the scripture is defining determines the date of when the Feast of First Fruits is celebrated. To summarize, the Sadducees always celebrate the Feast of First Fruits on a Sunday following the Feast of Unleavened Bread, while the Pharisees always celebrate it on Nisan 16th.

Not only is understanding how each sect interprets scripture important, but is equally important to know which sect was in charge of the Temple practices during Jesus' lifetime. If the High Priest was from the order of Pharisees, then the Feast of First Fruits would have been celebrated on Nisan 16th regardless of which Gregorian day it landed during the week. If the High Priest was a Sadducee, then the celebration would have occurred on a Sunday. Reading in Matthew 26:3, we are told that Cai'aphas is the High Priest. The Gospel of Luke in Chapter three verse two seems to imply two high priests were present: An-nas and Cai'aphas. Thankfully, the Gospel of John clarifies that An-nas was the father-in-law of Cai'aphas who was the High Priest (John 18:13). From their names alone in scripture, it would be impossible to discern the religious sect of either An-nas or Cai'aphas. Thankfully, the first-century, Jewish historian,

Josephus wrote about both these men in his work, <u>The Antiquities of the Jews</u>.

According to Josephus, An-nas officially served as High Priest for ten years between the timeline of 6A.D. to 15 A.D. He was removed from power by the Roman procurator Gratus. While having been officially removed from office, he remained one of Israel's most influential Sanhedrin leaders, because he was the true power behind his five sons and his son-in-law, who individually were also appointed to the position as High Priest over the years. Josephus specifically records that An-nas and his family belonged to the sect of Sadduccess.[28] It is extremely unlikely that An-nas would have given his daughter in marriage to a Pharisee, when the two sects had such opposing views of economic status and scriptural interpretation. Therefore, the occurrence of both names implies the ruling class of the Temple during Jesus' lifetime would have been the Sadducees.

By the time Josephus wrote his historical narrative in the late first century regarding the fall of Jerusalem in 70 AD, the Jewish Sanhedrin had established the concept that the Feast of First Fruits would always observed on Nisan 16 and Pentecost on Sivan 6.

> "Josephus went through a rather lengthy explanation that the Sabbath of Lev. 23:11 meant the first day of Unleavened Bread, not Saturday. Thus, apparently some time before the destruction of the Temple, the practice of observing First Fruits and Pentecost on Nisan 16 and Sivan 6 was in place…"[27]

Josephus' prolonged justification of the timing for the Feast of First Fruits, while indicating the practice of celebrating on Nisan 16th was in effect, also exemplifies it was not the only interpretation of Scripture used by the Jews. Had Nisan 16th been the only method used by the Jews, Josephus would not have had to explain the difference between the interpretation of which Sabbath Scripture implied because everyone would have known only one interpretation and celebrated at the same time. Josephus seems to almost argue his point, as if refuting other Jewish scholars who still held to the practice of interpreting or celebrating on the Sunday. Sadly, the majority of Bible scholars and commentators are quick to affirm the Feast of First Fruits has always been observed on Nisan 16th, when there is obvious historical evidence to the contrary. These scholars wrongly assert because Nisan 16th was the date for Feast of First Fruits, it must therefore have been the date Jesus rose from the grave. Nonetheless, since the Sadducees were in control of Temple worship practices during Jesus' lifetime, the sixteenth of Nisan would only have been recognized as the Feast of First Fruits if this date corresponded with the Sunday after the Feast of Unleavened Bread. If the crucifixion transpired on a Wednesday or Thursday, Nisan 16th would not have been the date for the Feast of First Fruits.

Therefore, the understanding of the Sadducees' timeline is essential to correctly determining the date of the resurrection of Jesus Christ. Also crucial is the historical fact that during the lifetime of Jesus, the Pharisaical calendar principles securing the Feast of First Fruits to Nisan 16th and Shavuot to Sivan 6th were not in place. Thus, commentaries or notes in study Bibles which firmly report the Feast of First Fruits is a fixed date to Nisan 16th, while correct to some extent, are woefully inaccurate for the calendar and timeframe during Jesus' life. It is highly probable that the Feast of First Fruits was celebrated on the Sunday following the Feast of Unleavened Bread because the Sadducees were in control of the Temple. In a week with a Friday crucifixion, Sunday would be Nisan 16th. However, in a week with a Wednesday crucifixion, the corresponding Sunday would be Nisan 18th, and a Thursday crucifixion would correlate to a Sunday on Nisan 17th.

Spiritual Relevance

Jesus as The First Fruits

The Feast of First Fruits revealed aspects of Jesus Christ who would be the "First Fruits" of God's redemptive plan. On this feast, Israel was to bring before the Lord the "first" of the harvest grain. By offering the harvest to God before any man could eat of it, Israel was acknowledging the source of all their blessings including a 'natural' harvest of grain was from God.

Israel was described as a first-fruits of God's harvest in the Book of Jeremiah 2:3. Similarly, Christians are especially dedicated to God in the manner of first fruits, as it is written in James 1:18, "of His own will He brought us forth by the word of truth, that we might be a kind of firstfruits of His creatures." The day of the wave sheaf or omer is significant for God's people today, because it commemorates the ascension of Jesus Christ and His acceptance by the Father as the "first of the firstfruits" of the redeemed of God.

Early in the morning of His resurrection, Jesus appeared unto Mary Magdalene. It was during this meeting that Jesus informed Mary that He was going to ascend to His Father before returning to His disciples. His ascension into Heaven on the day of His resurrection was to fulfill the wave-sheaf offering, which was waved by the High Priest before the

Lord. The acceptance of the first fruit sanctified the remaining harvest sheaves, for if the firstfruit be holy, the lump is also holy" (Romans 11:16).

> "₁₇Jesus saith unto her [Mary Magdalene], Touch me not; for I am not yet ascended to my Father: but go to my brethren, and say unto them, I ascend unto my Father, and your Father; and to my God, and your God."
> John 20:17

As the wave-sheaf offering was being performed by the Levitical priests in the earthly Temple during the morning, Jesus was simultaneously being accepted by the Father. For Jesus alone as High Priest of the Melchizidek Order was able to wave the offering (Himself) before the Lord in the Heavenly Tabernacle.

> "₁₁But **Christ being come an high priest** of good things to come, **by a greater and more perfect tabernacle, not made with hands,** that is to say, not of this building; ₁₂Neither by the blood of goats and calves, but by his own blood he **entered in once into the holy place**, having obtained eternal redemption for us."
> Hebrews 9:11

Alfred Edersheim in his book entitlted <u>The Temple: Its Ministry and Services</u> ellaborated on the uniqueness of the two different types of first fruits preseted before the Father in Heaven by Jesus Christ. One was Jesus Himself as the first fruits of all mankind resurrected from the dead; the other was the presentation of the first harvest Jesus obtained when rising from the dead: the resurrection of the Old Testament saints from Sheol's Paradise who were transported to Heaven. Since the firstfruits wave-offering was a type of peace offering in the Torah, Jesus' presentation of the resurrected saints to the Father enhances another spiritual layer to the depth of Romans 5:1, which states "therefore being justified by faith, we have peace with God through our Lord Jesus Christ." Jesus not only made peace between God and man, but His first offering in the Temple was a peace offering. He presented before Heaven's altar the first of resurrected men and women signifying His firstfruits of the spiritual harvest. Verses in the Book of Matthew, chapter twenty-seven, confirm the Old Testament saints had not only risen but appeared to many in Jerusalem as testimony to their resurrection from the dead. Interestingly, there is no mention of the resurrected saints appearing or remaining in Jerusalem after Jesus' ascension to the Father, indicating their ascension with Him.

> "Here the apostle clearly links the firstfruit offering with the resurrection of Yeshua our Mashiach. Yeshua's resurrection was like a 'wave offering' presented before the Father as the 'firstfruits' of the harvest to come! Moreover, Yeshua presented His firstfruits offering to the Father on this day: The tombs also were opened. And many bodies of the saints who had fallen asleep were raised, and coming out of the tombs after his resurrection they went into the holy city and appeared to many."[29]

After being presented before God, Jesus returned to Earth to spend the next forty days with His disciples. Scripture records later on the same Sunday as His pre-dawn resurrection, Jesus appeared to other disciples and eventually to ten in the Upper Room. Between the interval of Jesus' appearance to Mary Magdalene in the graveyard and His appearance to the apostles, God, the Father, accepted Him as the "First Fruits" from the dead.

> "₂₀But now is ***Christ risen from the dead, and become the firstfruits of them that slept [are dead]***. ₂₁For since by man came death, by man came also the resurrection of the dead. ₂₂For as in Adam all die, even so in Christ shall all be made alive. ₂₃But every man in his own order: ***<u>Christ the firstfruits</u>;*** afterward they that are Christ's at his coming."
> 1 Corinthians 15:20-23

Additionally, a wave-offering before the Lord did not require the sacrifice to be consumed or destroyed on the altar. Priests literally lifted up the holy vessel containing the grain or fine flour made from the grain to present it to the Lord. Then, the grain or flour was given to the Levite families as food. A comparison can be made between this sacrificial concept and the Lord Jesus Christ as well. For the Lord Jesus is the portion of fine grain (or food) waved before God and given to the Lord's people for sustenance. Jesus described His own body at the Last Supper as "bread." His bread is nourishment for His followers who are part of His royal priesthood.

> "₅***Ye also, as lively stones, are built up a spiritual house, an holy priesthood,*** to offer up spiritual sacrifices, acceptable to God by Jesus Christ. ₆Wherefore also it is contained in the scripture, Behold, I lay in Zion a chief corner stone, elect, precious: and he that believeth on him shall not be confounded. ₇Unto you therefore which believe he is precious: but unto them which be disobedient, the stone which the builders disallowed, the same is made the head of the corner, ₈And a stone of stumbling, and a rock of offence, even to them which stumble at the word, being disobedient: whereunto

also they were appointed. ₉But ***ye are a chosen generation, a royal priesthood,*** an holy nation, a peculiar people; that ye should shew forth the praises of him who hath called you out of darkness into his marvelous light."
1 Peter 2:5-9

Just as the omer of fine flour became the physical bread for the Levitical families, Jesus is the bread for Christians who are "a royal priesthood." Jesus' sheaf arose to become the spiritual bread of life, which would be given to His people, and all those who partake of Him, eating daily from His bread are revived, restored, and resurrected.

Pentecost the Second Fruits Harvested

While Jesus is the original First Fruits of the harvest raised from the dead, the second harvest began on Pentecost, during which the Holy Spirit was poured out upon the disciples (Acts 2:1-4). With the outpouring of the Holy Spirit on Believers, they became eternally identified with the firstfruits harvest of Jesus.

> "₂₃And not only they, but ourselves also, which ***have the firstfruits of the Spirit***, even we ourselves groan within ourselves, waiting for the adoption, to wit, the redemption of our body."
> Romans 8:23

> "₁₈Of his own will begat he us with the word of truth, that ***we should be a kind of firstfruits of his creatures***."
> James 1:18

Verse 41 in Acts chapter two reports that 3,000 people were baptized on Pentecost into the eternal life Jesus Christ offers to all who will believe on Him. Therefore, the spiritual symbology of the Feast of First Fruits can be summarized in the receiving of life from the dead, with Christ rising first from the grave. Jesus represents the first harvest from the power of sin and death during the Feast of First Fruits. The impact of Feast of First Fruits on Pentecost is not only a timeline demarcation counting from the day of First Fruits fifty days to the day of Pentecost, but also reflects a spiritual conveyance of the Jesus' spiritual power and the freedom from death to His Believers. The timeline for the second harvest wasn't just a single day almost 2,000 years ago when over 3,000 people were filled with the Holy Spirit. The second harvest of souls began on the day of the Pentecost and continues until the day of Jesus' second coming, allowing everyone alive the chance for redemption. Jesus extends His harvest blessings to Believers (the second harvest), and they received power from on High through the Holy Spirit to continue the ministry of Jesus on the Earth (Acts 1:4-1:8 to 2:1-4).

CHAPTER 7

THE LAST SUPPER DILEMMA

The Last Supper vs. Seder Supper

It is important for those having participated in the traditions of men who are now returning to the Scripture to rightly discern between fact and fiction. Although there are many practices and teachings commonly held within various denominational and nondenominational Christian churches, such as the Seder Supper, many of these customs have nothing to do with Bible scriptures directly. Ignorantly, many Christians have believed the practices of the Seder Supper are reflective of the Last Supper consumed by Christ. In trying to honor Jesus' last meal, they have mistakenly fallen from the Gospel of Grace and are in fact usurping the authority of Scripture by exalting the traditions of man above God's word.

Many understand from the Bible that during the lifetime of Jesus Christ, the Second Temple in Jerusalem was intact. Sacrifices were offered at the Temple in accordance with the Mosaic Law, including the sacrifice for the birth of Jesus, two turtledoves (Luke 2:22-24). Temple ordinances determined the Jewish calendar, and sacrificial lambs for Passover could still be offered. As a result of the Temple being operational during the lifetime of Jesus Christ, there was no Seder Supper ritual. The Passover meal during Jesus' life was kept solely in conjunction with the Law of Moses memorial of the Exodus outlined in the Torah. The lamb was slain by the Levitical priests then roasted on the night of Nisan 15th, consumed with bitter herbs and unleavened bread.

Upon the destruction of the Second Temple in 70 A.D. by the Romans, the ability to continue sacrificial practices regarding the Passover lamb ceased. The Jewish priesthood was scattered, and the identity of the Jewish religion was in danger of completely dissolving. As a result, the Sanhedrin, specifically the Pharisees sect, instituted rudimentary practices for honoring the journey from Egypt in the Book of Exodus that would commemorate the traditional Passover meal. Gamaliel II wrote the first documented source of a Seder Supper in 80 A.D. when he commented on the *Haggadah*.

> "Anyone who has not said these three words on Passover has not discharged his duty, and these are they: pesach, matzah and maror. Pesach ('Passover') – because the Allpresent passed over the houses of our ancestors in Egypt. Matzah ('unleavened bread') – because our ancestors were redeemed in Egypt. Maror ('bitter herbs') – because the Egyptians made the lives of our ancestors bitter in Egypt."[30]

Since 80 A.D. additional clarifications to the rituals have been added, which have culminated in the present day Seder Supper experience. "Seder" is a Hebrew word meaning "order," because the meal ceremony followed an established sequence of liturgical recitations and ritual foods, which narrate the Passover saga. This ritualistic sequence was governed by an instructional guide called the *Haggadah*.

Later in this book, further explanation is given regarding the primary difference of the Afikomen, or unleavened bread, used in the Seder Supper (which replaced the original memorial Passover Meal) and the leavened bread used during the Last Supper. In a Seder Supper, as in the Passover Meal, unleavened bread is the only allowed form of bread to be served. Per Torah restrictions, all chametz would have been removed from the house before this meal was served. At the Last Supper, Jesus served leavened bread. Although leavened bread is the pinnacle difference between the Seder Supper and the Last Supper, other significant differences between these two meals are also noticeable. For example the Seder Supper is held on Nisan 15th, while the Last Supper occurred on Nisan 14th. Hence, it is reasonable to conclude that anyone upholding the Seder Supper as a Christian practice does so ignorant of Jewish history and the biblically defined Last Supper.

Which Night: Nisan 13/14th vs. Nisan 14/15th

There are many details within the New Testament Scriptures that clearly identify which night the Last Supper was eaten. Many of these details hinge on identifying Torah Law restrictions for Nisan 15th and correlating these restrictions to events that happened during the night of the Last Supper. Associating similar Torah restrictions to events that happened the following day of the crucifixion also help to delineate the timeline. When considering all the Scriptural evidence, it becomes obvious that the night of the Last Supper occurred on Nisan 14th, when Nisan 13th changed to Nisan 14th. As such, this event could not have been the Mosaic Passover memorial meal, which must occur on the night of Nisan 15th as Nisan 14th gives way to Nisan 15th.

One of the events that transpired during the evening of the Last Supper is the washing of the disciples' feet by Jesus.

> "After that he [Jesus] poureth water into a basin, and began to wash the disciples' feet, and to wipe them with the towel wherewith he was girded."
> John 13:5

While there is symbolic washing of the hands in a Seder Supper, genuine washing or bathing is forbidden by the Torah on Nisan 15th. The restriction against washing derives from Sabbath restrictions for the feast day, outlined in Leviticus 23:7, "you shall do no servile work therein." While a weekly Sabbath forbids all work even cooking or maintaining a fire, a feast Sabbath allows for work to be performed that is directly associated to celebrating the feast, such as cooking the feast meal by roasting the Passover lamb over a fire. All other general work, not directly associated with the Feast, is strictly forbidden. This included washing or bathing. The washing of one's feet is considered servile work. Therefore, if Jesus had washed the disciples' feet on the night of Nisan 15th, He would have violated the Torah Law and not have been spiritually perfect. Since Scripture records Jesus was a spotless lamb, in order to avoid violating the feast day restrictions associated with Nisan 15th, the foot washing event must have occurred on Nisan 14th.

Another event recorded on the night of the Last Supper is the departure of Jesus and His disciples to the Garden of Gethsemane after the meal. All four Gospels record Jesus' journey to the garden (Matthew 26:36, Mark 14:32, Luke 22:39, John 18:1). The following verse from Exodus clearly describes that forbiddance of Jews to leave their homes on the night of Nisan 15th, when the Passover lamb was eaten.

> ₂₂And ye shall take a bunch of hyssop, and dip it in the blood that is in the bason, and strike the lintel and the two side posts with the blood that is in the bason; ***and none of you shall go out at the door of his house until the morning.*** ₂₃For the Lord will pass through to smite the Egyptians; and when he seeth the blood upon the lintel, and on the two side posts, the Lord will pass over the door, and will not suffer the destroyer to come in unto your houses to smite you. ₂₄And ye shall observe this thing for an ordinance to thee and to thy sons for ever."
> Exodus 12:22-24

Therefore, if the Last Supper had been held on Nisan 15th, Jesus and His disciples would have been forbidden to leave the Upper Room to travel to the Garden of Gethsemane. Knowing conclusively they traveled that night assures once again that the night in question must have been Nisan 14th. Similarly, the Gospels also record that it was during this night Jesus was taken before the High Priest and the Sanhedrin. Even if one were to presuppose Messiah could travel on the night of Nisan 15th, there could be no such travel for the Sanhedrin which strictly observed the ordinances of Moses. No member of the Pharisee or Sadducee high council would have left his home on the first night of the Feast of Unleavened Bread, let alone the High Priest himself. Thus, the restriction of travel for Nisan 15th clearly alludes to these events occurring on the night prior to the holy feast day.

In addition the Gospel of John in chapter thirteen witnesses to the events of the Last Supper as being "before the Feast of the Passover" (John 13:1). On this night, the Apostle John records the events and opinions of the disciples regarding Jesus encouraging Judas to leave after dinner:

> "₂₉And some of them thought, because Judas had the bag, that Jesus had said unto him, buy those things that we have need of *against [before] the feast*; or that he should give something to the poor."
> John 13:29

Torah Law prohibits the purchasing of merchandise on a Sabbath. Since the disciples knew Jesus did not break Sabbath law, it would be unreasonable for them to presume Jesus was sending Judas to purchase items on the annual Sabbath feast day of Nisan 15th. Subsequently because Scripture records the disciples believed Jesus sent Judas to purchase items **before** the Feast. The logical conclusion is then the Last Supper transpired on Passover, Nisan 14th.

Additionally, the Gospel of John records events that happen the morning following the Last Supper. Among these events was Jesus being taken to Pontius Pilate.

> "₂₈Then led they Jesus from Caiaphas unto the hall of judgment: and it was early; and *they themselves went not into the judgment hall, lest they should be defiled; but that they might eat the passover.*"
> John 18:28

The bold emphasis in the scripture above highlights the fact that the Sanhedrin did not want to defile their bodies. If they had defiled themselves, they could not have eaten of the Passover lamb during the Feast of Unleavened Bread on the night of Nisan 15th. This important detail in the Gospel of John underscores the fact that the prior night events (of the Last Supper) must have occurred on Nisan 14th.

Moreover, after the crucifixion, Joseph of Arimathea is said to have purchased a linen shroud.

> "$_{46}$And he **bought** fine linen, and took him down, and wrapped him in the linen, and laid him in a sepulchre which was hewn out of a rock, and rolled a stone unto the door of the sepulchre."
> Mark 15:46

The word for "bought" in the scripture above is the Greek word "agorazo" which means to purchase.^{31} To buy or sell merchandise was forbidden by Torah Law on Annual Sabbaths and weekly Sabbaths. Therefore, the act of purchasing linen to wrap the body of Jesus could not have been performed on Nisan 15th by a devout Jew. Thus, this action places additional emphasis of the death of Christ occurring on Passover day, Nisan 14th.

Many Christians argue Jesus consumed the true Passover meal, and use His statement in Luke 22:15 to justify their opinion, "with desire I have desired to eat this Passover with you before I suffer." However, those using this opinion have overlooked the details of the meal that Jesus served. The original Passover meal was eaten on the night of Nisan 15th, as Nisan 14th turn to the 15th. This memorial meal consisted of the Passover lamb, bitter herbs, and unleavened bread. All leaven was to be removed from the Jewish home before the Feast of Unleavened Bread in accordance with Torah Law (Exodus 12:15, 13:7). Therefore, Messiah could not eat leavened bread during the Last Supper meal if this dinner were to have occurred on the night of Nisan 15th.

"₂₆And as they were eating, Jesus took bread (Strong's #740), and blessed *it*, and brake *it*, and gave *it* to the disciples and said, Take, eat: this is my body."[31]
Matthew 26:26

"₂₂And as they did eat, Jesus took bread (Strong's #740), and blessed, and brake it, and gave to them, and said, Take eat: this is my body."[31]
Mark 14:22

"₁₉And he took bread (Strong's #740), and gave thanks, and brake it, and gave unto them, saying, This is my body which is given for you: this do in remembrance of me."[31]
Luke 22:19

Scripture in repeating detail identifies the bread eaten during the Last Supper as "leavened bread." The Strong's #740 indicated above is for the Greek word "artos," which is defined as a "raised loaf of bread."[31] There is a separate Greek word for unleavened bread (Strong's #106), "*azumos.*"[31] Since Jesus could not violate Torah Law, the details regarding the bread He served clarify the timeline to be on the night of Nisan 14th. Thus, the meal eaten at the Last Supper could not have been the genuine Mosaic Passover meal, memorializing the flight from Egypt.

The Last Supper Meal

Pondering the synoptic gospels account of the Last Supper and the account in the Gospel according to St. John, on the surface there has been the traditional understanding of a different interpretation in the timeline of events surrounding the Last Supper. The synoptic gospels seem to imply that Jesus ate the original "Passover meal," an event that occurs on the night of Nisan 15th while the timeline in the Gospel of John clearly indicates this dinner, commonly referred to as the Last Supper, took place on the night of Nisan 14th. Many Christian scholars over the years have dismissed the differences between the two contrasting accounts as not being significant enough to overcome the reality of the end product: Christ died for the sins of mankind and rose for our justification. Other Christians have used their limited interpretation of this seeming contrast to justify their misunderstanding of the timeline and have Jesus dying wrongly on Nisan 15th. Even worse, Jewish scholars and those with a spirit of antichrist have used this seeming contradiction to justify their opinion of the invalidity of the Last Supper and crucifixion events, which define the very Messianic ministry of Jesus Christ. However, upon deeper examination, the synoptic gospels and the Gospel of John do not contradict each other. In fact, the "differences" noted by many actually reinforce the ministry of Jesus Christ in the giving of the Gospel of Grace.

The Gospel of John clearly describes the events regarding the Last Supper to have occurred on Nisan 14th in the evening, followed immediately the next day on Nisan 14th by the trail and death of Jesus Christ. The synoptic gospels also give a timeline of events starting on Nisan 14th and when taken in their entirety completely agree with the Gospel of John. Consider the following scriptures:

> "[17]Now the *first day of the feast of unleavened bread* the disciples came to Jesus, saying unto him, Where

wilt though that we prepare for thee to eat the Passover?"
Matthew 26:17

"₂₀Now when the even was come, he sat down with the twelve ₂₁and as they did eat, he said, Verily I say unto you, that one of you shall betray me.
Matthew 26:20-21

"₁₂And the first day of unleavened bread, *when they killed the Passover [lamb]*, his disciples said unto him, Where wilt though that we go and prepare that thou mayest eat the Passover?"
Mark 14:12

"₁₇And in the evening he cometh with the twelve ₁₈And as they sat and did eat, Jesus said, Verily I say unto you, One of you which eateth with me shall betray me."
Mark 14:17-18

"₇Then came the day of unleavened bread, *when the Passover [lamb] must be killed.* ₈And he sent Peter and John saying, Go and prepare us the Passover, that we may eat."
Luke 22:7-8

Because the Torah is extremely definitive about which date the lamb should be killed (Exodus 12:6), the date of the events described in the synoptic gospels can be known to occur on Nisan 14th. Since the Jewish day begins at sunset, the synoptic gospels are accounting a dinner occurring on Nisan 14th. While there is some indication of a few hours between the request for a location by the disciples in where to eat and Jesus' gathering with them to eat the Last Supper, there is no indication that the disciples' question came early in the morning or that an entire day passed between these events. While some scholars argue the final meal was actually consumed the following night on Nisan 15th during the traditional Passover meal, in order to maintain this viewpoint, these scholars must disregard the details of scripture that clearly define the type of meal, specifically the bread, being consumed in the synoptic gospels.

> "$_{26}$And as they were eating, Jesus took bread (Strong's #740), and blessed *it*, and brake *it*, and gave *it* to the disciples and said, Take, eat: this is my body."[31]
> Matthew 26:26

> "$_{22}$And as they did eat, Jesus took bread (Strong's #740), and blessed, and brake it, and gave to them, and said, Take eat: this is my body."[31]
> Mark 14:22

> "$_{19}$And he took bread (Strong's #740), and gave thanks, and brake it, and gave unto them, saying, This is my body which is given for you: this do in remembrance of me."[31]
> Luke 22:19

In all these verses, the type of bread being consumed is a raised loaf of common bread, not unleavened bread. Torah clearly affirms no man shall eat leavened bread with the Passover lamb meal. In fact, Mosaic Law **required** unleavened bread to be eaten for the Passover meal consumed on Nisan 15th (see Exodus 12:8, 12:15, 12:18, 12:20, 13:6, 23:15, 34:18, Leviticus 23:6, Numbers 9:11, 28:17, Deuteronomy 16:3, 16:8). By the fifteenth day of Nisan, all leaven was to be removed from the Jewish home (Exodus

12:15, 13:7). Since Jesus neither could nor would violate Torah, the details regarding the bread He served clarify the timeline. The Last Supper must have occurred on the night of Nisan 14th and must exemplify a deeper meaning of His ministry, one which is not based on memorializing the past (events in Egypt) but reflect a prophetic future.

The word for bread as listed in the synoptic scriptures above is the Strong's #740, which the Greek word *"artos,"* literally meaning a raised loaf of bread.[31] There is a separate word for unleavened bread in Greek, Strong's #106, *"azumos"* which literally means unfermented, free from leaven, unleavened bread.[31] However, scripture never mentions the bread eaten during the Last Supper as being *azumos*. As demonstrated above, all the gospel accounts agree that it was leavened bread Jesus took and broke.

An astute scholar might argue, "wait a minute, that's a bold statement to make, stating **all** the gospel accounts agree that Jesus served leavened bread at the last supper because the Gospel of John does not clearly associate any bread or wine with the Last Supper. In fact, the only mention of food during John's account would seem to be the "sop" spoken of in chapter 13, verses 26-27." However, such a scholar would be wrong because he would have overlooked the prophetic announcement of the bread used for the Last Supper quoted in John 13:18:

> "I speak not of you all: I know whom I have chosen: but that the scriptures may be fulfilled, He that eateth bread (Strong's #740) with me hath lifted up his heal against me."[31]

The Gospel of John again reinforces that leavened bread or a raised loaf is being consumed during this final meal. This scripture while being descriptive of the bread at the Last Supper meal is also a prophetic scripture quoted from Psalms 41:9:

> "Yea, mine own familiar friend, in whom I trusted, which did eat of my bread (Strong's #3899), hath lifted up his heal against me."[31]

In examining the Hebrew word from the Strong's #3899 for the term bread used in Psalms 41:9, the word "lechem" is derived.[31] Lechem is the Hebrew word for a loaf of common bread, a leaven or raised loaf of bread; whereas (Strong's #4682) matstsah is the Hebrew word for unleavened bread.[31] Thus, both the Hebrew and Greek witnesses for the bread consumed during the Last Supper refer to a loaf of raised bread, or leavened bread.

Not only is leavened bread involved at the Last Supper in the initiation of the New Covenant, also referred to as the Eucharist or Holy Communion, but in every occurrence of the use of the word "bread" by Jesus in all the gospels, the Greek word artos (Strong's #740) is used.[31] Jesus **ALWAYS** identifies Himself as being the raised loaf. Never in the Bible does Jesus describe Himself as unleavened bread.

- He is the **True Bread of Heaven** (John 6:32)
- He is the **Bread of God** (John 6:33)
- He is the **Bread of Life** (John 6:35 and 6:48)
- He is **the Living Bread** which came down from Heaven (John 6:51)

- The bread that He gives is His flesh, given for the life of the world (John 6:51)

Jesus' very birthplace of Bethlehem also denoted His identification with raised bread. Bethlehem literally means "House of Raised Bread." Therefore, Jesus is from the House of Raised Bread, again reinforcing His spiritual association with raised bread instead of unleavened bread. Hence, the clarification of the use of leavened bread during the Last Supper is not a trivial fact. Its importance is reinforced in 1 Corinthians chapters 10 and 11. There is a crucial aspect of the Gospel of Grace revealed in understanding why leavened bread (a raised loaf) was broken by Jesus Christ at the Last Supper and why Jesus repeatedly stated He was a raised loaf of bread, distancing His ministry from unleavened bread. The difference between the types of bread is symbolic of the difference between the Mosaic Law and the Gospel of Grace.

To discover the mystery of the Gospel of Grace revealed in the types of bread, one needs to further examine the definitions for unleavened and leaven bread discussed in the bible:

Bread in Hebrew (Old Testament):

Lechem (Strong's #3899)[31] – noun: Leavened Bread (Raised Loaf)

Lechem's definition comes from the root word *lacham* (Strong's #3898)[31] which is a verb that has two primary meanings 1) to feed on; 2) figuratively this word means to fight, do battle, to make war, prevail, overcome.

> **Matstsah** (Strong's #4682)[31] – noun: Unleavened Bread
>
> The Matstsah bread definition comes from the root word *matsats* (Strong's #4711)[31], in the sense of greedily devouring for sweetness; it means milk, or to suck milk.[31]

After beholding the root meanings behind *lechem* and *matstsah*, it is no small significance that the New Testament teaches a delineation between the Mosaic Law and the Gospel of Grace describing this difference as "milk" and "strong meat."

> "[12]For when for the time you ought to be teachers, ye have need that one teach you again which be the ***first principles of the oracles of God***; and are become such as have ***need of milk***, and not of strong meat. [13]For ***every one that useth milk is unskillful in the word of righteousness: for he is a babe***. [14]But ***strong meat belongeth to them that are of full age***, even those who by reason of use have their senses exercised to discern both good and evil".
> Hebrews 5:12-14

One must understand what the "first principles of the oracles of God" are before he can proceed further. Scripture teaches that unto the Jews was committed *"the oracles of the God"* (Romans 3:2). The ***first principles*** defined literally mean "the first elements," or "something orderly arranged from the beginning," or "in an order of rank."[31] Thus, "first principles of the oracles of God" can only refer to the Mosaic Law.

Those operating under a "milk mentality" are intertwined in the Mosaic Law and have not come to the end of their own self-effort; rather they are still trying to fulfill the Law. "Sucking milk," the root behind the Hebrew for 'unleavened bread,' is indicative then of those people who are under the Mosaic Law or in a Mosaic Law based mentality. Anyone using "milk" is stated to be *unskillfull* (Strong's #552), which literally defined means "ignorant" or "inexperienced."[31] What are the milk drinkers or those following the Law of Moses ignorant of? The Word of Righteousness! The Strong's Greek word #3056 for *"word"* used above means: logos. The Logos is Jesus Christ, who scripture teaches was made flesh and dwelt among us (John 1:14). Therefore, law keepers are inexperienced with Jesus. The definition of "righteousness" (Strong's #1343) means "by implication of character" or "an act, specifically Christian justification, righteousness."[31] Thus, those who are entangled in the Mosaic Law are inexperienced with Jesus and are ignorant of their righteousness and justification in Him.

> "[17]For therein is the *righteousness of God revealed from faith to faith*: as it is written, The just shall live by faith."
> Romans 1:17

> "[21]But now the *righteousness of God without the law is manifested*, being witnessed by the law and the prophets; [22]Even *the righteousness of God which is by faith of Jesus* Christ unto all and *upon all them that believe*: for there is no difference: [23]For all have sinned, and come short of the glory of God; [24]Being justified freely by his grace through the redemption

that is in Christ Jesus: ₂₅Whom God hath set forth to be a propitiation through faith in his blood, to declare his righteousness for the remission of sins that are past, through the forbearance of God;"
Romans 3:21-25

"₂₁For he hath made him *to be* sin for us, who knew no sin; that *we might be made the righteousness of God* in him."
2 Corinthians 5:21

Those under the Mosaic Law or those mixing Law and Grace do not understand the fullness of the completed works of Jesus Christ. For the Law was designed to bring mankind to the end of himself and to the knowledge of Jesus Christ. Once the finished works of Jesus' are completely understood, Believers realize their identity in Christ. Believers who know they have been made righteous by the blood of Christ never return to the Mosaic Law (or works) for their redemption, justification, or sanctification. Believers must operate in the New Covenant by faith alone, which by its very nature is contrary to the Mosaic Law of works.

"₂₄Wherefore the law was our schoolmaster to bring us unto Christ, that we might be justified by faith. ₂₅But after that faith is come, we are no longer under a schoolmaster."
Galatians 3:24-25

Believers who have come to the understanding of the Righteousness in Christ are at the place of eating "strong meat" (Hebrews 5:12 & 14) because they know who they are in Jesus Christ and are ready to teach others the Gospel of Grace. These Believers have their identities established firmly in Jesus, and as such He nourishes them and matures them. The words used for "strong" and "meat" in Hebrews chapter five are outlined below:

Strong (Strong's #4731)[31] – Greek noun *"stereos"* meaning solid or firm, steadfast, referring to what is immovable, unchanging. Root word from verb (Strong's #2476)[31] "histemi" meaning to establish, to appoint, to covenant, to abide

Meat (Strong's #5160)[31] – Greek noun *"trophe"* meaning nourishment, food, maintenance. Root word from verb (Strong's #5142)[31] trepho meaning "I feed," "I nourish," to bring up, to make grow

It is easy to discern from the definitions above, the differences between milk and real food. Milk, symbolic of the Mosaic Law, was never given to sustain man's eternal life. A man existing solely on milk will be a carnal man, walking in the ways of his flesh and ruled by his behavior. Jesus is the raised Bread of Life, the unchanging truth, which will provide nourishment for the soul and cause maturity in your understanding of God. As Believers grow in the knowledge of God's Grace and understand their righteousness in Christ, old behavior patterns cease and they walk as spirit-filled men and women.

1 Corinthians 3:1-3 reinforce this concept, as the words *"were not able"* and *"neither yet now are ye able"* are derived from the Greek word "dunamai." Dunamai usually means, 'to be empowered, to show ability and power.' Carnal Christians lack spiritual power and the ability to overcome the flesh, exemplified by their jealousy and strife. The scripture states Paul could not speak to these Christians as "spiritual"

(Strong's Greek #4152), literally meaning from Thayer's Greek Lexicon *"relating to the realm of the Spirit, the invisible sphere in which the Holy Spirit imparts faith, reveals Christ."*[32] Thus, a Believer operating in the Spirit, is one whom the Holy Spirit has imparted faith and revealed Jesus. Having this knowledge, a man knows his identity in Christ and is empowered to live above the rudimentary principles of the Mosaic Law and flesh. By living above the flesh, the spiritual man eats real sustenance, strong meat. Correspondingly, people who do not have a complete revelation of the finished work of Christ Jesus are not operating in the spiritual realm and as a result are spiritually powerless to overcome the sins of flesh including sexual and physical addictions; fear and anxiety; depression, anger and bitterness; envy and jealousy; gossiping and lying, pride, or idolatry.

> "₁And I, brethren, could not speak unto you as unto spiritual, but as unto carnal, (*even as*) unto babes in Christ. ₂I have fed you with milk, and not with meat: for hitherto ye were not able (*to bear it*), neither yet now are ye able. ₃For ye are yet carnal: for whereas (*there is*) among you envying, and strife, and divisions, are ye not carnal, and walk as men?"
> 1 Corinthians 3:1-3

It is no coincidence that the leavened (raised) bread that Jesus took and broke at the Last Supper corresponds to the identical type of bread that Mel-chiz'ed-ek, King of Sa'lem brought as part of the ceremonial offering to Abraham. Mel-chiz'ed-ek was a High Priest of the God and operated in God's covenant of Grace as exemplified not only in the leavened bread and wine but in the oration he gives when addressing Abraham:

> "₁₈And ***Melchizedek*** king of Salem ***brought forth bread and wine***: and ***he was the priest of the most high God***. ₁₉And ***he blessed him***, and said, ***Blessed be Abram*** of the most high God, possessor of heaven and earth: ₂₀***And blessed be the most high God***, which hath delivered thine enemies into thy hand. And he [Abraham] gave him [Melchizedek] tithes of all."
> Genesis 14:18-20

Many scholars have determined that Mel-chiz'ed-ek operated under a benediction of Grace not only because He preceded the Mosaic Law, but also because his ministry was only one of blessings. The Mosaic Law presumed the strength of man to fulfill the Law; thus it stated, "thou shall…" and "thou shall not…" Within the Mosaic Law, man operated under a system of blessings and curses, which were dependent upon the man's behavior or performance to the Law. Basically, the Law was a system of "do good, get good" and "do bad, get bad." Sadly, within this system, no son of Adam was ever able to operated within only the blessings, because every man continued to sin. Therefore, the sacrificial system was given as part of the Mosaic Law to make atonement for the failures of man's ability to keep the Law perfectly. Therefore, while the Law was perfect and holy, man who was not holy or spiritually perfect could not keep the Law and through the sacrificial system was brought to the knowledge of his perpetual sinful state that required a divine Savior.

God in His great mercy and love for mankind found fault with the first covenant of Mosaic Law, not with the perfection of the covenant but with man's inability to keep the Law, which kept mankind in a cyclical state of cursing (see Hebrews 8:6-12). Thus, God instituted a new covenant mediated by Jesus, the Gospel of Grace, which is completely different. It is not founded on the strength of men to perform, but is based on the strength of God to provide. Within the Gospel of Grace, a Believer's behavior never determines covenant blessings or curses from God because The New Covenant of Grace only contains blessings. There is no curse associated for lack of performance. The New Covenant is based upon the behavior and performance of Jesus Christ alone, and those who enter into the New Covenant are there solely by the Grace of God through faith in Jesus. Since Jesus was flawless, He alone fulfilled the Mosaic Law perfectly, and Believers who accept Jesus enter into His righteousness before God. His righteousness is imputed to the Believer, and the Believer is eternally infused with the righteousness of God, which is in Christ Jesus (Romans 3:22 and 2 Corinthians 5:21). Whenever God looks upon the Believer, He sees only Jesus's righteousness, and as a result, eternal blessings flow to the Believer through Jesus. This is because Jesus bore the sins of mankind and was already cursed in His body by God on the cross making atonement for the sins of mankind. There can be no additional cursing for men who believe in Him. Thus, only blessings are available in the New Covenant of the Gospel of Grace.

> "$_6$But now hath he [Jesus] obtained a more excellent ministry, by how much also he is the ***mediator of a better covenant***, which was ***established upon better promises***. $_7$For if that first covenant had been faultless, then should no place have been sought for the second. $_8$For finding fault with them, he [God] saith, Behold, the days come, saith the Lord, when I will make a ***new covenant with the house of Israel and with the house of Judah***: $_9$Not according to the covenant that I made with their fathers in the day when I took them by the hand to lead them out of the land of Egypt;

because they continued not in my covenant, and I regarded them not, saith the Lord. ₁₀For *this is the covenant that I will make* with the house of Israel after those days, *saith the Lord; I will put my laws into their mind, and write them in their hearts*: and *I will be to them a God, and they shall be to me a people*: ₁₁And they shall not teach every man his neighbour, and every man his brother, saying, Know the Lord: for all shall know me, from the least to the greatest. ₁₂For *I will be merciful to their unrighteousness, and their sins and their iniquities will I remember no more."*
Hebrews 8:6-12

"₁₆For God so loved the world, that he gave his only begotten Son, that *whosoever believeth in him should not perish*, but have everlasting life."
John 3:16

"₁₃*If we believe not, yet he abideth faithful*: he cannot deny himself."
1 Timothy 2:13

During the meeting between Mel-chiz'ed-ek and Abraham, Mel-chiz'ed-ek simply blesses. He does not mention any consequences or curses to Abraham. There is no mention of performance requirements for Abraham before God's blessing would be bestowed upon him. The Mosaic Law involves both blessings (to those upholding the Law) and curses (for those who fail to perform it perfectly). The ministry of Mel-chiz'ed-ek is a ministry of divine blessing. The name of Mel-chiz'ed-ek transliterated means "King of Righteousness." He is also called the King of Sa'lem, which being interpreted is the Hebrew word (Strong's #8004) "shalem," meaning peace or peaceful. This word stems from the Hebrew word (Strong's #7999) shalam. Shalam connotates "be safe" and to "be free from fault." Therefore, the symbology behind the naming of Mel-chiz'ed-ek implies that The King of Righteousness makes one free from fault and provides peace with God. The Holy Spirit specifically refers to Jesus in the Book of Hebrews as a High Priest of the Mel-chiz'ed-ek Order. Jesus is the King of kings (1 Timothy 6:14-15; Revelations 17:14, 19:16), who has made Believers free from fault, free from sin. Believers now enter into the New Covenant of Grace, which contains only blessings from God.

Thus, there is a depth of wisdom in understanding the Hebrew roots behind leavened bread (that deep, nourishing knowledge of Jesus who went to battle and prevailed over sin, who upon continually feeding we are raised up, grown & matured) and unleavened bread (the milk or Mosaic law; the rudimentary instruction designed to bring a man to the end of his self-effort and recognize his need for a divine savior). Knowing that leavened bread is used by the Mel-chiz'ed-ek Order also helps one to understand the fullness of the symbolized for unleavened bread in the Old Testament. Similarly, additional wisdom is revealed in understanding the Greek definitions of leavened and unleavened bread and their symbology.

Bread in Greek (The New Testament):

Artos (Strong's #740) – A raised loaf, leavened bread; showbread (loaves consecrated to the Lord)

Artos' root word comes from the verb *airo* (Strong's #142) meaning to lift up, elevate, or raise up (literally and figuratively); to bear away what has been raised, to take away what was attached, to expiate sin: to loose or take away from another what was his; to appropriate; to take and apply to any use.

Within the very definition of Artos (raised up) is the picture of Jesus high and lifted up (John 3:14-15 and John 12:32). Also the root verb exposes the essence of Jesus being the expiation of man's sins. He has raise up sin from off of mankind and carried it. He has taken away that which was attached to men by their very nature, the nature of Adam, and loosed them from the burden of sin and death. He can appropriate to them His righteousness as He bears away their sins. Jesus is the amazing bread of life from the eternal House of Raised Bread in Heaven.

The Greek word for unleavened bread also has very deep meaning in the root word.

> **Azumos** (Strong's #106) – unleavened bread, unfermented, free from leaven
>
> Azumos is from two Greek words (Strong's #1) *"a"* (aleph) of Hebrew origin, the first letter of the alphabet, meaning figuratively Alpha, and used as a contraction meaning "without" and *zume* (Strong's #2219) meaning ferment, leaven.

Aleph in Hebrew is associated with "Father" (Abba). Its pictograph is of the ox (a symbol of the sacrificial animal). Aleph therefore is preeminent in its order and alludes to the indescribable mysteries of the oneness of God and God as a sacrifice (in Jesus). The word *aluph* (derived from the very name of this letter) means "Master" or "Lord." Thus, even in the Greek definition and understanding of azumos there is a Hebraic imprint. This symbolic reference testifies that without the lifting of the Lord (God's Grace), you can only have unleavened bread (the Law). The Mosaic Law is natural to a man. Men understand the concept of works: do good, get good; do bad, get bad. However in their most zealous works, men will never be righteous because as sons and daughters of Adam they inherently have sinful "DNA" that by its very nature prevents them from being righteous through self-effort. God's Grace independent of men's effort to perform righteously is the only true hope mankind has for rising out of this state of perpetual sin. God alone can lift mankind up, replacing their sinful nature, as He causes them to be reborn by His spirit. Without the Father reaching out to save humanity, we can never reach salvation by our own merit. Thus, azumos is the depiction of the Mosaic Law because it means, "being without or void of any lifting or raising up." Unleavened bread is void of the Father's leavning (or Grace). Those eating azumos (living under the Law) for their righteousness or sustenance can never rise above or overcome the Law because they continually focus on their own strength and effort. Only through Jesus, who alone was able to fulfill the Mosaic Law, can man ever be lifted up as righteous before God. It is through the Grace of God, righteousness is imputed to men by the efforts of Christ Jesus.

Therefore, while it is true that Jesus states in Luke 22:15, "with desire I have desired to eat this Passover with you before I suffer," it has been incorrectly interpreted that this statement affirmed Jesus actually ate the Mosaic memorial Passover meal on Nisan 15th. This interpretation is wrong because Jesus did not come to give the law. "For the law was given by Moses, but Grace and truth came by Jesus Christ" (John 1:17). Jesus came to give Grace and Truth, culminated in the New Covenant, a true spiritual Passover in the giving of His life for our life. Therefore, Jesus is not affirming a desire to eat the Mosaic Passover covenant meal with His disciples; instead, Jesus is expressing His great desire to institute the New Covenant, by which the disciples and all mankind will partake of His flesh and blood to receive everlasting life. Until this time in Jesus' ministry, the New Covenant while hinted at in His preaching had not been established. However, on this Passover night (Nisan 14th), the fullness of the spiritual analogies reflected in the first the Passover are concluded. There is no more reason for Messiah or His followers to keep the Mosaic Passover to remember the bondage in Egypt and God's deliverance from physical slavery. The true Passover lamb and New Covenant have come (Hebrews 8:6-12). The Bread of Life is raised up, and the curse of sin and death has forever passed over all those who partake of Jesus Christ.

In conclusion according to the Torah, the reason for the continuance of the Passover meal was to honor the memory of the night Israel was released from bondage. Thus, Jesus purposely did not break unleavened bread at the Last Supper Passover meal, to embrace this fateful night as a reenactment of the events in Exodus. Jesus was not interested teaching His disciples to remember Moses' law of deliverance from Egypt, for they clearly had those principles established in the Torah already. Instead, Jesus was instituting a New Covenant exemplified by new bread. Jesus' breaking of leavened bread during the Last Supper commemorated the New Covenant: the Gospel of Grace, which was now being given to men. This New Covenant replaced the Old Covenant of the Mosaic Law.

> "₆But now hath he obtained a more excellent ministry, by how much also he [Jesus] is the mediator of *a better covenant*, which was *established upon better promises*. ₇For if that *first covenant* had been faultless, then should no place have been sought for

the second. ₈For *finding fault* with them, he saith, Behold, the days come, ***saith the Lord, when I will make a new covenant*** with the house of Israel and with the house of Judah: ₉***Not according to the covenant that I made with their fathers in the day when I took them by the hand to lead them out of the land of Egypt***; because they continued not in my covenant, and I regarded them not, saith the Lord. ₁₀For ***this is the covenant*** that I will make with the house of Israel after those days, saith the Lord; I will put my laws into their mind, and write them in their hearts: and I will be to them a God, and they shall be to me a people: ₁₁And they shall not teach every man his neighbour, and every man his brother, saying, Know the Lord: for all shall know me, from the least to the greatest. ₁₂For ***I will be merciful to their unrighteousness, and their sins and their iniquities will I remember no more.***"
Hebrews 8:6-12

God found fault with the children of Israel who where unable to keep the Old Covenant which God says He instituted on the Feast of Unleavened Bread (Nisan 15th, *in the day* when He took them out of Egypt). Again here in Hebrews 8:9, "unleavened bread" is tied to the Old Covenant of Law. God found fault with this covenant because man could not keep it. Therefore, God established a better covenant; a New Covenant founded on better promises in which God would be merciful to man's unrighteousness and no longer attribute man's sins to him. The New Covenant would be established upon the broken body and blood of Jesus Christ, who taking all mankind's sins upon Himself exchanged them for His righteousness. God now imputes the righteousness of Christ to Believers as a result of Jesus mediating the New Covenant. Jesus never had any intention of breaking the old bread (unleavened bread) to feed His disciples the abiding Passover meal. Jesus came to give humanity new bread, better bread: the bread of life. The true bread from Heaven, raised up from the dead gives Believers eternal life. Hallelujah! Jesus came to give those who would believe "life and life more abundantly" (John 10:10). Jesus even compared the Kingdom of Heaven is compared to leaven not chametz. In Matthew 13:33 and Luke 13:20-21, Jesus stated the Kingdom of Heaven was like leaven that a woman took and mixed into three measures of flour. This doughy mixture of leaven and flour was obviously designed to become the woman's bread. Perhaps she only started with a little leaven, but eventually all the dough became leavened. If the Kingdom of Heaven is like leaven working through dough, let it come into your life and raise you up to a higher level.

Now that Believers have obtained the new bread, the raised bread of Jesus instituted at the Last Supper, let them partake of the Holy Communion properly. Let them not celebrate the Seder Supper as a reflection of Moses or the Last Supper with unleavened bread. Believers should never return to the milk of the Mosaic Law, the unleavened bread of the Old Covenant, which has passed away. Believers should press forward to consume the raised bread, the strong meat: the unchangeable, immovable truth of our righteousness in Christ Jesus which will nourish the soul and lead men out of the flesh into the invisible realm of the Holy Spirit who continually reveals Jesus as Christ to those who have ears to hear. The immovable truth of His Holy Communion consumes every enemy as the Believer partakes of the leaven of Jesus and dispels the doctrine of the Pharisees & Sadducees. As Believers feed on Jesus, the power of His finished work prevails in them. Just as the leaven permeated the three measure of flour and caused all the dough to be transformed, Jesus prevails over sickness, pain, pride and addictions. His raising bread of life releases heavy burdens and bondages of the enemy. Believers feeding on Him overcome every aspect of the flesh that has held them back. Rise up like new bread. Rise up with Him through partaking of His body and blood. Rise up to the knowledge of who you are in Christ Jesus, for Believers are now the Righteousness of God, and eternal life flows in and through them! The old unleavened bread has passed away, and behold Jesus makes all things new.

CHAPTER 8

Passover Week Detail of Events

Daily Details Defined

The Gospel of John outlines a timeline for the events of the week before Jesus Christ was crucified. He clarifies the timeline by beginning six days before the Passover. On that day, Jesus arrived at the house of Lazarus in Bethany.

> "₁Then Jesus six days before the Passover came to Bethany, where Lazarus was, which had been dead, whom he raised from the dead."
> John 12:1

The interpretation of the word "Passover" in this context should be read as Nisan 14th not Nisan 15th, which additional passages clarify. Therefore six days before Nisan 14th is Nisan 8th. Thus, Jesus arrived at Lazarus' house on Nisan 8th.

The Gospels of Mark (10:46-11:1) and Luke (19:1-11) explain Jesus traveled from Jericho to reach Bethany. In the Gospel of John, we read that the travel from Jericho to Bethany was to raise Lazarus from the grave. After raising Lazarus, Jesus withdrew and entered into a city called Ephraim (John 11:54), which was approximately five miles away from Bethany. The distance from Bethany to Jerusalem was a

Month of Nisan

Chart 14

		Day 6	Day 5	Day 4	Day 3	Day 2	Day 1	
Day	Nisan 7	Nisan 8 At Bethany	Nisan 9	Nisan 10 Selection of Lamb	Nisan 11	Nisan 12	Nisan 13	Nisan 14 Passover
Evening	Nisan 8	Nisan 9	Nisan 10	Nisan 11	Nisan 12	Nisan 13	Nisan 14 Passover	Nisan 15

little less than two miles, which is longer than the 4,000 cubits allowed for Sabbath travel for personal pleasure or business. The distance from Ephraim to Bethany also exceeded Sabbath travel restrictions.

Keeping in mind's timeline for starting events on Nisan 8th, weekly outlines of crucifixion and resurrection events have been provided. Each weekly chart is based on Jewish calendar days and cross-referenced to Gregorian days of the week. Details explaining scriptural contradictions and/or scriptural alignments for each outline have been provided. The charts clearly eliminate a crucifixion date being on Saturday, Sunday, Monday, and Tuesday, because it would not be possible to have a crucifixion on either of these days with the discovery of his resurrection occurring three days later on a Sunday. This results in only three remaining possibilities for consideration: Wednesday, Thursday, and Friday.

Each of these three remaining possible dates is examined in further detail, providing the arguments for or against that particular Gregorian day of week. It should be noted specific events such as Passover and Feast of Unleavened Bread are described by means of the Jewish calendar fixed date because they are directly associated to the monthly date by Torah law. As discussed earlier, the Feast of First Fruits does not have a specific date assigned to it in the Torah. The assigned date of Nisan 16th to the Feast of First Fruits was an additional restriction by the Pharisees late in the Second Temple or after it's destruction. Therefore during the lifetime of Jesus, under Sadducee reign of the temple, no fixed date would have been assigned to this Feast Day. Opinions for both the Pharisee and Sadducee's interpretations will be explored when appropriate for each of the remaining dates (Wednesday, Thursday, Friday).

The weekly charts ultimately confirm the Church's long held traditions of a Palm Sunday, the triumphant entry of Jesus into Jerusalem, followed by a crucifixion death date on Friday are not Biblical. It is mathematically impossible for these events to occur on these two Gregorian days during any week, given the Torah requirements for Nisan 10th and Nisan 14th. A Friday crucifixion always results in the triumphant entry occurring on a Monday, and a Palm Sunday triumphal entry into Jerusalem will always correspond to a Thursday crucifixion. Therefore, no matter how the weekly tables are construed, at least one aspect of Christian tradition is intrinsically wrong and totally out of line with the Bible.

Weekly Event Tables

Saturday Crucifixion:

As this calendar clearly demonstrates, it would be impossible for Jesus to die on a Saturday and be resurrected after three days with the discovery occurring on a Sunday morning.

Table 15

Gregorian Calendar Days				
Sun	Mon	Tues	Wed	Thurs
Jewish Calendar Days				
Nisan 8	Nisan 9	Nisan 10	Nisan 11	Nisan 12
Jesus Arrived in Bethany		Selection of Passover Lamb		
		(Ex 12:3, Mt 21:1-11)		
Night: Nisan 9	Night: Nisan 10	Night: Nisan 11	Night: Nisan 12	Night: Nisan 13
	Selection of Passover Lamb	Jesus returns to Bethany (Mt 21:17)		
	Jesus in Bethany (Jn 12:1-11)			

Saturday Crucifixion continued:

	Gregorian	Calendar	Days	
Fri	Sat	Sun	Mon	Tues
	Jewish	Calendar	Days	
Nisan 13	Nisan 14	Nisan 15	Nisan 16	Nisan 17
	PASSOVER **Weekly Sabbath***	Feast of Unleavened Bread*		Jesus' Resurrection Discovered
		(Lev 23:4-8)		(Mt 28:1, Mk 16:2)
	Jesus Dies at 3PM (Mk 15:34)			
Night: Nisan 14	**Night: Nisan 15**	**Night: Nisan 16**	**Night: Nisan 17**	**Night: Nisan 18**
PASSOVER **Weekly Sabbath***	Feast of Unleavened Bread*			

* No work allowed by Jewish Law

Sunday Crucifixion:

As this calendar clearly demonstrates, it would be impossible for Jesus to die on a Sunday and be resurrected after three days with the discovery occurring on a Sunday morning.

Chart 16

Gregorian Calendar Days				
Mon	Tues	Wed	Thurs	Fri
Jewish Calendar Days				
Nisan 8	Nisan 9	Nisan 10	Nisan 11	Nisan 12
Jesus Arrived in Bethany		Selection of Passover Lamb		
		(Ex 12:3, Mt 21:1-11)		
Night: Nisan 9	**Night: Nisan 10**	**Night: Nisan 11**	**Night: Nisan 12**	**Night: Nisan 13**
	Selection of Passover Lamb	Jesus returns to Bethany (Mt 21:17)		Weekly Sabbath*
	Jesus in Bethany (Jn 12:1-11)			

* No work allowed by Jewish Law

Sunday Crucifixion continued:

	Gregorian	Calendar	Days	
Sat	Sun	Mon	Tues	Wed
	Jewish	Calendar	Days	
Nisan 13	Nisan 14	Nisan 15	Nisan 16	Nisan 17
Weekly Sabbath*	PASSOVER	Feast of Unleavened Bread*		Jesus' Resurrection Discovered
	Jesus Dies at 3PM (Mk 15:34)	(Lev 23:4-8)		(Mt 28:1, Mk 16:2)
Night: Nisan 14	Night: Nisan 15	Night: Nisan 16	Night: Nisan 17	Night: Nisan 18
PASSOVER	Feast of Unleavened Bread*			

* No work allowed by Jewish Law

Monday Crucifixion:

As this calendar clearly demonstrates, it would be impossible for Jesus to die on a Monday and be resurrected after three days with the discovery occurring on a Sunday morning.

Chart 17

	Gregorian	Calendar	Days	
Tues	Wed	Thurs	Fri	Sat
	Jewish	Calendar	Days	
Nisan 8	Nisan 9	Nisan 10	Nisan 11	Nisan 12
Jesus Arrived in Bethany		Selection of Passover Lamb		Weekly Sabbath*
		(Ex 12:3, Mt 21:1-11)		
Night: Nisan 9	Night: Nisan 10	Night: Nisan 11	Night: Nisan 12	Night: Nisan 13
	Selection of Passover Lamb	Jesus returns to Bethany (Mt 21:17)	Weekly Sabbath*	
	Jesus in Bethany (Jn 12:1-11)			

* No work allowed by Jewish Law

Monday Crucifixion continued:

	Gregorian	Calendar	Days	
Sun	Mon	Tues	Wed	Thurs
	Jewish	Calendar	Days	
Nisan 13	Nisan 14	Nisan 15	Nisan 16	Nisan 17
	PASSOVER	Feast of Unleavened Bread*		Jesus' Resurrection Discovered
		(Lev 23:4-8)		(Mt 28:1, Mk 16:2)
	Jesus Dies at 3PM (Mk 15:34)			
Night: Nisan 14	Night: Nisan 15	Night: Nisan 16	Night: Nisan 17	Night: Nisan 18
PASSOVER	Feast of Unleavened Bread*			

* No work allowed by Jewish Law

Tuesday Crucifixion:

As this calendar clearly demonstrates, it would be impossible for Jesus to die on a Tuesday and be resurrected after three days with the discovery occurring on a Sunday morning.

Chart 18

	Gregorian	Calendar	Days		
Wed	Thurs	Fri	Sat	Sun	
	Jewish	Calendar	Days		
Nisan 8	Nisan 9	Nisan 10	Nisan 11	Nisan 12	
Jesus Arrived in Bethany		Selection of Passover Lamb	Weekly Sabbath*		
		(Ex 12:3, Mt 21:1-11)			
Night: Nisan 9	Night: Nisan 10	Night: Nisan 11	Night: Nisan 12	Night: Nisan 13	
	Selection of Passover Lamb	Jesus returns to Bethany (Mt 21:17)			
	Jesus in Bethany (Jn 12:1-11)	Weekly Sabbath*			

* No work allowed by Jewish Law

Tuesday Crucifixion continued:

	Gregorian	Calendar	Days	
Mon	Tues	Wed	Thurs	Fri
	Jewish	Calendar	Days	
Nisan 13	Nisan 14	Nisan 15	Nisan 16	Nisan 17
	PASSOVER	Feast of Unleavened Bread*		Jesus' Resurrection Discovered
		(Lev 23:4-8)		(Mt 28:1, Mk 16:2)
	Jesus dies at 3PM (Mk 15:34)			
Night: Nisan 14	Night: Nisan 15	Night: Nisan 16	Night: Nisan 17	Night: Nisan 18
PASSOVER	Feast of Unleavened Bread*			Weekly Sabbath*

* No work allowed by Jewish Law

Wednesday Crucifixion:

Chart 19

Gregorian	Calendar	Days		
Thurs	Fri	Sat	Sun	Mon
Jewish	Calendar	Days		
Nisan 8	Nisan 9	Nisan 10	Nisan 11	Nisan 12
Jesus Arrives in Bethany		Weekly Sabbath*		
		Selection of Passover Lamb		
		(Ex 12:3, Mt 21:1-11)		
Night: Nisan 9	Night: Nisan 10	Night: Nisan 11	Night: Nisan 12	Night: Nisan 13
	Selection of Passover Lamb	Jesus returns to Bethany (Mt 21:17)		
	Jesus in Bethany (Jn 12:1-11)			
	Weekly Sabbath*			

* No work allowed by Jewish Law

Wednesday Crucifixion continued:

	Gregorian	Calendar	Days	
Tues	Wed	Thurs	Fri	Sat
	Jewish	Calendar	Days	
Nisan 13	Nisan 14	Nisan 15	Nisan 16	Nisan 17
	PASSOVER	Feast of Unleavened Bread*		Weekly Sabbath*
		(Lev 23:4-8)		
	Jesus dies at 3PM (Mk 15:34)			Jesus rises from the Dead
Night: Nisan 14	Night: Nisan 15	Night: Nisan 16	Night: Nisan 17	Night: Nisan 18
PASSOVER	Feast of Unleavened Bread*		Weekly Sabbath*	

* No work allowed by Jewish Law

	Gregorian	Calendar	Days	
Sun	Mon	Tues	Thurs	Fri
	Jewish	Calendar	Days	
Nisan 18	Nisan 19	Nisan 20	Nisan 21	Nisan 22
Jesus' Resurrection Discovered (Mt 28:1, Mk 16:2)				
Night: Nisan 19	Night: Nisan 20	Night: Nisan 21	Night: Nisan 22	Night: Nisan 23
				Weekly Sabbath*

Wednesday Crucifixion:

The consideration of Jesus' crucifixion occurring on a Wednesday is not a new idea. Many Messianic Jews believe Jesus died on a Wednesday, because such a timeline would place the occurrences of His triumphant entry into Jerusalem and resurrection both on a Sabbath. This Wednesday crucifixion is also supported by other Sabbath day worshipping Christians such as the Seventh Day Adventists and the Church of Christ. Proponents view the Principle of First Mention for the Sabbath day of rest as the most highly significant aspect of the crucifixion week. All weekly events are thus interpreted from their Sabbath viewpoint, which basically summarized is "the two most defining prophesies (the selection of the Lamb and the resurrection) must have occurred on a Sabbath day." The only way for these two events to have occurred on a Sabbath is for the crucifixion of Jesus to have been on a Wednesday. Several early "Christian writings" also supported a Wednesday crucifixion date:

1. Clement of Alexandria (A.D. 150-220) wrote some Christians believed Christ was crucified on Wednesday, April 14, A.D. 28. {19th of Pharmuthi},[33]

2. Lactantius, a church historian who lived between 250-330 AD, placed Christ's crucifixion on Wednesday, March 23, A.D. 29,[34]

3. _The Narrative of Joseph_ (4th century) [The narrative of Joseph of Arimathaea], chapter 2 **(Considered Heresy by the Catholic Church)**

4. In *Acts of Pilate*, an early Christian apocryphal writing, there are manuscripts placing Christ's crucifixion on Wednesday, March 25, A.D. 33. **(Considered Heresy by the Catholic Church)**[35]

Clement recorded a Wednesday crucifixion for Jesus on April 14th in the year of 28 AD, however, calculations from the U.S. Naval Observatory identify the date of Nisan 14th (Passover) as April 28th. This correlates to a difference of two weeks between Clement's date and the astronomical moon necessary for a Passover, making it extremely unlikely for Clement to have been correct. A similar problem of astronomical relationship results in Lactantius' account of the crucifixion on Wednesday, March 23, 29AD. The U.S. Naval Observatory reports the vernal equinox for the year 29 AD occurred on March 22nd. It would be impossible for Nisan 14th to be one day after the vernal equinox since Passover occurs fourteen days after the new moon, and the new moon occurs approximately thirteen days after the equinox. For the year 29 A.D., Passover was estimated to be on April 18th. The difference between Lactantius' report of Passover and the astronomical account of Passover is 26 days. This difference is too substantial to be logical. Thus, Lactantius' account is also extremely improbable. It is also interesting to note Clement and Lactantius do not record the same Gregorian date or year for their proposed Wednesday crucifixion.

In addition to the above references regarding a possible Wednesday afternoon crucifixion, early Christian writers placed the Lord's Last Supper and capture on a Tuesday night.

1. the Didascalia Apostolorum (3rd edition), **(Considered Heresy by the Catholic Church)**

2. Epiphanius, Bishop of Salamis (AD 367-403) [see Didascalia Apostolorum] (translated by Hugh Connolly (Oxford: Clarendon Press, 1929), p. 181.] **(Considered Heresy by the Catholic Church)**

3. The Writings of Quintus Sept. Flor. Tertullianus with the extant works of Vicorinus and Commodiamus, in vol. 3, (Edinburgh: T & T Clark, 1895, pp. 388, 389 **(Considered Heresy by the Catholic Church)**

4. Ante-Nicene Fathers, vol 8, (Michigan, Wm. B. Eerdmans, 1955), p. 468. **(Considered Heresy by the Catholic Church)**

While supports of a Wednesday crucifixion claim a historical foundation for their position, the majority of evidence of record is not favorable. Of the early "Christian writings" that claimed a Wednesday crucifixion date, six of the eight pieces of literature or 75% of those writings were labeled heretical by the organized Church of their time. These writings were not labeled heresy for proposing a Wednesday crucifixion theory. Instead, the heresy label was given for doctrinal conflicts in these writings that undermined or contradicted the basic foundational principles of the Christian faith. Therefore, none of these six "early Christian writings" are considered legitimate or in agreement with Biblical principles. Since they do not uphold the basic Christian tenets of faith, they should be dismissed in their entirety as a factual Christian source of information. The other 25% of writings (Clement and Lactantius' writings) are implausible when astronomical calculations for the vernal equinox and Passover dates are determined. Thus in conclusion, only two of the eight "early Christian writings" documenting a Wednesday crucifixion were considered "real" Christians. Of these two authors, neither provides a Wednesday date that is in agreement with known astronomical phases of the moon necessary for Passover. Therefore, none of the early writings should be given any significant authority with regard to delineating a plausible Wednesday crucifixion.

A Missing Day

Additionally, there are other scriptural problems with a Wednesday crucifixion. One main problem results from a missing day. If Jesus arrived in Bethany on Nisan 8th, Wednesday night or Thursday morning, He could have eaten the famous dinner at Lazarus' house where Mary anointed Him with spikenard oil just after His arrival on either Nisan 8th in the evening or the following day of Nisan 9th in the evening.

If the position is taken Jesus arrived in Bethany on Wednesday night, Nisan 8th and ate dinner at Lazarus' home, then the following day should have seen Jesus traveling to Jerusalem for His Triumphant entry. However, this date would have been the eighth of Nisan, which would not be in agreement with Old Testament prophecies concerning the selection of the lamb on Nisan 10th. In addition, the entire day of Nisan 9th would be "missing" since scriptures record Jesus having the dinner followed by His trip to Jerusalem the following day. Since the evening of Nisan 8th is followed by the day of Nisan 8th and then again by the night and day of Nisan 9th both of which were not a Sabbath day of rest, such a timeline would have Jesus waiting for two days before traveling on Nisan 10th to Jerusalem to be selected as the lamb. The delay of two days would not be in agreement with John 12:12 which records the day after the dinner at Lazarus' house, Jesus entered Jerusalem.

If one maintains the position Jesus arrived on Thursday, Nisan 8th during the day, then dinner at Lazarus' house would occur on Nisan 9th in the evening. The following day would be Friday, Nisan 9th and should have Jesus entering Jerusalem. Again this date does not line up with the Exodus date for selection of the Passover lamb.

Sabbath Travel

Furthermore, a Wednesday crucifixion timeline would require Jesus to travel from Bethany on Saturday morning, Nisan 10th to arrive in Jerusalem for the triumphant entry. Since the distance from Bethany to Jerusalem is more than 4,000 cubits, this distance might be considered a violation of Torah Law. Jesus could not have violated Torah and still remained sinless. Therefore, one of two possibilities must exist. Either Jesus did not traveled beyond a Sabbath day's journey, meaning He did not have traveled from Bethany to Jerusalem on Nisan 10th, or the understanding of Sabbath travel restrictions requires additional review.

Proponents of the Wednesday crucifixion also are staunch supporters of a Sabbath triumphant entry into Jerusalem. Therefore, Jesus' not traveling on the Sabbath is excluded, and further examination of the potential Sabbath restrictions is required. While general travel restrictions are established on the Sabbath, not to exceed 4,000 cubits for business or personal pleasure; there is no travel restrictions for Jews seeking to attend worship services or travel to the local synagogue or temple. This exception is allowed because attendance at the synagogue or temple is considered part of the Sabbath ritual for honoring God. The Messianic Jewish Rabbinical Council Website provides information to Jews on how to practically apply Sabbath law, and includes historical and traditionally held values for Sabbath practices. They state that Judaism does not prohibit travel on the Sabbath to attend worship serves at a local synagogue or in sustaining contact with the synagogue community; although they note this travel must not be a substantial portion of daily events. The Messianic Jewish Rabbinical Council states that synagogue events are important to Sabbath worship, which is required to fulfill the commandment to keep the Sabbath.

Accordingly, Jesus could have traveled from Bethany to Jerusalem for worship at the Temple without violating Torah. This enables a triumphant entry by Jesus into Jerusalem on a Sabbath a real possibility, however it still would not explain the significant gap in weekly events for the missing day of either Nisan 8th, Nisan 9th, or both.

Feast of First Fruits Conflict

In a week with a Wednesday crucifixion, the Feast of First Fruits according to the Pharisaical interpretation of Scripture would have occurred on Friday, Nisan 16th. If Jesus had risen from the grave on Nisan 16th, He would not have been able to have risen on a Sabbath, as the Wednesday supporters uphold. Nor would He have been dead for seventy-two (72) hours as they demand. Therefore, proponents of a Wednesday crucifixion cannot believe in a Pharisaical interpretation of the Feast of First Fruits, because Jesus would not have been able to rise on this date since it was not a Sabbath. Thus, the Sadducee viewpoint regarding the Feast of First Fruits is the only possible explanation in a Wednesday crucifixion.

In a Sadducee interpretation, the Feast of First Fruits would have begun on Sunday, Nisan 18th. Because the Sadducees controlled the Temple during the lifetime of Jesus, it is plausible to believe that a Sadducee interpretation of the timeline for Feast of First Fruits is correct. However, since supporters of a Wednesday crucifixion uphold only a Sabbath resurrection, Jesus could not have risen from the dead on the Feast of First Fruits, Sunday, Nisan 18th. Therefore, the only way for a Sabbath resurrection to occur would have been to have Jesus rise at sunset, before the Feast of First Fruits. While Jesus would be alive before the Feast of First Fruits, He would not have risen on this feast date. Wednesday supporters don't see this technicality as a problem and believe Jesus could still legally be considered the First Fruits harvest held on the next day. Other Christian scholars believe Jesus' resurrection must have occurred on the Feast of First Fruits in order to fulfill the prophecy, and Christ could not have risen before this date. Consequently, in order to fulfill a Sabbath resurrection at sunset on Nisan 17th, neither the Pharisee nor Sadducee interpretation for Feast of First Fruits is upheld. It is probable that at least one Old Testament prophecy surrounding this feast remains unfulfilled on a Sabbath resurrection date.

Nisan 17th Symbolism, slightly possible but not during the morning

As mentioned above, in a Wednesday crucifixion, the Feast of First Fruits according to the reigning Sadducees sect would still have commenced on Sunday. Additionally, that particular Sunday would have been Nisan 18th. There are no Principle of First Mention or Progressive Mention themes in the Old Testament Scriptures associated with a date of

Nisan 18th. However, proponents of a Wednesday crucifixion believe there exists the possibility of Jesus' resurrection occurring on the Sabbath in the evening during the transition between the Sabbath and the first day of the week according to Matthew 28:1, which could possibly still fulfill the Nisan 17th symbolism if only just by moments.

Sabbath Resurrection

The Greek language in Matthew 28:1 could be indicative of an evening transition between the days of Nisan 17th and 18th. If the principle of an evening transition period were applied instead of the following morning daybreak on Nisan 18th, a Wednesday crucifixion could have Jesus raising on Nisan 17th late in the evening before the dawning of Nisan 18th. John Lemley has written a scholarly article entitled *"Was Opse Matthew's Oops"* in which he provides an extensive review of the Greek word *"opse"* (Strong's #3796) and its usage with regard to Matthew 28:1 and other biblical scriptures as well as additional non-biblical documentation. In each of the instances where the word *opse* was translated in the Bible, Mr. Lemley has determined it was always translated as "evening" or "late in the evening." The Septuagint also translated the word *"opse"* with reference to "the evening" in the Old Testament.

Mr. Lemley reported a similar pattern of the use of *opse* in non-biblical Greek writings. Therefore, he concludes if the translation for *opse* in all other contexts is 'evening,' its translation in Matthew 28:1 should also be "evening" instead of "end." Consequently, the reference to the dawning of the day in the Book of Matthew would present a picture not of the literal morning dawn, but the changing from one day into another day during the evening exchange. The passage below provides the translation for "opse" as evening and "dawn" as "changing of days" as translated by Mr. Lemley:

> "₁In the end **[evening]** of the Sabbath, as it began to dawn **[change]** toward the first day of the week, *came Mary Magdalene and the other Mary* to see the sepulcher. ₂And, behold, there was a great earthquake: for the angel of the Lord descended from heaven, and came and rolled back the stone from the door, and sat upon it. ₃His countenance was like lightning, and his raiment white as snow: ₄And for fear of him the keepers did shake, and became as dead men. ₅And *the angel answered and said unto the women, Fear not ye: for I know that ye seek Jesus, which was crucified. ₆He is not here: for he is risen*, as he said. Come, see the place where the Lord lay. ₇*And go quickly, and tell his disciples that he is risen from the dead;* and, behold, he goeth before you into Galilee; there shall ye see him: lo, I have told you. ₈*And they departed quickly from the sepulcher with fear and great joy; and did run to bring his disciples word.* ₉And as they went to tell his disciples, behold, Jesus met them, saying, All hail. And they came and held him by the feet, and worshipped him. ₁₀Then said Jesus unto them, Be not afraid: go tell my brethren that they go into Galilee, and there shall they see me. Matthew 28:1-10"[37]

Altering the traditional understanding of the Greek translation of *opse* in this verse significantly impacts the events of the story. This translation of *opse* causes Mary Magdalene and the other Mary to find Jesus' sepulcher empty on Saturday night instead of Sunday morning. It would also have Jesus appearing to the women on Saturday night. If read in this manner, a Wednesday crucifixion with a Saturday night resurrection could allow the Principle of First Mention theme of salvation on Nisan 17th to remain intact, even if just for a few minutes. It could also account for a Sabbath resurrection.

72 Hour Death Timeline Requirement

Proponents of a Wednesday crucifixion death timeline simultaneously support a literal interpretation of Jesus being dead for three days or seventy-two (72) hours of death. As the table below demonstrates, the major problem with this theory is that it results in Jesus being dead longer than three days and three nights.

Chart 20

Wednesday	Thursday	Friday	Saturday
Day: Nisan 14	Day: Nisan 15	Day: Nisan 16	Day: Nisan 17
Jesus dies at 3PM entombed before sunset			Jesus Alive before Sunset
Dead: Day 1	Dead: Day 2	Dead: Day 3	Dead: Day 4
Night: Thurs Nisan 15	Night: Friday Nisan 16	Night: Saturday Nisan 17	Sunday Nisan 18
Dead: Night 1	Dead: Night 2	Dead: Night 3	

To offset the fact Jesus would be dead four days and three nights, Wednesday crucifixion supporters believe only the time Jesus' body is in the tomb can be counted toward his death prophecy. The Wednesday timeline opinion is three hours shorter than Jesus' actual time of death. While most Christians calculate Jesus' death beginning on the cross as the start of Jesus' death timeline, Wednesday crucifixion observers claim Jesus' prophecy in the Gospel of Matthew being "in the heart of the earth" was a literal timeline calculating Jesus' death period not from his actual time of death on the cross but from the moment He entered "the earth" or was in the tomb. Their interpretation of scripture in this manner eliminates the nasty problem of Jesus being dead seventy-five (75) hours, longer than three days. They calculated His entombment at 6:00 PM on Nisan 14th until 6:00PM, literally seventy-two hours of time in the grave.

> "$_{39}$But he answered and said unto them, An evil and adulterous generation seeketh after a sign; and there shall no sign be given to it, but the sign of the prophet Jonas: $_{40}$For as Jonah was three days and three nights in the whale's belly; *so shall the Son of man be three days and three nights in the heart of the earth.*"
> Matthew 12:39-40

Thus, Wednesday proponents recognize the death timeline only beginning when Jesus' physical body was laid in the tomb. Their "physical body only" interpretation makes a Wednesday crucifixion avoid conflict with the commonly understood concept of a three-day and three-night timetable. Albert Barnes' commentary also supported the belief that "in the heart of the earth" meant from Jesus' entombment.

> "$_{40}$'In the heart of the earth.' The Jews used the word heart to denote the interior of a thing or to speak of being in a thing. It means here, to be in the grave or sepulcher."[38]

As explained earlier in this book in Chapter 5, The Sign of Jonah, a requirement for the death timeline to be seventy-two (72) hours proposed by Wednesday crucifixion supporters is not substantiated in scripture. In scriptures with similar terminology for counting days, especially three days or three days and nights, the timeline of events is longer than forty-eight (48) hours but less than seventy-two (72) hours, which accurately places the event to occur during the third day.

In addition, Wednesday supporters claim the requirement of Jesus' death must be based on His physical body being in *"heart of the earth,"* which they interpret to mean in the tomb. However, the phrase in "the heart of the earth" can mean more than just the physical grave. This terminology is also used in Old Testament scriptures to refer to the spirit or soul being in spiritual paradise or hell, located in the center of the Earth. The confusion in terminology or understanding of "Hell" arises from the way the Hebrew words "Sheol" and "queber" and the Greek words "Hades," "Tartarus," and "Gehenna" have been translated into English bibles. The English translation has the words "hell" or "grave" used almost interchangeably; however, in the original languages the concepts of "hell" and "the grave" are not the same.

The Hebrew word *"sheol"* is found in the Bible sixty-five times, translated as "the pit" (3 times), "the grave" (31 times), and "hell" (31 times); yet this word has a clear identity of the "spirit underworld" or spiritual holding place of the dead. Queber is the Hebrew word common for "grave" in the Old Testament and is used sixty-four times. It is translated "grave" (34 times), "sepulcher" (26 times) and "burying place" (4 times). While in English these two words are translated similarly as "grave," from the differences between how *Sheol* and *queber* are used in the original Scripture text, it is obvious that they are not the same concept. Sheol is always used in the singular sense and never used in a plural form, unlike queber, which repeatedly is used in a plural form, meaning multiple graves. The physical body is never referred to go to Sheol, but queber makes reference thirty-seven (37) times in scripture to the body going there. There is no reference to an individual having or owning Sheol, while an individual's queber is mentioned five times in the Old Testament. People are put into a queber by man thirty-three times in scripture, but no man is ever mentioned to put anyone into Sheol. Similarly, man is said to have dug a queber or owned a queber but never Sheol. There is no reference in scripture to man having ever physically touched Sheol, but five references of men touching a queber. Queber has a root verb associated with it named "quabar" which means to bury or be buried.

Several references are made in scripture about the difference between Sheol and the grave. The first one is found in the book of Genesis, chapter 50.

> "After Jacob died, Joseph had his body mummified, a process that took forty days, then took him back to Canaan for burial (Gen. 50:1-14). When we add to that the thirty days of mourning (Gen. 50:2-4), and the time it took to travel to Canaan for the funeral (Gen. 50:5-13), we see that it was several weeks after Jacob was *"gathered unto his people"* (Gen. 49:33) before his body was placed in the cave that served as his burial place. Considering that he had been dead for well over two months before his body was buried and that the Scriptures state that at the time he died he was *"gathered to his people"* (Gen. 49:33) is telling. This shows that at the time of physical death, when *"he*

yielded up the spirit," his soul immediately departed his body to be with Isaac and Abraham. This cannot be a reference to his body being gathered together with their bodies, as that did not take place for over ten weeks. This is strong proof that Sheol does not mean a burial place for the body, but is the place where the souls of the departed reside."[39]

Another reference in Isaiah, chapter 14, implies that communication takes place in Sheol/Hades between the inhabitants of that region. Since the dead physical body cannot speak, it is obvious that something other than a physical place of burial is being referenced.

"In Isaiah 14:4-20, we find the prophet foretelling the eventual defeat and death of the king of Babylon. The nation that would eventually send Judah into captivity will itself be defeated and its mighty king will find himself among *"the chief ones of the earth...the kings of the nations"* (Isa. 14:9) who preceded him in death. These are the kings of nations that he had conquered with the sword and ruled over with a cruel hand (Isa. 14:6). These same men will serve as a welcoming committee for this once great "world ruler" when he arrives in Sheol/Hades. In mock surprise, they will ask this once powerful king, *"Art thou also become weak as we? Are thou become like unto us?"* (Isa. 14:10). They then taunt him by pointing out that the pretentious display of magnificence that he had demonstrated as the king of Babylon now meant nothing (Isa. 14:11)."[39]

Those in this Scripture who are in Sheol encounter the reality of how helpless and hopeless they are. One of the boasts made by these kings against the King of Babylon is that their bodies have been placed in respective tombs, but he lacked honored because he lacked a respectable burial, *"But thou are cast out of the grave (queber) like an abominable* (despised) *branch...thou shalt not be joined with them in burial"* (Isaiah 14:18-20). Scripture states that the kings were not joined physically in burial so the conversation of this chapter must be occurring in a place beyond the grave, a spiritual place since the body and soul are in different places. The soul went to Sheol, while the body remained unburied (verse 20).

> "It is true that this is a prophetic passage; and there are various opinions as to the identity of the person in view here (verses 12-15 are commonly thought to refer to Satan, the power behind the Gentile kings). But, regardless of who this prophecy is about, or whether it has already been fulfilled or not, does not change the fact that Sheol and the grave are to be regarded as different places in this passage of Scripture."[39]

In the Book of 1 Samuel, another clear understanding of Sheol is provided, which separates its identify from the physical grave. The prophet Samuel died some time before this event. King Saul distraught by his estrangement from God sought out the witch of Endor to bring Samuel's soul back from the dead. Upon summing Samuel from the dead, Samuel conversed with King Saul and told Saul that Saul and his sons would be with him the next day (1 Samuel 28:15-19). As foretold, Saul and his sons died the next day in battle (1 Samuel 31:1-6); however, their bodies were not buried the day of their death. King Saul's body and those of his sons were taken by the Philistines and hung in Beth-Shan (1 Samuel 31:7-10). Valiant men from Jabesh-Gilead heard the news, went by night, and stole their bodies back. After taking Saul and his son's bodies to Jabesh, they were burned and their bones were buried. The timing of the final burial of King Saul and his sons is approximately three days after Saul died, maybe longer. Thus, they did not join Samuel in the physical grave on the day they died, but their souls went down to Sheol where the person (or soul) of Samuel was located. Since Samuel prophesized they would die and be with him the next day (1 Samuel 31:1-6) and Samuel was a prophet of the Lord, his words must come to pass. King Saul and his sons joined Samuel in Sheol the day they died and their bones were placed in a grave several days later. Obviously spiritual Sheol and the physical grave are not the same thing, nor are they in the same location.

> "Death and Sheol/Hades are linked together at least thirty-three times in the Scriptures. In these, we see a general distinction between the "outward man," which is the body and the "inward man," which is the soul (cf. II Cor. 4:16). In this sense, death, or the grave, claims the physical part of man, the body, while Sheol/Hades claims the separated, spiritual part of man, the soul. This is exactly the meaning of Psalm 16:10: *"For Thou wilt not leave my soul in Hell* (Sheol); *neither will Thou suffer Thine Holy One to see corruption."* In his Pentecostal address, Peter left no room for doubt that this was a prophetic pronouncement concerning the time between the Lord Jesus Christ's death on the Cross and His resurrection. First, he quoted Psalm 16:8-11 (Acts 2:25-28) and then made direct application of verse 10 to Christ (Acts 2:31). Not only was the Lord Jesus' soul not left in Sheol/Hades, but neither was His body left to rot in the grave. That Peter used Hades, the place of Sheol, in this quotation shows that they are identical in meaning."[39]

The significance of Psalm 16:8-11 cannot be minimized because these verses identify that Jesus' soul was in Sheol immediately upon death while His body was later placed in the grave. A Wednesday timeline demanding a physical body entombment of seventy-two (72) hours is not substantiated by this prophetic verse. In fact, Psalms 16 would seem to imply that Jesus' death timeline was based spiritually on His time in Sheol, not His physical presence in the queber or tomb.

> "When we speak of the heart of something, we are not referring to that which is superficial or only skin-deep. Symbolically, the heart signifies the innermost character, feelings, or inclinations of a man... When used figuratively in the Scriptures, the word "heart" is used in a similar fashion, thus the heart of the earth gives reference to something much deeper than a simple place of burial for a man's body barely under the surface of the earth. That it is said that before His ascension the Lord Jesus first descended *"into the lower parts of the earth"* (Eph. 4:9) affirms this. In a Psalm of thanksgiving for being delivered from death, David makes reference to this by distinguishing between Sheol/Hades (rendered grave in the KJV) and Queber (rendered pit in this passage) (Ps. 30:1-3)."[39]

After the cross, the souls of those who die "in Christ" do not go to Sheol/Hades but to Heaven to be present with the Lord (2 Corinthians 5:8), because of the work of Jesus Christ's death and resurrection. However, before Jesus' finished work, all souls went to Sheol, either to a place of torment and punishment or to Abraham's bosom/paradise, as exemplified in Jesus' narrative of Lazarus and the Rich

Man in Luke 16:14-31. Jesus told the thief on the cross, "this day you shall be with me in Paradise (Hades)" indicating that Jesus' soul would go to Sheol, not that the thief would be buried with Jesus in the tomb.

Thus, from New Testament Scriptures we understand that Jesus' death on the cross, while excruciating and horrible, was not the worst aspect of His death and substitutionary position for our sins. In addition to the grave, Jesus also had to experience Hades and separation from God. The entrance of one's soul into either Hell or Paradise was immediate upon one's physical death. Thus, Jesus' soul would have immediately entered Sheol when He died on the cross, and a timeline for Jesus to be spiritually in the *"heart of the earth"* would have begun at 3:00 PM when He died. Jesus told the thief on the cross that the two of them would be together in Paradise, indicating the location of His soul immediately upon death.

> "$_{42}$Then he [the thief] said, "Jesus, remember me when you come into your kingdom. $_{43}$Jesus answered him, "Truly I tell you, today you will be with me in paradise."
> Luke 23:42-43

The word "paradise" translated above in verse forty-three (43) according to Thayer's Greek Lexicon conveyed the concept of "Eden" or the portion of Sheol/Hades, which was the abode of the righteous souls awaiting the resurrection. Jesus after His death was in the lowest parts of the earth not only physically (in the tomb) but also spiritually in Paradise located in Sheol. Therefore, Wednesday supporters who demand a limited biblical interpretation of Jesus' physical body entombment to derive at a seventy-two hour timeline for death are taking the most extreme and legalistic viewpoint possible. Simultaneously, Wednesday proponents must exclude the obvious spiritual references and symbolism of Jesus being in Sheol located the "heart of the earth" to maintain their position. The prophecies in Psalms 16 and Matthew 12, reaffirmed in fulfillment in Acts chapter 2, are intertwined and should not be divided exclusively to support any singular position, but rather need be taken in context and relationship to each other to derive at the correct understanding of which portion of Jesus (His physical body or His soul) was being referenced to be prophetically in the heart of the earth three days and three nights. Delineating exactly which one of these two different aspects, spiritual or physical, the prophecy was declaring while somewhat open for interpretation does not conclusively support a seventy-two hour mandated physical entombment perspective. Consequently, the Wednesday crucifixion timeline can only be substantiated if viewed from an extremely legalistic stance of seventy-two (72) hours, based solely upon the physical entombment of Jesus's body and not His actual time of death or the length of time His soul was in Sheol, which would have been seventy-five (75) hours.

A Conflict of Death Prophecy Timelines

A possible conflict in the timeline of Jesus' prophecies regarding His death is apparent in a Wednesday crucifixion. While most Wednesday supporters focus the entirety of their resurrection arguments around Matthew 12:40, the other eleven self-prophecies given by Jesus regarding his death timeline seem to be completely neglected. In a Wednesday crucifixion as mentioned above, proponents insist on a legalistic seventy-two hour itinerary of death beginning in the tomb. This timeline requires Jesus to rise at exactly the same second He was entombed. Any second after the seventy-two hour timeline would cause Jesus' resurrection to literally occur on the fourth day. A seventy-two hour and one second timetable would cause the resurrection to technically happen on the forth day, as it would extend past a literal three days or seventy-two hours. While it is not impossible for God to cause a resurrection at a precise moment, Wednesday supporters cannot account for the factual death of Christ being at least seventy-five hours. Seventy-five hours is certainly longer than three days. There are eleven prophecies given by Jesus that required Him to rise on the third day.

>Matthew 16:21, "be raised again the third day"
>
>Matthew 17:23, "and the third day he shall be raised again"
>
>Matthew 20:19, "and the third day he shall rise again"
>
>Mark 8:31, "and after (Strong's 3326) three days rise again"
>
>Mark 9:31, "he shall rise the third day"
>
>Mark 10:34, "and the third day he shall rise again"
>
>Luke 9:22, "and be raised the third day"
>
>Luke 13:32, "and the third day I shall be perfected"
>
>Luke 18:33, "and the third day he shall rise again"
>
>Luke 24:7, "and the third day rise again"
>
>John 2:19, "in (Strong's 1722) three days I will raise it up"

Listed above are references to the Strong's Concordance Greek words for the prepositions preceding "three days."[40] Explanation of these Greek words helps to clarify that the concept was not meant to be "after" three days or seventy-two hours but "within" a three-day timeline, occurring on the third day. The Greek word corresponding to "after" (Strong's #3326) is also translated "on the" in two other Scriptures, and "in" (Strong's #1722) literally translated means "inside" or "within" something.[40] The use of "in" is significant because it summarizes the concept of within the third day Christ would be resurrected.

Rising seventy-five hours after His death on the cross does not fulfill Jesus' prophecies to rise on the third day. Any specific application of "death" by these eleven prophecies to reference only Jesus' time in the physical grave cannot be obtained, and Scriptures would have to be "added to" in order to arrive at such a conclusion from just these eleven prophecies. Clearly Wednesday supporters must dismiss these prophecies in preference of the seventy-two (72) hour entombment theory, because two death timelines cannot be mutually supported. A Wednesday death timeline requires Christ to be dead seventy-five hours but imputes only seventy-two hours of His total death time in the grave toward the three-day resurrection. The other, more literal, view of Scriptures concludes the total amount of time deceased must exceed two days (or forty-eight hours) but cannot exceed three days (or seventy-two hours). The last viewpoint is the only perspective, which has Jesus rising within the third day timeline. If perhaps Wednesday supporters had Jesus rising from the grave at 3:00 PM, the possibility would exist for a resurrection occurrence in the third day that did not extend beyond seventy-two hours of death. However, there is no support for a 3:00 PM resurrection on a Saturday within the remaining Biblical passages.

Anointing Difficulties

Finding the tomb empty on Saturday night might explain a Nisan 17th resurrection theme, but it would not explain other scriptural conflicts in either Matthew or with the other gospels for the events that ensued shortly thereafter. If one presumed the women found the Lord's tomb empty and Jesus appeared to them on Saturday night, the record of them in the other gospels returning the following Sunday morning to anoint His dead body with spices would not make logical sense. A surprise Sunday morning discovery of an empty tomb has no explanation under this Saturday "evening discovery" theory.

In the Gospel of Mark 16:1-5, scripture details Mary Magdalene, Mary the mother of James, and Salome arrived very early in the morning on Sunday, *"at the rising of the sun."* This event obviously does not happen at sunset on Saturday night because of the specific wording "at the rising of the sun." Therefore, if Mary Magdalene had already seen the risen Christ on Saturday night, it should not have surprised her to find the tomb empty still at dawn Sunday morning.

The Gospel of Luke 24:1-10 also records similar timing and events for Mary Magdalene and Mary the mother of James. It is chronicled that they came bringing spices to anoint Jesus' dead body on Sunday morning. Again, the question would remain as to why Mary Magdalene and the other Mary would bring spices for a dead man that they had already seen alive and risen on the previous Saturday night.

The Gospel of John 20:1 reports that Mary Magdalene went to the tomb "when it was **yet dark**." The translation for the English word *"yet"* (Strong's 2089) is derived from the Greek word *"eti"* whose literal translation means "still as a degree of time," or "now," or "after that."[40] The word "dark" is derived from "scotia" (Strong's #4653) meaning dimness.[40] This translation would mean that the time was twilight (either early morning or late evening). Since the day is recorded as "the first day," the timeline must be correctly interpreted as Sunday morning during twilight just before the sunrise, not Saturday night.

Even though discrepancies arise between the Gospel of Matthew and the other gospels, proponents of a Wednesday crucifixion remained undeterred stating the Matthew account could be resolved as a different account of the resurrection, since the scriptures seem to imply several different versions of eyewitness accounts. However, supporters holding this "different eye-witness" account theory neglect the fact that Scripture has only one author, The Holy Spirit. These accounts are all based solely from the Holy Spirit's direction and thus all the scripture should harmonize completely.

The Guard Question

While a different perspective may account for Matthew's version of resurrection events, other events in the timeline within Matthew's own account do not support an evening resurrection theory.

> "[10]Then said Jesus unto them, Be not afraid: go tell my brethren that they go into Galilee, and there shall they see me. [11]Now when they [the women] were going, behold, some of the watch came into the city, and shewed unto the chief priests all the things that were

> done. ₁₂And when they were assembled with the elders, and had taken counsel, they gave large money unto the soldiers, ₁₃Saying, **Say ye, His [Jesus'] disciples came by night,** and stole him away while we slept. ₁₄And if this come to the governor's ears, we will persuade him, and secure you. ₁₅So they took the money, and did as they were taught: and this saying is commonly reported among the Jews until this day."
> Matthew 28:10-15

Basically summarizing Matthew's events: after the women left the empty tomb rejoicing, the guards also left to report to the Jewish Sanhedrin that Jesus' tomb was empty. The Sanhedrin gave the soldiers advice in verse thirteen to say,"*His [Jesus'] disciples **came by night** and stole him*" while they were sleeping. The Greek word for night in this verse is "nux" (Strong's #3571) which means literally "night" or "midnight."⁴⁰ Therefore, it would be impossible for Jesus' disciples to have come at midnight and stolen His body if He resurrected before sunset (at approximately 6:00 PM) without any earlier watch taking notice of the empty tomb, because the stone had been rolled away. For the Sanhedrin to suggest such a grand lie would be believed by the general population is extremely doubtful.

Such an understanding of the scriptures would require the soldiers to state Jesus' disciples arrived during the previous night, before these particular soldiers were even on duty. It would not make sense for these late afternoon guards to claim the disciples took Jesus' body on someone else's watch at midnight. Neither would it make sense for the guards on the second watch not to have noticed an empty tomb long before the current guards were on duty. For the Sanhedrin to encourage afternoon guards to say they had fallen asleep on their watch, which resulted in Jesus' disciples stealing his

225

body at midnight does not even appear logical. Roman guards were divided into four watches for the night; therefore, a Roman soldier would only be on duty for three hours at a time. Jewish watches of the night were only four hours long. If the Sabbath resurrection is correct, then the guards that found the tomb empty and reported to the Sanhedrin would not have been the same soldiers on shift at midnight.

Thus, the more realistic interpretation of Matthew 28:10-15 would be the most direct or literal interpretation. The soldiers reporting the empty tomb to the Sanhedrin were the same soldiers responsible for the midnight watch. These soldiers could assert they had accidently fallen asleep on duty at midnight while Jesus' body was stolen. Such a tale proposed by the Sanhedrin would have been believable if the guards who were on duty during the midnight watch were the one's reporting Jesus' body went missing while they slept. Thus, the assertion of an evening resurrection prior to Jesus missing body in early morning would not be in agreement with the Matthew 28:10-15 scriptures.

Summary

In summary, the principle problems regarding a Wednesday crucifixion are only resolved

1. If one maintains the position of a missing day or two in the Scriptural timeline of events for Nisan 9th is not a problem, and

2. If Jesus arose from the grave before sunset on the Sabbath, Nisan 17th, and

3. If the prophetic scriptures in Psalms 16, Matthew 12:40, and Acts 2 literally required seventy-two (72) hours of physical body entombment and could not have been referring to Jesus' spiritual position in Sheol, and

4. In Jesus' prophecy for being dead three days and three nights in Matthew 12:40 outweighs the other eleven prophecies He gave stating He would rise "on the third day" or "in three days," and

5. If the Old Testament prophecy concerning Jesus' resurrection on the Feast of First Fruits remaining unfulfilled is not a problem, and

6. If the Matthew account for the Greek *"opse"* is a different personal eyewitness completely separate from the other gospel accounts, which are in unison, regarding a Sunday morning resurrection, and

7. If Mary Magdalene who knew Jesus was alive on Saturday night still went searching for Him on Sunday morning to anoint His body for burial, and

8. If the interpretation of events in Matthew 28:10-15 are twisted to imply the soldiers blamed the previous watch but still took responsibility for finding the empty tomb upon waking from their accidental sleep during the day (as this watch would have been on duty during the evening at 6 PM when Jesus rose from the grave).

Thus, a Wednesday crucifixion requires a lot of "if's" to resolve contrasting scriptures. Even trying to justify contrasting scriptures, at least one of the Old Testament prophecies is not truly fulfilled because Jesus does not rise from the dead on the Feast of First Fruits, but rises the day before the sheaf offering was to be waved. Additionally, an evening resurrection is inconsistent with the other three gospel accounts, which clearly place events before the sunrise of the first day of the week. Even assuming Matthew's gospel is an independent account, the timeline should still be reasonably consistent with the other scriptures because the same inspirational influence, the Holy Spirit, is the ultimate author of all the gospels. It remains extremely doubtful all scriptures can harmonize completely to fulfill a Wednesday crucifixion date. Therefore, a Wednesday crucifixion resulting in a Sabbath sunset resurrection witnessed by Mary Magdalene is not accurate and contradicts or subverts too many other scriptures to be reflective of the truth.

Thursday Crucifixion outlined on next page.

Thursday Crucifixion:

Chart 21

Gregorian Calendar Days				
Fri	Sat	Sun	Mon	Tues
Jewish Calendar Days				
Nisan 8	Nisan 9	Nisan 10	Nisan 11	Nisan 12
Jesus Arrived in Bethany	Weekly Sabbath*	Selection of Passover Lamb		
		(Ex 12:3, Mt 21:1-11)		
Night: Nisan 9	Night: Nisan 10	Night: Nisan 11	Night: Nisan 12	Night: Nisan 13
Weekly Sabbath*	Selection of Passover Lamb	Jesus returns to Bethany (Mt 21:17)		
	Jesus in Bethany (Jn 12:1-11)			

* No work allowed by Jewish Law

Thursday Crucifixion continued:

	Gregorian Calendar Days			
Wed	Thurs	Fri	Sat	Sun
	Jewish Calendar Days			
Nisan 13	Nisan 14	Nisan 15	Nisan 16	Nisan 17
	PASSOVER	Feast of Unleavened Bread*	Weekly Sabbath*	Jesus' Resurrection Discovered
	Jesus dies at 3PM (Mk 15:34)	(Lev 23:4-8)		(Mt 28:1, Mk 16:2)
Night: Nisan 14	Night: Nisan 15	Night: Nisan 16	Night: Nisan 17	Night: Nisan 18
PASSOVER	Feast of Unleavened Bread*	Weekly Sabbath*		

* No work allowed by Jewish Law

Thursday Crucifixion:

Opponents of a Thursday crucifixion refute the possibility of a Thursday crucifixion date primarily based on the current Jewish calendar restrictions and fixing of dates. The first argument of dispute involves the current Jewish calendar forbidding consecutive holy convocation and weekly Sabbath days. A Thursday crucifixion would result in the Feast of Unleavened Bread occurring Thursday night to Friday night followed immediately by the weekly Sabbath, which would transpire from Friday night to Saturday night. This would place the holy convocation day (for Unleavened Bread) and the weekly Sabbath in consecutive order (occurring back to back) during the week. Hillel II's calendar does not allow for consecutive Sabbaths in a week. Therefore, people examining the current Jewish calendar firmly state Thursday is automatically excluded as a possibility based on Jewish calendar principles. However, as mentioned in Chapter 1 of this book, during the lifetime of Jesus, the Jewish calendar was not the same calendar that exists today. It was based solely on Torah practices and did not forbid specific convocation dates to prevent consecutive Sabbaths. The Jewish calendar during Temple times was based on viewing the first sliver of the new moon. Therefore, it is highly possible that any Gregorian day of the week could have a holy convocation day, depending on the alignment that year for the first sliver of the moon.

Another resistance to a Thursday crucifixion revolves around the current Jewish calendar not documenting any Thursday Passover date. If one uses the current Jewish calendar to regress back to 26-33 A.D., no Passover date is found to ever transpire on a Thursday. However, as mentioned in the Jewish calendar section, the current Jewish calendar is based on Hillel II's mathematical equations and restrictions to avoid consecutive Sabbaths, which did not formally exist during the lifetime of Jesus Christ. To understand the current restrictions in the Jewish calendar for dating Passover, Rabbi Menachem Posner posted a comment on the chabad.org site, which clarified Passover could never occur on "Sunday, Tuesday or Thursday evenings." Therefore, according to Hillel II's tradition, Nisan 15th, Unleavened Bread can never occur on Thursday evening, which is why there is no Jewish calendar regression for Passover occurring on a Thursday. Yet once again, the emphasis on Hillel II's calendar cannot overshadow the truth that during Temple times this particular pharisaical calendar was not the governing principle for the Jewish nation's reckoning of time. During Temple times, the Jewish calendar was based on the Sanhedrin sighting of the moon in Jerusalem. Nothing but God's ordinance in the Old Testament determined the calendar. There is no evidence of mathematical calculations or rules to prevent consecutive Sabbath days from ancient times. At best, the traditions from which Hillel II based his calendar have origins back to around 70 AD during the destruction of the Second Temple, almost forty years after Jesus' crucifixion.

The last opposition to a Thursday crucifixion date surrounds the fixing of the Feast of First Fruits to a Nisan 16th date. It is a known fact Hillel II's additional regulations for establishing the Feast of First Fruits on Nisan 16th was based on the Pharisaical interpretation of Scripture. It is also known in history that the Pharisees were not in control of Jewish temple worship during the lifetimes of John the Baptist or Jesus Christ. Instead the Sadducees were the ruling party and High Priests of those times. The Sadducees interpreted Scripture regarding the Feast of First Fruits to begin always on a Sunday, the date after the weekly Sabbath. If the current Jewish calendar affixing Nisan 16th to the Feast of First Fruits was hypothetically in place during Jesus' lifetime, opponents of a Thursday crucifixion date state Jesus would not have fulfilled the prophecies regarding the Feast of First Fruits because He would have risen from the grave after this date on Nisan 17th. However, because Nisan 16th was not a requirement for the Feast of First Fruits during the lifetime of Jesus, it is not a deterring factor against a Thursday crucifixion date. A Jewish calendar based on sighting the moon could allow for Passover, Nisan 14th to occur on any Gregorian day of the week, including a Thursday with the Sadducee Feast of First Fruits occurring on Sunday, Nisan 17th. Since Jesus lived during the Second Temple and Temple practices determined the calendar, it could be possible to have a Thursday Passover followed on Friday by the Feast of Unleavened Bread even if not reflected on current Jewish calendar regressions or presently allowed due to Hillel II's restrictions. Thus, one cannot simply look to current Jewish calendar practices for the truth of the practices maintained during the Second Temple and believe they are equivalent, since they are not. Excluding a Thursday crucifixion date because of one's lack of historical knowledge and changes to the Jewish calendar system is not a legitimate justification for eliminating of this day. A Thursday is a viable Gregorian date for the crucifixion of Jesus Christ.

No Missing Day

A Thursday crucifixion has no Sabbath travel restriction problems evidenced in other days of the week. It also exhibits no missing days of inactivity on Nisan 8th or 9th that could not be easily understood. On a Thursday crucifixion, Jesus would have arrived in Bethany on Nisan 8th, Friday afternoon. Friday evening and Saturday (day) would have been the Sabbath, a day of rest. Obviously, the famous dinner at Lazarus' house could not have been held on the Sabbath night (Friday night) because of the Torah restrictions regarding preparing or cooking food. Accordingly, when the Sabbath ended, a large dinner would have been prepared on Saturday night. The following day, Sunday, would have been Nisan 10th and would be in agreement with the timeline of events in the gospels for Jesus' triumphal entry into Jerusalem after the meal at Lazarus' house. A triumphant entry into Jerusalem on Nisan 10th would fulfill the Old Testament prophecies associated with the selection of the Passover Lamb on Nisan 14th. Thus, in a Thursday crucifixion date, the event timeline in the New Testament remains intact without any discrepancies or missing of days while simultaneously fulfilling all the Old Testament prophecies.

Nisan 17th Symbolism – Fulfilled in the morning

On a Thursday crucifixion with a Sunday resurrection, Jesus would be dead literally for three days and three nights without any manipulation of the timeline to account for Jesus being dead either too long (as in a Wednesday death) or too short (as in a Friday). Additionally, a Thursday crucifixion on Nisan 14th would result in a Sunday resurrection occurring on Nisan 17th. Knowing the Principles of First Mention and Progressive Mention uphold Nisan 17th as a date in the history of the world for new beginnings (Noah's Ark) and in Israel's specific history (the parting of the Red Sea in exodus from Egypt; eating of the new grain in the Promise Land; restoration of true worship in the Temple in 2 Chronicles, and events in the Book of Esther). Biblically, Nisan 17th has repeatedly represented salvation, deliverance, restoration and redemption. It is no surprise that Jesus would have risen triumphantly over death on Nisan 17th. Since the Sadducees were the reigning authority of the Second Temple, the Feast of First Fruits would have been celebrated on the day after the weekly Sabbath, which in a Thursday crucifixion would have been on Sunday, Nisan 17th. Therefore, the symbolism associated with Nisan 17th throughout the Old Testament culminated in a Thursday crucifixion.

Chart 22

Thursday	Friday	Saturday	Sunday
Day: Nisan 14	Day: Nisan 15	Day: Nisan 16	Day: Nisan 17
Jesus dies at 3PM			Jesus Alive before Sunrise
Dead Day 1	Dead Day 2	Dead Day 3	
Night: Nisan 15	Night: Nisan 16	Night: Nisan 17	
Dead Night 1	Dead Night 2	Dead Night 3	

Timing of Death

Thursday is the only date within a Gregorian week that completely harmonizes all the Scriptures, both the Old Testament prophecies and further restrictions given in New Testament prophecies by Jesus. It provides a death timeline spanning three days and three nights, if the calculation of Jesus' death occurs from the moment of death on the cross and not the placement of His body in the tomb. As mentioned during the Wednesday crucifixion explanation of events, there is a significant difference between the timeline of death on the cross and placement in the tomb, approximately three hours. The difference isn't just a calculation of time; it is a difference in interpretation of scripture in Psalms 16 and Acts 2. In a Thursday crucifixion, the death timeline would start from the moment Jesus' soul entered Sheol in the 'heart of the earth" and not three hours later when his physical body entered the queber (tomb). Either way, even if one started the timeline from Jesus' entombment, Jesus would have died on the cross and been entombed on a Thursday, which logically must count for the day He died. Just as if a person is born at 12:01 AM or at 11:59 PM on July 1st, the date of birth is July 1st. So too it is with death. If a person died at 12:01 AM or at 11:59 PM of July 1st, the date of the person's death would be the same. A Thursday crucifixion results in three days of death (or daylight portions of death), which include Thursday (Nisan 15), Friday (Nisan 16), and Saturday (Nisan 17). It also results in three nights of death (or nighttime portions of death), which are Thursday night (Nisan 15), Friday night (Nisan 16), and Saturday night (Nisan 17). Since Jesus rises before dawn of Nisan 17th, the day portion for Sunday (Nisan 17) cannot be counted because until sunrise the time is still in the night of Nisan 17. Therefore, Jesus' death spans three Jewish days and three Jewish nights, in agreement the calendar God created.

> 3:00 PM Nisan 14th to 3:00 PM Nisan 15th = 24 hours
>
> 3:00 PM Nisan 15th to 3:00 PM Nisan 16th = 24 hours
>
> 3:00 PM Nisan 16th to 6:00 AM Nisan 17th = <u>15 hours</u>
>
> Total   63 hours

Additionally, the timeline for death is approximately sixty-three (63) hours, which literally allows Jesus to rise on "the third day." Therefore, Jesus' eleven prophecies specifically stating He would rise on "the third day" or "in three days" and His prophecy in Matthew 12:40 are completely harmonized without any manipulation of scripture. There is also no necessity for a strict legalistic interpretation requiring a seventy-two (72) hour entombment before the Scriptures can be synchronized. If Scriptures are believed literally for the time of death, a Thursday crucifixion unifies all the prophecies.

Additionally a Thursday crucifixion does not require a sunset resurrection like a Wednesday crucifixion. Thus, there is no major conflict between any of the Gospel accounts for the crucifixion regarding the timing of the women appearing at the tomb or the guards on duty. In a Thursday crucifixion, the guards responsible for watching the tomb during the night watch when Jesus arose from the dead would have been the guards reporting to the Sanhedrin in the morning. These guards could have been believed if they lied and reported they had fallen asleep on duty, neglecting their post, which allowed the disciples to steal the body.

Therefore, in conclusion the resistance to a Thursday crucifixion based upon the current Jewish calendar or any regressions using Hillel II's equations would not be biblically or historically accurate. A Passover on Thursday would have been possible and even probable during the Second Temple, which based its calendar on sighting the new moon. A Thursday crucifixion provides for a resurrection on the Feast of First Fruits while simultaneously fulfilling the Sunday discovery and the Nisan 17th symbolism. It also allows for the guards' lie to be believed. Jesus' prophecies concerning rising in three days or on the third day combined with His prophecy of being dead three days and three night is literally fulfilled in a Thursday crucifixion week. No manipulation of Scriptures or extreme legalism is required for understanding a Thursday crucifixion, and daily events are completed without any missing day(s) in the New Testament timeline. Also, there is no discrepancy for the triumphant entry into Jerusalem on Nisan 10th, which would have occurred on a Sunday. While Sabbath supporters refuse to embrace the selection of the Passover Lamb or Jesus' resurrection on a Sunday, New Testament scriptures strongly corroborate a timeline that indicates God who rested on the Sabbath began a new thing within creation by the resurrection of His Son on a Sunday. This concept of God beginning a new thing in creation is not recent. The prophet Jeremiah proclaimed in 31:22 that God would create a "new thing" on the Earth. Isaiah also prophesizes that God proclaiming, "Behold, I will do a new thing; now it shall spring forth; shall ye not know it?" (Isaiah 43:19). A new beginning represented by a resurrection on the first day of the week would not conflict with God being the God of the Sabbath, especially if one applies the spiritual concept of Sabbath discussed in the calendar section of this book.

Friday Crucifixion:

Chart 23

	Gregorian	Calendar	Days	
Sat	Sun	Mon	Tues	Wed
	Jewish	Calendar	Days	
Nisan 8	Nisan 9	Nisan 10	Nisan 11	Nisan 12
Jesus Arrived in Bethany		Selection of Passover Lamb		
Weekly Sabbath*		(Ex 12:3, Mt 21:1-11)		
Night: Nisan 9	Night: Nisan 10	Night: Nisan 11	Night: Nisan 12	Night: Nisan 13
	Selection of Passover Lamb	Jesus returns to Bethany (Mt 21:17)		
	Jesus in Bethany (Jn 12:1-11)			

* No work allowed by Jewish Law

Friday Crucifixion continued:

	Gregorian	Calendar	Days	
Thurs	Fri	Sat	Sun	Mon
	Jewish	Calendar	Days	
Nisan 13	Nisan 14	Nisan 15	Nisan 16	Nisan 17
	PASSOVER	Feast of Unleavened Bread*	Jesus' Resurrection Discovered	
		(Lev 23:4-8)	(Mt 28:1, Mk 16:2)	
	Jesus dies at 3PM (Mk 15:34)	Weekly Sabbath*		
Night: Nisan 14	Night: Nisan 15	Night: Nisan 16	Night: Nisan 17	Night: Nisan 18
PASSOVER	Feast of Unleavened Bread*			
	Weekly Sabbath*			

* No work allowed by Jewish Law

Friday Crucifixion
(The Good Friday Traditional Viewpoint):

While celebrated by Christianity from as early as the fourth century as the date of Jesus' crucifixion, there are many problems with a crucifixion happening on a Friday afternoon. The primarily problem of a Friday crucifixion lies in Jesus' self-prophecy in Matthew 12:40 of being dead three days and three nights:

> "₃₉But he answered and said unto them, An evil and adulterous generation seeketh after a sign; and there shall no sign be given to it, but the sign of the prophet Jonas: ₄₀For as Jonah was three days and three nights in the whale's belly; *so shall the Son of man be three days and three nights in the heart of the earth.*" Matthew 12:39-40

Chart 24

Friday	Saturday	Sunday
Day: Nisan 14	Day: Nisan 15	Day: Nisan 16
Jesus dies at 3PM		Jesus Alive before Sunrise
Dead Day 1	Dead Day 2	
Night: Nisan 15	Night: Nisan 16	
Dead Night 1	Dead Night 2	

Recalling the section on the Jewish calendar, a twenty-four day is divided into two twelve-hour sections, of night and day. The twenty-four "day" begins at sunset with night. Night lasts until the following sunrise, which starts the "day" (or daylight) portion of the twenty-four hour "day." With Jesus' death occurring on a Friday afternoon, the number of Jewish days dead, including His date of death, would be two days: Nisan 14th (Friday) and Nisan 15th (Saturday). However, this computation would only be correct if time was counted from His death on the cross. A calculation of time from entombment as many Christian scholars propose would have only one date of death, Saturday. The number of nights Jesus would be dead would also be two: Nisan 15th (Friday) and Nisan 16th (Saturday). Since Jesus' resurrection occurred before the sunrise on Sunday, it could not be counted for a day of death because the "day" portion of Nisan 16th would begin after sunrise. Therefore, a Friday crucifixion only describes at most two days and two nights of death, not the prophesized three days and three nights in Matthew 12:40.

There have been many attempts over the years to justify the calculation of "a day" or "a night" by Gregorian standards. However, Jesus was the Jewish Messiah speaking to the nation of Israel and his Jewish disciples. He would not have referenced time by a Roman or Gregorian calendar, but would have used His Father's (God's) calendar, the Jewish calendar from the Torah. Scholarly commentaries have also attempted to dismiss the lack of time Jesus was dead in Matthew 12:40 by implying it didn't mean a literal three days and three nights but was rather speaking a Jewish expression or idiom. Their position maintains Jesus spoke in "rounded numbers" and any part of a day counted for an entire day.

> "The period during which Jesus was to lie in the grave is here expressed in round numbers, according to the Jewish way of speaking, which was to regard any part of a day, however small, included within a period of days, as a full day (See 1 Samuel 30:12-13, Esther 4:16, Esther 5:1, Matthew 27:63-64)"[41]

It should be noted that **all** the famous Christian commentators presupposed from tradition Jesus died on a Friday and rose on a Sunday. Therefore, their commentaries are skewed to justify a Friday crucifixion because of their personally held bias for this date as their foundation for a timeline. Every attempt was made by them to minimize or discount discrepancies within the Scriptures to support a Friday to Sunday death timeline. This writer has no problem with scholars concluding any part of the day of death, even though it was only several hours instead of the whole day, could be counted as a day of being dead. Under this mentality, whether Jesus died on a Wednesday, Thursday, Friday at 3:00 PM on the cross, that particular day would be the date from which His death timeline began. This writer has agreed to apply this concept when counting time, as reflected in all the paragraphs explaining death timelines proposing both a literal interpretation of death starting at the cross and a legalistic seventy-two hour mentality. However, as mentioned above, even calculating the date of death on Friday, there are at a maximum only two days and two nights of death possible.

Ironically, Christian commentators presupposing the Jesus "rounded number of days" theory also state in their commentaries that the phrase "in the heart of the earth" was actually a reference to Jesus being in His sepulcher (see note in Wednesday crucifixion timeline). If these commentators combined their two theological positions regarding the any portion of a day being dead with their "in heart of the earth" meaning in the sepulcher to calculate the time for Jesus' death, they would obtain only one Jewish day, Nisan 15th. Because Christ would have been in the grave mere moments before Nisan 15th or during the transition of Nisan 14th to Nisan 15th, the daylight portion of Nisan 14th would be highly questionable to be included as a "day" and only the daylight portion of Nisan 15th would qualify as a "day" of death. The night of Nisan 15 and Nisan 16 would also still qualify, giving a total period of death for one day and two nights.

Thus, the timeline for a Friday crucifixion is at most thirty-nine (39) hours. As mentioned in the chapter, The Sign of Jonah, there is no Biblical example of a thirty-nine hour period of time qualifying for the description of three days and three nights or on the third day. If the death timeline were calculated from entombment, the maximum hours would be thirty-six (36) hours.

3:00 PM Nisan 14th to 3:00 PM Nisan 15th = 24 hours

3:00 PM Nisan 15th to 6:00 AM Nisan 16th = <u>15 hours</u>

Total 39 hours max

While a Friday crucifixion does cover three different portions of Jewish days: Nisan 14th (Friday), Nisan 15th (Saturday), and Nisan 16th (Sunday), these periods do not cover three days and three nights of time. A Friday crucifixion scenario would have to presume Jesus did not mean literally what He said regarding "three days and three nights" in Matthew 12:40, and the Greek words translated "days" and "nights" were metaphorical for a general concept of a Gregorian day. Considering the numerous other literal prophetic timelines Jesus fulfilled to become God's Passover lamb, it is doubtful His prophetic statements in the Gospel of Matthew would be based on generalities or idiom concepts. A more literal interpretation is the most logical and strait forward understanding of the Scriptures. Jesus meant what He said and was not speaking in idioms regarding the prophecy in Matthew 12:40. He would indeed be dead for three days and three nights, yet rise on the third day. To necessitate this interpretation of Scriptures, Jesus must be dead longer than 48 hours and less than seventy-two hours.

Travel Restrictions and A Missing Day

The Gospel of John records six days before the Passover (Nisan 8) Jesus arrived in Bethany. In a Friday crucifixion week, Nisan 8th is a Sabbath. Therefore, this scenario would require Jesus to travel from Ephraim to Bethany on the Sabbath. Because the distance is approximately 14 miles, it exceeds Torah Law travel restrictions of 4,000 cubits. Since we know Jesus the Christ was without sin, He could not violate the Torah, including Torah travel restrictions for personal travel on a Sabbath. Therefore, Jesus could not have arrived in Bethany on Nisan 8th in a Friday crucifixion week.

If one assumed Jesus arrived at night on Nisan 8th to Bethany instead of during the day, Jesus' travel would have occurred on Nisan 7th thus not violating Torah, which would be acceptable. However, this proposed timeline of events would require the dinner at Lazarus' house specially prepared for Christ to occur on Nisan 9th after the Sabbath rest. Because the scriptures articulate a series of successive events, having dinner on the night of Nisan 9th would place Jesus's immediate travel to Jerusalem for His triumphal entry on the next date, Nisan 9th. Such a timeline would not be in agreement with New Testament scriptures or Old Testament prophecies. If Jesus was in Bethany on the night of Nisan 8th and retained a triumphant entry to Jerusalem on Nisan 10th, the scriptures would be required to skip a full day of activity on Nisan 9th. However, the New Testament Scriptures do not insinuate a missing day in the timeline, and this would not the best conclusion of the interpretation of scriptures. Therefore, it is highly unlikely either of these Nisan 8th or 9th Bethany dinner scenarios is possible. Thus it provides Scriptural doubt to a Friday crucifixion.

Nisan 17th Symbolism - Absent

Furthermore, a Friday crucifixion would result in the Feast of First Fruits celebration occurring on Nisan 16th by either the Sadducee or Pharisee calculation because it would be the first day (Sunday) of the week following the Feast of Unleavened Bread, Nisan 15th. Unlike Nisan 17th where a clear theme of salvation, deliverance, and new beginnings has been biblically established, there is no indication of any particular theme associated with Nisan 16th in Old Testament scriptures. Nisan 16th has no historical value indicating redemption to Israel and would not correspond to God's Principle of First Mention and the Progressive Mentions of Nisan 17th in the Bible.

The Preparation Day

Additionally, supporters of a Friday crucifixion believe the *"day of preparation"* was the Friday before the weekly Sabbath since they propose the weekly Sabbath coincided with the holy convocation Sabbath.

> "[62]Now **the next day, that followed the day of the preparation**, the chief priests and Pharisees came together unto Pilate, [63]Saying, Sir, we remember that that deceiver said, while he was yet alive, After three days I will rise again. [64]Command therefore that the sepulcher **be made sure until the third day**, lest his

disciples come by night, and steal him away, and say unto the people, He is risen from the dead: so the last error shall be worse than the first. ₆₅Pilate said unto them, Ye have a watch: go your way, make it as sure as ye can. ₆₆So *they* went, and *made the sepulcher sure, sealing the stone, and setting a watch.*"
Matthew 27:62-66

As a result of their interpretation of *"the day of preparation,"* the next day would have been on one of the highest holy days for the nation of Israel, Nisan 15th. Since this particular Sabbath would have been a combination of the weekly Sabbath and the Feast of Unleavened Bread, many events for the general assembly of Israel would have been required not to mention the preparation for the Feast of First Fruits. This double sacred day makes it unlikely for the chief priests and Pharisees to have taken the time out of their required religious tasks and prayers on Nisan 15th to seek Pilate to seal Jesus' tomb.

Additionally, much fuss has been made over the "High Sabbath" recorded in John 19:31. Some scholars have argued the qualifications for a "High Sabbath" require the day to consist of both an annual holy convocation day and a weekly Sabbath. Many understand this concept based on Jewish tradition that became effective after Hillel II's calendar change. There is no historical evidence that the Apostle John knew the terminology for "High Sabbath" required the day to have two corresponding Sabbaths. It is just as reasonable for the Apostle John to denote the holy convocation day of Unleavened Bread on Nisan 15th as a "High Sabbath" to distinguish its occurrence within the week separate from the weekly Sabbath on Friday. Thus, the argument that a "High Sabbath" must only be a holy convocation day occurring on a weekly Friday Sabbath is unsubstantiated during the first century.

Therefore, because of the many scriptural contradictions, it is impossible for a Friday crucifixion to be in agreement with all the Scriptures.

1. Jesus' death timeline of thirty-six (36) to thirty-nine (39) hours is less than other the biblical examples of an event occurring "on the third day" which hold that events must be over two days (48) hours and under seventy-two hours, and

2. The inability to fulfill the prophecy of "three days and three nights" of death as prophesized by Jesus in Matthew 12:40, and

3. The discrepancy of a possible Torah travel violation on Nisan 8th, and

4. A missing day in the sequence of events recorded in the New Testament, often documented by commentators, and

5. The lack of fulfillment of the Nisan 17th symbolism for redemption and new beginnings identified prophetically in Old Testament Scriptures.

Furthermore, as mentioned earlier in the beginning narrative of weekly events, it is impossible for Christianity to uphold a Sunday triumphant entry date for Jesus in Jerusalem with a Friday crucifixion. The weekly events for a Friday crucifixion would require a Monday triumphal entry date to Jerusalem. Therefore, Christians upholding the traditional "Good Friday" death date cannot simultaneously support a "Palm Sunday" and be in agreement with the Bible. The

Gregorian Friday crucifixion timeline does not literally fulfill all the Scriptures associated with the death and resurrection of Jesus Christ and events surrounding His last earthly week. Subsequently, it cannot be an accurate day for His death.

Comprehensive List of Weekly Events & Prophetic Scriptures

To harmonize all the Old Testament prophecies with the events recorded in New Testament Scriptures without having any missing days or Torah violations and to include the Principle of First Mention and the Principle of Progressive Mention for Nisan 17th, only one Gregorian day of the week unifies the Scriptures. Therefore, the following comprehensive list of weekly events and cross-referenced prophetic Scriptures was based on a Thursday crucifixion.

A reader comparing gospel accounts of the resurrection should be aware that Luke has a tendency to list events by subject rather than in a sequence of time. This grouping by event or subject instead of outlining events in a chronological order is evident in Luke's account of the baptism of Jesus. Luke tells the story of John the Baptist, his sermons, his preaching for repentance by baptism, and his baptizing of the multitude in the Jordan River. Then Luke reports King Herod arrested John the Baptist and put him in prison, because John had rebuked Herod for his marriage to Herodias. The other gospels acknowledge John baptized Jesus in the Jordan River before John was shut up in prison. John's martyrdom immediately followed his imprisonment.

Nevertheless, after mentioning the imprisonment of John the Baptist, Luke continued by stating, "When all the people were baptized, it came to pass that Jesus also was baptized; and while He prayed, the heaven was opened. And the Holy Spirit descended in bodily form like a dove upon Him" (Luke 3:21-22). Therefore, it is obvious Luke is stating John baptized Jesus in the presence of the multitude before John's imprisonment. However, Luke mentions this incident only after speaking about the ministry of the Lord Jesus Christ. Thus, Luke categorized the ministry of John the Baptist as one subject, then explained the ministry of Jesus Christ without regard or acknowledgement to the overlapping timeline of these two ministries or the chronological order of events. When examining events leading up to the crucifixion and resurrection of Jesus, Luke tends to narrate a whole subject before shifting to another. The arrangement of events by subject does not contradict the other biblical accounts of events; but rather demonstrates Luke's unique style of writing. Understanding Luke's writing technique helps better clarify the timeline of events during Christ's Passion Week.

Nisan 8th – would begin on Friday

Day

Jn 12:1	Jesus arrives at Lazarus' home in Bethany

Nisan 9th – Sabbath

Jesus would rest on the Sabbath according to law in Lazarus' home.

Evening

Ex 31:14-15	No work allowed on the Sabbath

Day

Ex 31:14-15	No work allowed on the Sabbath
Ex 16:29	Travel restricted on the Sabbath for personal pleasure or work; allowed for temple worship
Josh 3:4-5	Travel restriction is defined as 4,000 cubits total, or about 6,000 feet (a little over 1 mile). See page 246
Jn 11:18	Travel from Bethany to Jerusalem was a little less than 2 miles

Nisan 10th - Selection of the Lamb – Sunday

Evening

Jn 12:2	Jesus has dinner at Lazarus' home, specially prepared for Him
Jn 12:3	Mary anoints Jesus' feet with spikenard oil

Day

Mt 21:1-7	Jesus sends to Bethphage for donkey
Mt 21:1-11; Mk 11:1-12 Lk 19:28-44 Jn 12:12-19	Triumphant entry into Jerusalem
Mk 11:11 Lk 19:47	Jesus enters the Temple
Lk 19:41-44	Jesus weeps over Jerusalem
Mt 21:17	Goes to Bethapage

Cross- Referenced Prophecies & Scriptures

Song of Sol 1:12	While the king sitteth at his table, my spikenard sendeth forth the smell thereof.
Ex 12:3	Speak ye unto all the congregation of Israel, saying, In the **tenth day of this month** they shall take to them every man a lamb, according to the house of their fathers, a lamb for an house:

Nisan 10ᵗʰ - Selection of the Lamb (continued)
Cross- Referenced Prophecies & Scriptures:

Ps 118:26	Blessed be he that cometh in the name of the LORD: we have blessed you out of the house of the LORD.
Zech 9:9	Rejoice greatly, O daughter of Zion; shout, O daughter of Jerusalem: behold, thy King cometh unto thee: he is just, and having salvation; lowly, and riding upon an ass, and upon a colt the foal of an ass
Ex 12:5	Your **lamb shall be without blemish**, a male of the first year: ye shall take it out from the sheep, or from the goats:
Jer 35:17	Therefore thus saith the LORD God of hosts, the God of Israel; Behold, I will bring upon Judah and upon all the inhabitants of Jerusalem all the evil that I have pronounced against them: because I have spoken unto them, but they have not heard; and I have called unto them, but they have not answered. Thus Jesus weeps over Jerusalem because this prophecy will be fulfilled.
Gen 22:8	And Abraham said, My son, **God will provide himself a lamb** for a burnt offering: so they went both of them together
Duet 16:5-7, Num 9:13-14	All Jewish males must appear in Jerusalem for Passover
Jn 1:29	The next day John seeth Jesus coming unto him, and saith, **Behold the Lamb of God**, which taketh away the sin of the world.

Nisan 10th - Selection of the Lamb (continued)
Cross- Referenced Prophecies & Scriptures:

Heb 9:14	How much more shall the blood of Christ, who through the eternal Spirit offered himself *without spot* to God, purge your conscience from dead works to serve the living God?
1 Ptr 1:19	But with the precious blood of Christ, *as of a lamb without blemish and without spot*

With the Sabbath ended, a large dinner in Jesus' honor could commence. Jesus ate the evening meal at the home of Lazarus, Mary & Martha in Bethany. During supper, Mary anointed Jesus' feet with spikenard ointment and wiped his feet with her hair. Jesus stated in verse seven that Mary had held onto this oil prophetically to symbolically anoint him before his burial.

Nisan 11th

Evening

Mt 21:17; Mk 11:11	Jesus goes to Bethany to lodge

Day

Mt 21:19-22; Mk 11:13	Fig Tree cursed
Mt 21:12-17; Mk 11:15-18; Lk 19:45-48	Jesus cleanses the Temple
Lk 19:47	Jesus teaches in Temple
Mk 11:18; Lk 19:47	Scribes & Priest desire to destroy Christ

Cross- Referenced Prophecies & Scriptures:

Mt 26:55; Mk 14:49; Lk 22:53	Jesus spends the 10th, 11th, 12th, 13th of Nisan in the Temple being "examined" for any spiritual defect.
Ex 12:3-6	Lamb taken into the house and kept for examination of blemish (Nisan 10th -13th)
Jer 7:11	Is the house of God become the den of thieves?
Isa 56:7	Mine house shall be called a house of prayer
Psalm 69:9	Zeal of God's house ate Christ up

Nisan 12th

Evening

Lk 21:37	Jesus abides at Mt of Olives

Day

Mt 21:28-23:39, Mk 12:1-44,	Jesus teaches in Temple
Mk 11:20-26; 13:1-37	Fig Tree Found withered
Lk 20:9-21-4, Mt 24:1-51; Mt 24:1-51; Mk 13:1-37; Lk 21:5-36	Olivet Discourse
Mt 26:3-4; Mk 14:1-2 Lk 22:1-6; Jn 11:47-53	Scribes & Priest conspire to capture Christ

Nisan 12th (continued)
Cross-Referenced Prophecies & Scriptures:

Mt 26:55; Mk 14:49; Lk 22:53	Jesus spends the 10th, 11th, 12th, 13th of Nisan in the Temple being "examined" for any spiritual defect.
Ex 12:3-6	Lamb taken into the house and kept for examination of blemish (Nisan 10th-13th)
Psalm 2:2	Gather against Christ
Isa 5:1-7	A reflection Jesus' parable of the vineyard
2 Chr 36:16	A reflection on Jesus' parable of mistreating the Lord's servants/messengers
Isa 8:14-15	Christ the stumbling block and rock of offense to Israel
Isa 28:16; Psalm 118:22	Jesus the chief cornerstone
Dan 2:44	Jesus' kingdom has no end
Jer 26:18	Jesus' prophecy of Jerusalem's destruction
Joel 2:1-2	Judgment day foretold

Nisan 13th

Evening

Mt 26:6-11; Mk 14:3-9	Simon the Leper's House in Bethany, unnamed woman anoints Jesus' head

Day

Mt 26:6-9; Mk 14:3-16; Lk 22:3-30	Jesus teaches in Temple
Mt 26:14-16; Mk 14:10-11; Lk 22:3-6	Judas seeks to betray Christ
Mt 26:17-91; Mk 14:12-16; Lk 22:7-30	Preparation for Last Supper

Nisan 13th (continued)
Cross- Referenced Prophecies & Scriptures:

Ex 29:7	High Priest's head anointed with oil
Lev 8:12	High Priest's head anointed with oil
Esther 3:9-12	Ha'man for silver betrays Israel to death – symbolic of Judas betrayal of Jesus
Ps 133	Blessings of God commanded to flow like oil on the High Priest's head
Mt 26:55; Mk 14:49; Lk 22:53	Jesus spends the 10th, 11th, 12th, 13th of Nisan in the Temple being "examined" for any spiritual defect.
Ex 12:3-6	Lamb taken into the house and kept for examination of blemish (Nisan 10th -13th)
Zech 11:12	Jesus betrayed for 30 pieces of silver

Interesting fact: 13 Nisan was April 1st in 1920: The day the Nazi Party formally emerged.

Nisan 14th Passover

Evening

Mt 26:26-29; Mk 14:22-25; Lk 22:14-23	Last Supper/New Covenant
Jn 13:1-20	Upper Room Events - Washing of Disciples Feet
Mt 26:21-25; Mk 14:18-21; Jn 13:21-30	Betrayal announced
Mt 26:30-56; Mk 14:26-52; Lk 22:39-42	Garden of Gethsemane
Mt 26:47-56; Mk 14:43-50; Lk 22:47-53; Jn 18:1-27; Jn 19:14-15	Arrest & Trial of Jesus at Midnight
Mt 26:69-75; Mk 14:66-72; Lk 22:54-61	Peter denies Jesus

Nisan 14th Passover (continued)

Day

Mt 26:47-56; Mk 14:43-50; Lk 22:47-53; Jn 18:1-27	Midnight: Jn 19:14-15 Arrest & Trial of Jesus
Mt 27:1-2; Mk 15:1-15; Lk 23:1-25; Jn 18:28-19:16	Trial before Herod & Pilate
Isa 53:4-5; 1Peter 2:24; Mt 8:16-17; Mt 27:26; Mk 15:15; Jn 19:1	Jesus scourged for our physical healing
Mt 27:22-26; Mk 15:25-26	Crucifixion starts 9AM
Mt 27:45; Mk 15:33; Lk 23:44-45	Noon the sun goes dark until 3PM

Nisan 14th Passover (continued)

Day

Mt 27:50; Mk 15:34-37; Lk 23:46; Jn 19:28-30	Jesus dies on cross at 3PM
Mk 16:1; Lk 24:54-56	Women buy spices & prepare to anoint Jesus' body
Jn 19:31-36	Not a bone broken in Jesus
Mt 27:57-58; Mk 15:42-46; Lk 23:50-53; Jn 19:38-40	Joseph of Arimathea pleads for Jesus body, prepares Jesus' body for burial by wrapping it in new linen.
Mt 27:57-66; Mk 15:42-47; Lk 23:50-56; Jn 19:38-42	Jesus in tomb before sunset
Mt 12:40	First day of death in tomb

Nisan 14th Passover (continued)

Cross-Referenced Prophecies & Scriptures:

Gen 3:15	Prophecy of Satan wounding Jesus but Jesus conquering and overcoming Satan
Gen 14:18	Last Supper Foreshadowed – Melchizedek Priesthood
Ex 11 & 12	Selection of Lamb, death of Lamb
Duet 21:22-23	To die on wood (tree)
Lev 17:11	Life is in the blood, given to make atonement for man
Jer 31:31-34	A New Covenant would be given by God to Israel and would be based entirely on His effort, not man's works
Zech 11:12	Judas betrayed Christ for 30 pieces of silver
Zech 13:7	Disciples abandon Christ
Duet 16:5-7	Passover lamb to be sacrificed outside the city gates of Jerusalem
Psalm 41:9	He who ate with me, lifted up his heal against me
Dan 9:26	Messiah foretold to die
Gen 3:15	Satan bruises Jesus' heal; Jesus bruises Satan's head
Midnight: Jn 19:14-15	Cross reference with Angel of Death in Egypt at Midnight 12:29
Isa 50	Scourging foretold; beard plucked out
Isa 53	Scourging & death foretold
Psalm 22	Crucifixion Foretold
Zech 11:13	30 pieces of silver cast to the potter's field
Psalm 55:12-14	Betrayed by Peter

Nisan 14th Passover (continued)
Cross- Referenced Prophecies & Scriptures:

Zech 12:10	Jews will mourn killing Christ whom they pierced
Ex 12:46; Num 9:12-	Not a bone to be broken in the Lamb
Rom 3:23-24; 1 Jn 1:7	Christ blood made atonement
Isa 50:3	Sun to hide its face in mourning
Psalm 35:11-12	False witnesses against Christ
Psalm 69:21	Gave Jesus vinegar to drink
Psalm 22:17; Psalm 34:20	No bones broken in Jesus
Psalm 35:19	Jesus hated without a cause

The word given in Deut 21:22-23 as "tree" is "*'ets*" in Hebrew, which means can mean tree or any plank or stick of wood. In fact, the root of this word is the verb "to shut" which implies planks of wood used for doors or windows rather than representing living trees.

Nisan 15ᵗʰ – Feast of Unleavened Bread

Evening

Mt 27:58-60	Jesus in the tomb
Mt 12:40	First night of death in tomb

Day

Mt 27:58-60	Jesus in the tomb
Mt 27:62-66	Sanhedrin ask Pilate to seal Jesus' tomb
Mt 27:66	Tomb seal & guard set
Mt 12:40	Second day of death in tomb

Cross- Referenced Prophecies & Scriptures:

Ex 23:14-15	Feast of Unleavened Bread starts
Ex 12:46	The Passover lamb shall not go out of the house
Ex 12:10	The Passover lamb shall be roasted with fire, nothing to remain by morning
Mt 12:40	The Son of Man 3 days/3 nights in the heart of the Earth
Psalm 16:10	Jesus' soul was in Sheol; body in the grave
Eph 4:9	Jesus descends to the lowest parts of the Earth
Dan 6:17	Stone sealed with signet ring so it could not be broken by order of the King

Nisan 16th – Weekly Sabbath

Evening

Mt 27:58-60	Jesus in the tomb
Mt 12:40	Second night of death in tomb

Day

Mt 27:58-60	Jesus in the Tomb
Mt 12:40	Third day of death in tomb

Cross- Referenced Prophecies & Scriptures:

Ex 31:14-15	No work allowed on the Sabbath
Mt 12:40	The Son of Man 3 days/3 nights in the heart of the Earth

Nisan 17th – Resurrection/New Covenant Begins

Evening

Mt 27:58-60	Jesus in the Tomb
Mt 12:40	Third Night of Death

Day

Mk 16:2; Lk 24:1-3; Jn 20:1	Jesus alive before sunrise
Mt 28:2	Great earthquake & angels at tomb
Mt 28:1; Mk 16:1-2; Lk 24:1	Women come to anoint Jesus' body
Mt 28:1-01; Mk 16:1-18; Lk 24:1-49; Jn 20:1-23;	Discovery of Jesus' resurrection
Jn 20:14-17	Jesus appears to Mary Magdalene
Mt 28:11-15	Guards tell Sanhedrin of Jesus' open tomb; guards bribed
Mt 27:52-53	Dead saints rise with Christ
Jn 20:17	Jesus ascends to His Father in Heaven
Lk 24:13-45	Jesus walks with disciples to Emmaus
1 Cor 15:5	Jesus appears to Peter

Nisan 17ᵗʰ – Resurrection/New Covenant Begins Cross- Referenced Prophecies & Scriptures:

Mt 12:40	The Son of Man 3 days/3 nights in the heart of the Earth
Gen 8:4	Noah's Ark Rested
Ex 14:21-30	Crossed Red Sea
Joshua 5:12	Eat for the first time from the Promise Land harvest
Esther 8:1-11	Delivered from annihilation
Acts 2:27; 13:35-37	Jesus's body did not see corruption
Psalms 16:10	For thou wit not leave my soul in Sheol; neither wilt though suffer thine Holy One to see corruption
Psalm 22	Death & Resurrection of Christ
Isa 26:19	Dead to rise with Christ
Psalm 68:18	Jesus led captivity away (resurrected Old Testament saints)
Psalm 49:15	God to redeem Him from the grave
1 Corin 15:3-4	Christ rose the third day
Ex 23:14-16; Duet 16:16-17 Lev 23:9-14	Feast of First Fruits; No one shall appear before the Lord empty
1Cor 15:20-23; Ro 8:29	Jesus is the First Fruits

Nisan 17th – Resurrection/New Covenant Begins Cross- Referenced Prophecies & Scriptures
(continued)

Dan 7:13-14	Jesus' kingdom has no end, dominion over all creation

Psalms 16:10 has two different facets of prophecy – one is spiritual as Jesus' soul will not be left in Sheol, the spiritual holding place (Paradise) and the other is physical as Jesus' body would not be left to rot in the grave either. Thus, both Jesus' soul and body are prophesized to be raised from the dead.

Nisan 18th

Evening

Mk 16:9-18; Lk 24:34-45; Jn 20:19-25	Jesus appears to Apostles again, Thomas not present

CHAPTER 9

THE CONCLUSION

God is the most intentional being that has ever and will ever exist. Every thing (every thought, emotion, word, and action) He does has purpose. Nothing is done accidentally or haphazardly. Eternal power and purposefulness inundate every word spoken by God; each declaration unveils His divine master plan of Jesus.

Complete within Himself, God lacked for nothing; yet within that completeness was a heart overflowing with love for the children He would create. All God's resources have been focused on the restoration of mankind, which He foretold in our darkest hour amidst the beauty of Eden. His promises were reiterated over and over again: line upon line, and precept upon precept, until their fulfillment at Golgotha on the cross. God's love enabled Him to set aside a portion of His heavenly glory to enter mortality and dwell with mankind. After becoming human, Jesus gave His back to Roman lashes, His hands to iron nails, His brow to thorny piercings, His holy blood to the ground, and His life to the grave. God gave everything He was to redeem you back, to restore His children to their rightful positions and inheritance.

Amazingly, the entire story of redemption is revealed within God's prophetic calendar. Each holy convocation date uncovers a particular aspect about the master plan ministry of Jesus Christ. When examining God's calendar for mankind, it is essential to remember how this chapter began: God is the most intentional being that exists, and all His intentions in this creation revolve around humanity. God's calendar does not exalt some pathetic need for selfish pleasure requiring worship from men on specific dates. Instead, His calendar is a type of dress rehearsal for mankind, which through past observances prepared people for the glorious intervention of Jesus on our behalf. Interestingly, God gave a calendar to mankind not based on a solar timeline. His prophetic announcements are heralded by a lunar schedule, standing in opposition to the various characteristics of a solar calendar.

Man's natural wisdom proclaims the "sun" is responsible for all life on Earth and declares its astronomical chart to be the most accurate method of calculating time for Earth. Yet, in reality, God's "Son" is the source of all life. Jesus has created all things, both invisible and visible and holds creation together. Jesus is the most accurate method of determining time, because He began time and will one day stop it.

> "$_{16}$For by Him [Jesus] were all things created, that are in heaven, and that are in earth, visible and invisible, whether they be thrones, or dominions, or principalities, or powers: all things were created by Him, and for Him: $_{17}$And He is before all things, and by Him all things consist."
> Colossians 1:16-17

Just as the moon doesn't shine in and of itself but simply reflects the light of the sun, the difference between the solar and lunar calendars are spiritually representative of the difference between the 'unregenerate heart' of a natural man and the 'new heart' of a saved man. Unregenerate hearts believe they are the center of their universe, emotionally, mentally, and physically speaking. As a result, they view the creation revolving around their hedonistic needs. In an unregenerate worldview, humanity is the pinnacle of random evolution. Because it celebrates a universe without God, man is placed center-stage. Thus, in this paradigm, man's natural wisdom is the highest form of understanding, and as such, everything orbits around man's intellect. As one might expect, from this perspective, the solar calendar prevails, because it exalts man's highest scientific knowledge regarding astronomical calculations involving time. Natural man in his fallen state is often unaware of the higher wisdom available in the universe, a wisdom that created the scientific world and leads science to the end of itself.

Whereas a calendar based on the moon, spiritually symbolizes an acknowledgement that creation doesn't revolve around mankind's fallen intellect or man himself (as typified by the solar calendar). Instead, life in creation hinges on the real "Son," the Son of God. Just as the moon does not create light, but only reflects the sun's light; mankind has been created in God's image to reflect the Son of God in creation. Even though God's prophetic calendar is lunar, it doesn't begin with the full moon, or the image of a man reflecting the fullness of Christ immediately. Instead, God begins at the new moon, or the dark of the moon when no light can be seen. Spiritually, this symbolizes the darkest hour for humanity, after Adam's ultimate betrayal of God in Eden creates sin's isolation of mankind from God. In that gloomiest hour, the sliver of first light is seen, like the dawning of the new moon. Humanity sees its first glimmer of hope, given graciously by God, as He proclaims the first prophetic announcement of Jesus:

> "₁₅I will put enmity between the [Satan] and the woman, and between thy seed and her seed [Jesus]; it shall bruise thy head, and thou shalt bruise heal."
> Genesis 3:15

Thus, the first day in the lunar calendar begins at the first sliver of the new moon, corresponding to the first sliver of hope for mankind's redemption given in Eden. The moon's phases have a spiritual representation for humanity as well. They serve as a portrait of the continuing prophetic announcements throughout the Old Testament declaring the Savior's coming arrival and ministry. Each prophecy builds line upon line, one upon another, until the fulfillment of God's promise is culminated in Jesus's sacrifice at the full moon. The phases of the moon waxing (or growing) to the full moon depict the timeline of history building up to its crescendo in Christ. It is no coincidence that Passover always occurs on a full moon, because it is when the "fullness of time was come" (Galatians 4:4) that Jesus Christ appeared.

Nonetheless, it wasn't Jesus' birth that saved humanity, but His death that redeemed mankind. His death occurred precisely at the revelation of the full moon on Nisan 14th, and His body laid in the tomb on Nisan 15th that first night under a full moon. The fullness of the spiritual glimmer of hope referenced in Eden had finally come, and the lunar calendar in its moon phases reflect this spiritual truth. As an appreciation of the understanding of God's prophetic calendar forms within the saved soul, even the moon's phases echo the glory of God's prophetic promises. For it was under a full moon, Jesus knelt in the Garden of Gethsemane for the Father's will to prevail, and under a full moon, Jesus lay buried in a tomb awaiting resurrection from the dead.

Not only is God's prophetic calendar lunar, but it also starts in the spring, changing man's original calendar from the birth of Adam in the autumn to a rebirth from Jesus' ministry in the spring. Spring has always been celebrated as a season of new life throughout all cultures of the world. Thus symbolically, God's prophetic calendar replaced the "Fall" of Adam with new life in Jesus' during spring. New spiritual life has come with the first full moon of the spring; new life has come to a world too long held captive by the wintery season of sin. Where death, darkness, and lack of provision once prevailed during the harshest season, a new season of bountiful harvest is now celebrated, bringing life and abundance back to the children of God.

Although the solar calendar bases its calculation of time on sunlight, the lunar calendar revolves around the True Light of creation, expressed in Genesis 1:3, "and God said, Let there be light: and there was light." The light that shone on the first day of creation was not our sun or any solar celestial body; because the Scriptures record the creation of the celestial heavenly bodies (the sun, moon, and stars) occurred on the fourth day (Genesis 1:14-18). Therefore, the light that shone on the first day of creation will remain long after our sun stops shining. In fact, in the Book of The Revelation of Jesus Christ to St. John, the Apostle John records in chapter 21:23 that after the passing away of the old heaven and old Earth, when the New Heaven and New Earth are created, there will be no need of the sun or the moon to give light upon the city of New Jerusalem for "the glory of God did lighten it, and the Lamb [Jesus] is the light thereof." Thus, eventually after the second coming and millennial reign of Jesus Christ, neither the lunar calendar which prophetically announced the Savior's coming and ministry nor the solar calendar which exalted the fallen nature of man will be required. Instead, the glory of God in Christ Jesus will be eternally, all-sufficient for Believers who dwell with Him in the New Jerusalem.

However, before that time prevails, there remains at least two dates on God's prophetic calendar awaiting fulfillment. If you will recall from the first chapter of this book, God declared seven holy convocation feasts in addition to His Sabbath as high holy days on His calendar. The number seven is extremely significant because it biblically represents the concept of completion, again signaling God will bring a close to His calendar after all the events revealing Jesus have been completed. The day will come when time itself will be folded up and a new "reality" will prevail as eternity begins (Hebrews 1:10-12).

The list of the seven holy convocation feasts announced in Leviticus chapter twenty-three, verses five through thirty-four, are as follows:

- Passover: (Nisan 14th)
- Feast of Unleavened Bread (Nisan 15th & 21st)
  - 1st and 7th days are holy convocations
- Feast of First Fruits
- Pentecost (Shavuot)
- Feast of Trumpets: Rosh Hashanah (Tishri 1)
- Day of Atonement (Tishri 10)
- Feast of Tabernacles (Tishri 15 & 22)
  - 1st and 7th days are holy convocations

These prophetic high holy days are part of the great mystery of duality. Each holy convocation date represents a literal time with a specific event associated for the Jewish nation while simultaneously symbolically depicting an eternal spiritual truth and application in Jesus' ministry for all mankind, which would be accomplished once and for all on that particular feast date. Prophetic calendar dates having a one-time, spiritual event associated with them include Passover, the Feast of First Fruits, Pentecost, Rosh Hashanah and the Day of Atonement. One example of the great mystery of duality is revealed in Passover. Passover occurred on Nisan 14th and had a literal physical fulfillment for the Jews in Egypt. It was completed on the natural level on the day Israel was redeemed from slavery under Pharaoh and escaped the judgment of God upon Egypt by the plague of death. Passover also has a single, spiritually eternal event associated with it accomplished by Jesus Christ. On Passover, Nisan 14th, the Lamb of God was slain on the cross to provide redemption for every person wanting to escape the slavery of sin and destruction of death from God's everlasting judgment against sin. According to the Book of Hebrews, Jesus' sacrifice was a single event that is eternally complete for all mankind throughout all generations. Never again will Jesus be required to die for the sins of mankind. Thus, Nisan 14th serves not only as a literal natural day in Egypt but as the eternal date salvation was obtain by Christ on the cross for Believers. If one observed all the events in God's prophetic calendar as dress rehearsals for Jesus' ministry, one can better understand the duality of the physical events coinciding to their eternal, spiritual counterpart.

Examining God's calendar from a purely spiritual standpoint, several single prophetic calendar dates stand out as being eternally completed by Jesus during His first incarnation, death and resurrection. In addition to the Passover, Jesus fulfilled the Feast of First Fruits on Nisan 17th, when He rose triumphantly from the grave. On this date, He ascended to appear before the Father's heavenly throne with His first fruits, the saints resurrected from the dead accompanying His resurrection. Similarly, the day of Pentecost was also fulfilled after the resurrection of Christ. After His ascension to heaven, Jesus sent the promise of the Father, the Holy Spirit, to indwell Believers. Ever since that memorable day, new Believers continue to receive the promise of the Father as the Holy Spirit indwells and empowers them to continue the ministry of reconciliation.

It is also highly probable that Tishri 1, the Feast of Trumpets, was fulfilled during the first coming of Jesus Christ as His birth date. Because Jesus is referred to as the last Adam, He could likely have been born on the same date Adam was thousands of years ago. The birth of the new Adam on the same date would provide additional symbolic emphasis on Jesus' humanity and His rightful entitlement to the inheritance of all the blessings and authority originally bestowed upon the first Adam. Many Christian commentators have speculated that Jesus could have been born during the Feast of Tabernacles because the name of the feast implies a dwelling of God with mankind and is alluded to in the Book of John, chapter 1:14. However, because the Feast of Tabernacles has the additional requirement for all Jewish males to present themselves before the Lord in Jerusalem, Joseph (Jesus' earthly father) would have been required to be in Jerusalem, not Bethlehem for this feast. Since it is scripturally documented Joseph was in Bethlehem at Jesus' birth, he could not have been in Jerusalem fulfilling the Feast of Tabernacles' requirement. Therefore, it is more plausible for Jesus to have been born on Tishri 1 than during the Feast of Tabernacles. If Jesus did fulfill Tishri 1 during His first incarnation, then only one single-event prophetic date remains unfilled on God's calendar, which is Tishri 10th, the Day of Atonement.

The Day of Atonement will be a single date in the history of mankind. The entire sixteenth chapter of Leviticus is dedicated to describing the Day of Atonement's symbolic physical application. It is a date in which the nation of Israel will be cleansed from all their sins before the Lord (Leviticus 16:30). According to the Book of Romans, Believers have already received the spiritual fulfillment of this day, because we have "received the atonement" (Romans 5:11). The ninth chapter of the Book of Hebrews also confirms the Day of Atonement has been fulfilled for Believers, specifically referring to this day in verses seven and twenty-five, and alluding to its spiritual application by Jesus in verses eight through twenty-eight. Yet the possibility remains that at some future date during the month of Tishri, the Lord Jesus will physically return to redeem the nation of Israel as a literal spiritual counterpart to the Day of Atonement prophesized in the Book of Romans 11. For there remains the prophecy of the nation of Israel to "look upon me [Jesus] whom they have pierced" and mourn in repentance (Zechariah 12:10). It is highly likely according to God's pattern of fulfillment in all the other feast dates, that on Tishri 10, Israel will finally behold and accept their Messiah, Jesus Christ, at His second coming and bring closure to this date once and for all.

While Scripture clearly identifies the fulfillment of some of the singular events on God's prophetic calendar, it is interesting to note that two of the Lord's feasts are declared to contain two holy convocation dates within the week-long feasting period: The Feast of Unleavened Bread and the Feast of Tabernacles. Although each feast date portrays a particular aspect of the ministry of Jesus, these two particular feasts have additional significance associated with their fulfillment as emphasized by the number of days (seven) associated with the feast. As mentioned earlier, the number seven is biblically symbolic of completeness and perfection.

When one counts the additional holy convocation days for these two weeklong feasts, the number of total holy feast days listed in Leviticus chapter twenty-three equals nine. The number nine also symbolizes divine completeness and conveys the meaning of finality. Christ died at the ninth hour of the day, making the way of salvation open to everyone. There are also nine fruits of the Holy Spirit listed in the Book of Galatians chapter five and nine gifts of the Holy Spirit listed in 1 Corinthians chapter twelve. Thus, the significance of divine completeness is reiterated in God's prophetic calendar. Only after the entire ministry of Jesus has been visibly unveiled to mankind on the feast dates will God's calendar be complete.

The two specific high, holy convocation days celebrated within the week of the Feast of Unleavened Bread and the Feast of Tabernacles are the first and last days of the feast. Because the number seven indicates a perfect completion, these two feasts seem to indicate that prophetic events within these feasts events will require additional time for "completion" rather than occurring as a single event seen in other feasts dates like Passover and Pentecost.

The significance of the Feast of Unleavened Bread having two dates is conveyed within the two types of bread used during the two historical Passovers that began this celebratory feast. Originally, as mentioned in chapter seven of this book, the bread eaten at the first Passover, the Mosaic Passover, was unleavened bread and representative of the giving the Law. The Old Covenant of Law lasted approximately 1,400 years before Jesus established the New

Covenant of Grace on the second historical Passover during the "Last Supper." Therefore, there is a beginning date and an ending date for the Old Covenant, which simultaneously is the beginning date of the eternal New Covenant. Jesus alone was capable of fulfilling the Law, and its fulfillment was a significant part of His redemptive work and ministry. Only upon its fulfillment could the New Covenant be instituted. Thus, the holy convocation days for the week of the Feast of Unleavened Bread are spiritually symbolic of the Old and New Covenants and have been fulfilled. The first date of Unleavened Bread represented the beginning of the Mosaic Law. The last date in the Feast, a holy convocation, represented the completion of the Law and the eternal beginning of the Covenant of Grace. Therefore, the Feast of Unleavened Bread is another feast completely fulfilled by the first incarnation of Jesus Christ.

The Feast of Tabernacles also has two holy convocation days within its week. According to John 1:14, "And the Word was made flesh, and dwelt among us (and we beheld his glory, the glory as of the only begotten of the Father) full of grace and truth." The Greek word "dwelt" has the same meaning as "tabernacle" in Hebrew. It conveys the image of God dwelling or living with His people. Because we know that Jesus was Emanuel, "God with us," and came bodily to dwell with the sons of men during His first incarnation, the first day of the holy convocation dates for the Feast of Tabernacles has been fulfilled. However, there remains another day, the last date, within this feast awaiting fulfillment. This dates is representative of another period of time in which God will dwell again with His people on Earth. Scripture provides the answer to the spiritual symbology of the second holy convocation date in the millennial reign of Jesus. On a particular date in the future, Jesus will return and eventually begin His thousand-year reign, dwelling with men on Earth. This event will complete the second holy convocation day for Tabernacles, dwelling with mankind and closing out the "week" of tabernacles. However, until that time, the last day of the Feast of Tabernacles remains unfulfilled.

When interpreting scripture is it important to understand that God does not necessarily consider time as man does. The Book of 2 Peter in chapter three verse eight declares, "Beloved, be not ignorant of this one thing, that one day *is* with the Lord as a thousand years, and a thousand years as one day." Interestingly, God has operated within man's understanding of the dates of His prophetic calendar with regard to prophetic announcements for those calendar dates. God has repeatedly performed His ministry events exactly on the Jewish date and month He prophesized the event to occur. Yet, there are numerous instances where God's timeline for the length of days, weeks, or even years is exponential to man's traditional understanding of a day, a week, or a year. One such example is found in the ninth chapter of the Book of Daniel. Daniel proclaimed prophetically that seventy weeks was assigned to the nation of Israel for their sin. Biblical scholars and historians have proven these "seventy weeks" were not a literal timeline of seventy weeks consisting of seven days in each week. Instead, over 480 years existed between Daniel's first week and his sixty-ninth week. Furthermore, there has been almost a two-thousand year comma in the Book of Isaiah (chapter 61:1-2). It was these two verses Jesus quoted in the synagogue in Nazareth when He suddenly stopped in the middle of a verse two and closed the scroll. Jesus' actions of closing the scroll indicate a heavenly time gap between the declaration of the Good News of deliverance, healing, and freedom for mankind that began verse two and "the day of vengeance" and wrath of the Lord at the end of the same verse.

Therefore, as you examine God's prophetic calendar for future events, understand the timing between events may very, but the date of the event's occurrence is eternally fixed to the specific Hebrew month and day assigned to it by God in Leviticus. This is because God has declared in the Book of Isaiah that He foretells events to mankind so that we will know He has performed them when they happen, and that the events are not random acts or acts performed by a false idol or men.

> "₃*I have declared the former things from the beginning; and they went forth out of my mouth, and I shewed them; I did them suddenly, and they came to pass.* ₄Because I knew that thou art obstinate, and thy neck is an iron sinew, and thy brow brass; ₅*I have even from the beginning declared it to thee; before it came to pass I shewed it thee*: lest thou shouldest say, Mine idol hath done them, and my graven image, and my molten image, hath commanded them. ₆Thou hast heard, see all this; and will not ye declare it? I have shewed thee new things from this time, even hidden things, and thou didst not know them. ₇They are created now, and not from the beginning; even before the day when thou heardest them not; lest thou shouldest say, Behold, I knew them."
> Isaiah 48:3-7

It is of value to note that changes have occurred within the man-made Jewish calendar as a result of Hillel II's fixed dating system. Hillel II's calendar is estranged from God's original calendar, which was based on the sighting of the new moon in Jerusalem. As a result of these human changes to the understanding of the Jewish calendar dates, the actual date of Tishri 10th observed by men may vary from God's calculation of that day in the future, because God is not bound to the errors introduced by men into the calendar. Instead, God eternally abides in the Truth of His revealed word. Understanding the changes in man's observation of calendar dates and God's proclaimed timeline gives new insight as to why Jesus stated no man would know the day or the hour of His return. For even if a man understood Tishri 10th as the Day of Atonement; due to current changes in the Jewish calendar calculation, Tishri 10th may not be observed on its correct date according to God's word. This could cause the prophecy for the Day of Atonement to appear askew and make it seem to land on a different date observed by man, such as on Tishri 8th or Tishri 12th. Although God in His mercy may allow that date to line up with the day on Hillel's calendar. Nevertheless, one can be completely assured that the Day of Atonement will indeed come on God's established calendar date of Tishri 10th just as He prophesized, and Israel as a nation will have their sins removed on that day. Regardless of our current understanding of that particular date, whether it appears to be too early, too late, or right on time to us, the dating on God's eternal calendar will never be wrong. For unlike mankind, God has never added or dropped days in the calendar to correct for mathematical error. God knows precisely which day it really is. He also understands today's correlation to the prophetic timeline He gave man thousands of years ago. We may error on the understanding of time, but God will not.

God is systematically unveiling Jesus before humanity, performing eternally significant events on His high holy days as a method of validating who He is and what He has promised to do for mankind. Nine individual dates within

God's calendar lay the foundation for the times or seasons in which God will fulfill world-changing events through Jesus. The events surrounding Passover, the two dates for Unleavened Bread, Feast of First Fruits, Pentecost, Tishri 1, and the first half of the Feast of Tabernacles were fulfilled by the occurrences of Jesus' life, death, resurrection, and ascension. Over three-fourths of God's prophetic calendar is completed, only two dates await fulfillment!

For Christians, "the Passover still takes place today."[42] Believers are still entering into the Kingdom by the blood of the Passover Lamb of God. The Grace of God is continuously poured out upon humanity because of Jesus' death and resurrection. Through the covering of His holy blood upon their souls, Believers are protected eternally from the wrath of God. A perpetual Pentecost and Day of Atonement also exists for Christians, as they are daily indwelt and infilled by the Holy Spirit, being empowered for the ministry of reconciliation, and all their sins have been eternally atoned. Believers, indwelt by the Holy Spirit, are also tabernacling with God. Thus, Believers live continually in the prophetic dates already fulfilled on God's calendar.

The final two dates awaiting fulfillment by Jesus at His second coming are the Day of Atonement for the nation of Israel and the final day in the week of the Feast of Tabernacles, when God will once again dwell with mankind, for a thousand years. While Jesus said no man would know the day or hour of His return, He assured us that we should be able to discern the signs (Matthew 24:32-33). Again in 1 Thessalonians chapter five, Paul reiterates that Believers should not be ignorant of the times or seasons for the return of Christ. For although to the unregenerate world, Jesus will seem to come like a thief in the night, Believers are not walking in the darkness without knowledge and should know of His coming day.

> "₁But of the times and the seasons, brethren, ye have no need that I write unto you. ₂For yourselves know perfectly that the day of the Lord so cometh as a thief in the night. ₃For when they shall say, Peace and safety; then sudden destruction cometh upon them, as travail upon a woman with child; and they shall not escape. ₄*But ye, brethren, are not in darkness, that that day [the day Jesus returns] should overtake you as a thief.* ₅Ye are all the children of light, and the children of the day: we are not of the night, nor of darkness. ₆*Therefore let us not sleep, as do others; but let us watch and be sober."*
> 1 Thessalonians 5:1-6

Part of the watchfulness commanded to Believers is to understand the signs of the seasons, which should serve to encourage and comfort their hearts. What God has promised (the return of Jesus) will be accomplished, and Believers shall live together physically with Him eternally. To accomplish the task of watchfulness, Believers must not alter God's word for their own comfort or interpretation, or they are in danger of missing the divine revelation of Jesus. Nor can they afford the luxury of maintaining the traditions of men above the Word of God, which has occurred continually over the centuries with the dismissal of the application of God's calendar for the church, especially during the celebration of events surrounding Jesus' crucifixion and resurrection.

When the Church intentionally removed its anchor of time away from God's ordained calendar (the Jewish calendar) for the benefit of the solar calendar to independently celebrate "Easter," it displaced the value and symbology of God's word and lost enormous evidence for faith in God's word. Not only does this distancing from God's calendar negatively impact a Christian's ability to comprehend the depth of Divine endurance and the deeper revelation of Christ, but also it adversely affects our ability to understand future prophecies. This is why Believers must return to the purity of God's word for their guidance. It is also why the Bible encourages them in the Book of Romans to renew their minds with God's word (Romans 12:1-3). Believers are called to transform their natural understanding of the world, even of time itself, through the Word of God. They are encouraged to study God's word to rightly divide it (2 Timothy 2:15), because within the Word of God is the revelation of God's heart for mankind, His redemptive plan of love in Jesus, and the timeline for climaxing world events.

Hidden within God's prophetic calendar is His great love story for us. All His interactions in creation revolve around mankind, the center of His affection. Don't miss out on the opportunity to comprehend these prophetic events and gain a glimpse of the Divine because of misleading traditions of men within the Church. Study to show yourself approved, remembering you are called to be Children of Light who are not caught unaware by the second coming of Jesus.

> "[35]Watch ye therefore: for ye know not when the master of the house cometh, at even, or at midnight, or at the cockcrowing, or in the morning: [36]lest coming suddenly He find you sleeping.
>
> [37]And what I say unto you, I say unto all, **WATCH!**"
> Mark 13:35-37 *(bold emphasis added)*

Bibliography & Further Study:

Introduction

1. Hartill, J. Edwin *Principles of Biblical Hermeneutics*. Grand Rapids, MI: Zondervan, 1960, pg 70, 73.

CHAPTER 1

2. Judaism 101 Website - http://www.jewfaq.org/

3. Rabbi Bushwick, Nathan. *Understanding the JewishCalendar*. Moznaim Publishing Corp. 1989, pg 51

4. Rich, Tracey. The Jewish calendar from website http://www.jewfaq.org/calendar.htm

5. Strong, James. *Strong's Exhaustive Concordance of the Bible.* Madison, NJ: 1890. **Public Domain**

6. Barnes, Albert. *Albert Barnes Commentary on the New Testament*, revised edition (1873), notes on Colossians 2:16-17. **Public Domain**

7. Bingham, Joseph. *Antiquities of the Christian Church.* London: H.G. Bohn, 1856, p. 1149. **Public Domain**

8. Bingham, Rev. R. *The Works of The Reverend Joseph Bingham.* Oxford: The Oxford University Press. Volume 7, 1855. **Public Domain**

9. Jeremias, Joachim. *The Eucharistic Words of Jesus*. London: S.C.M. Press, 1966

10. Eusebius, Schaff, ed., *Church History*. **Public Domain** Christian Classic Ethereal Library (CCEL) http://www.ccel.org/

11. Time & Date Calendar - Julian Calendar website: http://www.timeanddate.com/calendar/julian-calendar.html

12. Time & Date Calendar - Gregorian Calendar website: http://www.timeanddate.com/calendar/gregorian-calendar.html

13. Hapgood, Isabel F. *The Service Book of the Holy Orthodox Catholic Apostolic Church*. New York, Association Press, 1906.

CHAPTER 2

14. Rosen, Ceil and Rosen, Moishe. *Christ in the Passover, Why This Night is Different.* Chicago, IL: Moody Press, 1978, pg 27.

15. Pink, Author W. *Gleanings in Exodus.* Chicago, IL: Moody Press, 1922. **Public Domain**

16. Anatolius. *The Paschal Canon of Anatolius of Alexandria.* Section 11, 270- 280 AD. **Public Domain**

17. *Jewish Encyclopedia.* 1906. **Public Domain.** *www.JewishEncyclopedia.com,* Entry for: *Passover.*

18. Edersheim, Alfred. *The Life and Times of Jesus Messiah.* Chapter 6. Originally Published 1883; **Public Domain**: Republished in Grand Rapids, MI: Christian Classics Ethereal Library. Wm. B. Eerdmans, 1953.

19. *Jewish Encyclopedia.* 1906. **Public Domain** *www.JewishEncyclopedia.com,* Entry for: *Passover Sacrifice.*

20. Flavius Josephus. *Antiquities of the Jews.* 14. 4. 3. **Public Domain**

21. Flavius Josephus. *The Jewish War.* 6.9.3 pages 422-427. **Public Domain**

CHAPTER 3

22. Strong, James. *Strong's Exhaustive Concordance of the Bible.* Madison, NJ: 1890. **Public Domain**

CHAPTER 4

23. Brown, Driver, Briggs and Gesenius. *Hebrew and English Lexicon,* New York: Snowball Publishing, September 2010. Entry for 'Ararat.'

24. *Smith's Bible Dictionary Online,* entry term: "watch" http://www.biblestudytools.com/dictionaries/smiths-bible-dictionary/watches-of-night.html

25. Anatolius. *The Paschal Canon of Anatolius of Alexandria.* Section 11, 270- 280 AD. **Public Domain**

CHAPTER 6

26. R.W. Research, *Feasts and Holidays of the Bible* pamphlet #455X. Torrance, California: Rose Publishing, 2004.

27. McCall, Thomas S. Th.D. *"The Mystery of the Date of Pentecost".* The July 1995 Levitt Letter. www.levitt.com/essays/pentecost
See website: www.levitt.com

28. Josephus, **Antiquities of the Jews** book 20, chapter 9, section 1. **Public Domain**

29. Edersheim, Alfred. *The Temple: Its Ministries and Services*. Peabody, MA: Hendrickson Publishers. 1994.

CHAPTER 7

30. Mishnah, Pesachim 10:5

31. Strong, James, *Strong's Exhaustive Concordance of the Bible.* Madison, NJ: 1890. **Public Domain**

32. Thayer, Joseph H. *Thayer's Greek Lexicon.* New York, NY: Harper & Brothers. 1886. **Public Domain**

CHAPTER 8

33. Clement of Alexandria, *The Ante-Nicene Fathers, vol. 2, ed*. Alexander Roberts and James Donaldson {Michigan: Wm. B. Eerdmans Pub. Co., 1956}, p. 333.

34. Christensen, Arne Soby. *Lactantius the Historian (An Analysis of De Mortibus Persecuturum)*, Copenhagen, Denmark: Museum Tusculanum Press, 1980}, p. 116, note 176, no. 46.

35. Cross, J.E. Two Old English Apocrypha and their Manuscript sources: *The Gospel of Nicodemus* and *the Avenging of the Savior*, ed. (Cambridge, Cambridge University Press, 1996), p. 138.

36. Messianic Jewish Rabbinical Council Website: **Shabbat Page**. http://ourrabbis.org/main/halakhah-mainmenu-26/shabbat-mainmenu-30

37. Lemley, John. Article: *"Is Opse Matthew's Oops,"* PDF can be viewed at http://cog-ff.com/audio/Major-Prophets/friendsofsabbath.org/Further_Research/Lemley/lemley_index.htm

38. Barnes, Albert. *Albert Barnes Commentary on the New Testament*, revised edition (1873), notes Matthew 12:40. **Public Domain**

39. Bedore, W. Edward. **The Berean Bible Institute, Articles.** Article Title: *Hell, Sheol, Hades, Paradise, and the Grave.* **www.bereanbiblesinstitute.org** PDF article cited at www.bereanbibleinstitute.org/HellSheolHadesParadiseandtheGrave.pdf

40. Strong, James, *Strong's Exhaustive Concordance of the Bible.* Madison, NJ: 1890. **Public Domain**

41. Jamieson, Robert; Fassette, A.R. and Brown, David. *Jamieson, Fassette, Brown Commentary on the Whole Bible.* Grand Rapids, MI: Zondervan; commentary on Matthew 12:40. 1871. **Public Domain**

CHAPTER 9

42. Bartlett, David Lyon and Taylor, Barbara Brown. **Feasting on the Word: Preaching the Revised Common Lectionary, Lent Through Eastertide, Year B, Volume 2.** Westminster John Knox Press: Kentucky; 2008, page 261.

Other Reference Materials

Abrahams, Israel. *Soncino Babylonian Talmud, Hagigah Tractate.* New Jersey: Talmudic Books, 2012; section 17a.

Barnes, T.D. *Constantine and Eusebius,* Harvard, 1981. Contains information about the Council of Nicaea.

Barnhart, Robert K. *The Barnhart Concise Dictionary of Etymology.* New York, NY: HarperCollins Publishers Inc., 1995.

Black, Vicki K. *Welcome to the Church Year: An Introduction to the Seasons of the Episcopal Church.* Harrisburg, PA: Church Publishing, Inc., 2004.

Bond, Helen. Article entitled: *Joseph Caiaphas: In Search of a Shadow.* Senior Lecturer in New Testament Language, Literature and Theology; University of Edinburgh, April 2005. From her book: *Caiaphas: Friend of Rome and Judge of Jesus?* Westminster: John Knox, 2004. Available online at: http://www.bibleinterp.com/articles/Bond_Joseph_Caiaphas.shtml

Davies, Norman. *Europe: A History.* New York, NY: HarperCollins Publishers Inc., 1998

Encyclopedia Britannica; entry for Sadduccee
http://www.britannica.com/EBchecked/topic/515862/Sadducee

Gerlach, Karl. *The Antenicene Pascha: A Rhetorical History.* Leuven, Belgium: Peters Publishers. 1998. p. 18, 21.

Other Reference Materials

Josephus, Flavius. *Josephus Complete Works, translated by William Whiston.* Grand Rapids, MI: Kregel Publications. 1981.

Josephus. *Antiquities of the Jews*; 3,10.15; 16,6.2; 18,2.1; 18, 4.3; and 20, 9.1

Tanner, Norman P., SJ, ed., *Decrees of the Ecumenical Councils,* (London: Sheed and Ward; Washington. D.C: Georgetown University Press. 1990). 2 volumes: v. 1. Nicaea I to Lateran V, v. 2. Trent to Vatican II. Includes the documents in the original Greek and/or Latin text, a reproduction of *Conciliorum oecumenicorum decreta*, and English translations.
Available online at http://www.fordham.edu/halsall/sbook2.asp

Hertzberg, Arthur. *Judaism.* New York, New York: Geeorge Braziller Inc. 1961

Jewish Encyclopedia. The unedited full-text of the 1906 Jewish Encyclopedia from the website *www.JewishEncyclopedia.com,* ©2002-2011. Entry: Calendar.

The Jewish Calendar
http://www.hebrew4christians.com/Holidays/Calendar/calendar.html

Lemley, John. *Ministerial Forum,* article *"High Day Sabbaths,"* Minneapolis: Evangelical Free Church of America Ministerial Association.
PDF can be viewed at http://cog-ff.com/audio/Major-Prophets/friendsofsabbath.org/Further_Research/Lemley/lemley_index.htm

Other Reference Materials

Odom, Robert L. *__Sabbath and Sunday in Early Christianity.__* Washington D.C.: Review & Herald Publishing Association. 1977

Robinson, George. *__Essential Judaism: A Complete Guide to Beliefs, Customs, & Rituals.__* New York: Pocket Books. 2000.

Steinsaltz, Adin. *__The Essential Talmud.__* Lanham, MD: Powman & Littlefield Publishers Inc. 1992.

Strassfeld, Michael. *__The Jewish Holidays: A Guide & Commentary.__* New York: Harper & Row Publishers. 1985.

Water, Mark. *__Understanding the Resurrection of Jesus Made Easy,__* Hendrickson Publishers. 2005.

Wigoder, Geoffrey. *__The Student's Encyclopedia of Judaism.__* New York: New York University Press. 2004

World Council of Churches' Website: Towards a Common Date of Easter.
http://www.oikoumene.org/en/resources/documents/wcc-commissions/faith-and-order-commission/i-unity-the-church-and-its-mission/towards-a-common-date-for-easter.html

INDEX OF ILLUSTRATIONS AND CHARTS

		Page #
Illustration 1	Hebrew Day	12
Illustration 2	Passover Door	70
Chart 1	Comparison of Jewish/Roman/Gregorian Hours	13
Chart 2	Hebrew Days of the Week	14
Chart 3	Jewish Day to Gregorian Day	15
Chart 4	Jewish Religious Calendar	18
Chart 5	Jewish Required Pilgrimages	29
Chart 6	Opinion #1	48
Chart 7	Opinion #2	49
Chart 8	Joshua's Promise Land Timeline	105
Chart 9	Traditional Good Friday Crucifixion/Resurrection Timeline	119
Chart 10	Biblically Correct Crucifixion/Resurrection Timeline	120
Chart 11	Correlating Scriptures	128
Chart 12	Sadducees' Feast of First Fruits	148
Chart 13	Pharisees' Feast of First Fruits	150
Chart 14	From Bethany to Passover	189
Chart 15	Saturday Crucifixion Week	192
Chart 16	Sunday Crucifixion Week	194
Chart 17	Monday Crucifixion Week	196
Chart 18	Tuesday Crucifixion Week	198

Chart 19	Wednesday Crucifixion Week	200
Chart 20	Wednesday Days Dead	211
Chart 21	Thursday Crucifixion Week	230
Chart 22	Thursday Days Dead	236
Chart 23	Friday Crucifixion Week	240
Chart 24	Friday Days Dead	242

TOPICAL INDEX

Abib, see Nisan

Abraham, 3-4, 58-64, 177-178, 180, 215, 218, 254

Abrahamic Lamb, see Lamb

Adam, 17, 19, 27, 94, 115, 123-124, 156, 178, 182-183, 275, 278

Adar I, 18-19, 21-22, 24, 112, 114-115

Adar II, 18, 21-22

Ahasuerus, King of Persia, 110-111, 113-115

Akedah, 34

An-nas, 150-151

Anatolius of Alexandria, 52, 117, 289, 290

Angel of Death, 45, 48-49, 51, 64, 83, 264

annual Sabbath, see High Sabbath

anointing, 61, 142, 223

Ante-Nicene fathers, 204, 291

antichrist, 7, 109, 167

anti-Semitic, 35, 37-38

artos, see bread

authority, 2, 29, 33, 37, 113, 159, 205, 236, 278

Av, 18

azumos, see bread

Babylon, 20, 215-216

Babylonian, 19-20, 293

Barnes, Albert, 28, 212, 288, 292-293

belly of the Earth, 129

Bethlehem Ephratah, 73-74

Bethlehem Zebulum, 73-74

Bishop of Laodicea, 52, 117

body of Christ, 33

bones, 76, 217, 265

bread,
    artos, 166, 170-171, 181-182
    azumos, 166, 170, 182-183
    Bread of Heaven, 106, 171
    Bread of Life, 106, 123, 157, 171, 176, 182, 184, 186-187
    common bread, 169, 171
    manna, 102-106
    matzah, 160
    unleavened bread, 46-48, 51-52, 54-57, 79, 84-89, 103-105, 138, 140, 151, 160-161, 165-167, 169-174, 181-187, 280

Bread of Heaven, see bread

Bread of Life, see bread

Byzatine Empire, 24

Caesar, Julius, 38

Caiaphas, 139, 164, 293

calculation of
    calendar, 38, 275, 284
    day, 8
    death timeline, 118, 236, 243
    month, 15, 22

calculation of
    moon, 24
    Passover, 36, 204
    week, 14
    year, 16-19, 25

calendar, 7-8, 19, 92, 145, 152, 192-2-1, 230-231, 240-241
    Gregorian, 15, 17, 38-40, 243, 289
    God's, 7, 9, 11, 19-20, 25-26, 28, 35, 37, 128, 271-280, 283-287
    Jewish, 5, 7, 14-18, 20-28, 31, 35, 93, 118, 128, 136, 139, 147, 159, 189, 190, 232-234, 237-238, 242-243, 283, 286, 288, 294
    Julian, 38-40, 289
    lunar, 20, 24, 35, 38, 139, 238, 271, 274-275
    prophetic, 5, , 11, 20, 271, 279-280, 282-283
    solar, 38, 271, 273, 275, 286

Calvary, see Golgatha

Catholic church, 31, 34, 37-39, 202-204, 289

Chag he-Aviv, 21

chametz, see leaven

Church, Christian church, 6, 35, 159, 288

Clement of Alexandria, 202-204, 291

common bread, see bread

Council of Nicaea, 35, 38, 40, 293-294

Council of World Churches, 38

creation, 9-11, 16-17, 19-20, 34, 66, 93, 239, 270, 272-273, 275,

creation, (continued) 287

crucifixion, 1, 5-6, 29, 31, 58, 62-63, 78, 90, 118, 120, ,135, 139, 147, 152-153, 161, 165, 167, 189-190, 192-213, 220, 224, 227-247, 249-251, 262, 264, 286

David, King, 10, 74, 131, 218

dawn, see sunrise,

Day of Atonement, Yom Kippur, 23, 27, 29, 276-279, 284-285,

death, 19, 30-31, 34, 36, 44-45, 47-49, 61, 63, 65, 67, 69-72, 76-84, 90, 93, 94, 105, 109-110, 113-127, 129, 135-137, 140, 156, 158, 165, 167, 182, 184, 190, 211-222, 235-239, 2424-245, 249-250, 260, 263-264, 266-269, 274-275, 277, 285

diaspora, 22, 24

Didascalia Apostolorum, 203-204

doorposts, 44, 46, 50-51, 61, 64, 69, 71-72

dunamai, 176

Easter, 34-40, 42, 286, 295

Eastern Orthodox Church, 34, 39-40

Edersheim, Alfred, 72, 74-75, 154, 289, 291

Egypt, 31, 34, 42-46, 48-57, 61-62, 64-65, 69-72, 83-85, 87, 95-97, 102, 131, 143, 160, 166, 170, 179, 184-185, 235, 264, 277

Elul, 18

Epiphanius, Bishop of Salamis, 204

ereb, see evening

Esther, Book of, 20, 22, 109-115, 132-133, 243, 260, 269

299

Esther, Queen, 110-113, 115, 121, 125, 132-133, 235

Ethanim, see Tishri

Eucharist, see Holy Communion

Eusebius, 35, 288, 293

evening, ereb, 8-11, 15, 43, 45, 47-50, 77, 96-97, 103, 105, 117, 130, 162, 167-168, 189, 205-206, 209-210, 223-224, 226, 228, 233-234, 252-253, 255-257, 259, 261, 266-268, 270

Exodus, Book of, 4, 11, 14, 19-20, 32, 41, 44-45, 47, 50-51, 53-54, 56-57, 64-66, 69, 72, 77, 79-81, 83-84, 86, 93-100, 102-103, 105, 121, 130, 144-146, 160, 162-163, 165, 168-169, 184, 289

exodus, 43, 49, 50, 62, 67, 71, 81, 93-95, 99-100, 121, 160, 184, 206, 235

Feast of First Fruits, 20, 27, 29, 104-105, 118, 120, 141-142, 144-145, 148-153, 158, 190, 207-208, 227-228, 233-234, 236, 238, 247-248, 269, 276-277

Feast of Ingathering, see Feast of Tabernacles,

Feast of Tabernacles, Sukkot, 28-29, 276, 278-282, 285

Feast of Trumpets, 29, 276, 278

Feast of Unleavened Bread, 29, 42-43, 46, 51-52, 55, 57, 83, 85-87, 103, 139-141, 144-145, 149-150, 152, 163-165, 167, 185, 190, 193, 195, 197, 199, 201, 231-232, 234, 241, 247-248, 266, 276, 279-281

Feast of Weeks, see Pentecost

fire, 22, 27, 46, 54, 57, 59, 79-80,

fire (continued) 86-87, 89, 146-147, 162, 266

First fruits, firstfruits, 20, 104, 115-117, 142-144, 153-157, 278

Friday, 14-15, 77, 119, 128, 136-138, 140, 148, 152, 189-190, 206-207, 211, 232, 234-237, 240-250, 252

Ga-ma'-il-el, 24

Gamaliel II, 160

Gehenna, 213

Gethsemane, garden of, 162-163, 261, 274

Gil'-gal, 102

Golgotha, 63, 76, 271

Good Friday, 242, 249

Gospel of Grace, 159, 167, 172-173, 175, 178-179, 184

Grace, 6, 19, 67, 91, 125, 146, 174-179, 181-183, 280-281, 285

grave, 2, 30, 94, 115, 117, 119-120, 129, 135, 152, 158, 188, 207, 212-214, 216-219, 222, 227-228, 234, 243-244, 266, 269-271, 277, 293

Gregorian calendar, see calendar

Ha'man, 109-114, 260

hades, 129, 213, 215, 217-219, 292

Haggadah, 160

hametz, see leaven

harvest, spiritual, 155, 158

heart of the Earth, 127, 129, 135,

heart of the Earth (continued), 212-213, 218-220, 237, 242, 244, 266-267, 269

heaven, 8-9, 30, 32, 59-60, 100, 106, 109, 123-124, 146, 153-155, 171, 178, 182, 186, 210, 218, 251, 268, 272, 275, 278

hell, 113, 123, 213, 217, 219, 292

Henry, Matthew, 72

heresy, 202-204

Hermes, 31-32

Herod, King, 250, 262

Heshvan, 18

Hezekiah, King, 107-108

High Priest, 69, 78, 80, 109, 124, 141, 150-151, 153-154, 163, 177, 181, 233, 260

High Sabbath, 103, 117, 137-139, 149, 248

Hodesh moon, 15

Holy Communion, Eucharist, communion, 31, 33, 34, 171, 186,

holy convocation, 22, 24-29, 43, 46, 56-57, 83, 86-87, 104, 137-138, 141, 149, 232, 247-248, 271, 276, 279-281

Holy Spirit, 9, 11, 30, 33, 37-38, 72, 87, 116-117, 124, 146, 157-158, 177, 181, 186, 224, 228, 251, 278, 280, 285

House of Hillel, 24

Irenaeus, 33

Isaac, 3-4, 34, 58-62, 64, 215

Iscariot, Judas, 89-91, 138, 163-164, 259-260, 264

Israel, 10-11, ,16, 20, 23-24, 27, 34, 37, 44-51, 56, 58, 61, 63-65, 67-69, 71-74, 77-78, 83-87, 94-

Israel (continued), 111, 113, 119, 121, 124, 137-128, 130, 133, 142-143, 146, 151, 153, 179-180,184-185, 235, 243, 247-248, 253-254, 258, 260, 264, 277, 279, 282, 284-285

Iyar, 18-19

Jericho, 71, 102, 188

Jermias, Jocachim

Jerusalem, 12, 16, 24-25, 29, 41-42, 67-68, 73-76, 146, 151, 155, 159, 188, 190, 202, 205-207, 233, 235, 239, 246, 249, 252-254, 258, 264, 275-276, 278, 283

Jesus, 1-2, 4-6, 12-13, 19-20, 26, 28, 30-31, 33-34, 37-38, 47-48, 58, 62-64, 67-72, 75-76, 78-81, 88-94, 101, 105-106, 108-109, 113-129, 135-140, 144, 146-147, 150-159, 161-172, 174-179, 181-188, 190, 192-203, 205-213, 217-228, 230-246, 248-282, 284-289, 294, 296

Jesus' passion, 31,34,36, 251

Jew, Jewish nationality, 11, 16, 19, 22, 24-25, 28-29, 31, 34-37, 44, 48-49, 53, 55, 57, 61, 63, 65-68, 72-75, 77, 83, 88-89, 91-93, 100, 109-110, 112-115, 118, 128, 132, 139-141, 145-146, 149, 151-152, 160-162, 165, 167, 169, 173, 202, 206, 212, 225, 233, 243, 254, 264, 276-278, 290-292, 294-295

301

Jewish calendar, see calendar

John, the Apostle, 30, 48, 138, 163-164, 166-168, 170, 189, 248, 275

John, the Baptist, 233, 250-251, 254

Jonah, 127, 133, 212-213, 242, 245

Joseph of Arimathea, 165, 202, 263

Joseph, father of Jesus, 74, 278

Joseph, son of Israel, 96, 214

Josephus, Flavus, 49, 77, 151-152, 289-291, 294

Joshua, 10, 71, 73, 102-105, 121-122, 269

journey, Sabbath's day, 206

Judaism, 6, 37, 288, 294, 295

Judas, see Iscariot, Judas

Julian calendar, see calendar

King of Persia, see Anhasuerus

Kislev, 18

Lactantius, 202-204, 291

lamb
  Abrahamic Lamb, 58-65
  Lamb of God, 4, 62-63, 65-67, 76, 82, 254, 277, 285
  Passover Lamb, 5, 31, 42-43, 47-48, 51, 53, 57, 61-64, 66, 69, 72, 76-78, 81, 84, 103, 105, 117, 160, 162, 164-165, 169, 184, 192, 194, 196, 198, 200, 206, 230, 235, 239-240, 245, 264, 266, 285
  Spotless Lamb, 4, 162

Lamb of God, see Lamb

Last Supper, 30-31, 47-48, 138, 156, 159, 161-168, 170-172,

Last Supper (continued), 177, 184, 186, 203, 259, 261, 264, 280

Lazarus, 188, 205-206, 218, 235, 246, 252-253, 255

Leaven, chametz, hametz, 46-47, 50, 52-56, 77, 84-86, 89-91, 95, 161, 165, 169, 171-172, 177, 182, 184, 186

lechem, 171-173

Levitical priesthood, 78-79, 107, 124, 141, 154, 157, 160

lintel, 44, 53, 64, 69, 71-72, 163

Lord's Passover, see Passover

Luke, the Apostle, 250-251

Magdalene, Mary 122, 153-155, 210, 223, 227-228, 268

manna, man'-na, see bread

Mary, mother of Jesus, 74

matstsah, 88, 171, 173

matzah, see bread

Melchizedek, 109, 124, 178, 264

messiah, 30, 34, 37, 68, 72-75, 78, 89, 117, 126, 128, 149, 163, 165, 184, 243, 264, 279, 289

Micah, Prophet, 74-76

midnight, 13, 34, 45, 48-51, 94-95, 225-226, 261-262, 264, 287

Migdal Eder, 72-75

Milk, 88-89, 143, 173-174, 176-177, 181, 186

mishnic, 74

missing day, 205, 207, 227, 234, 239, 246, 249-250

Mor'de-ca-i, 112-113, 115

morning watch, 99-101

Mosaic Law, 87-89, 103, 159, 161, 166, 169, 172-181, 183-184, 186, 280

Moses, 56, 65, 86, 95-101, 103, 130, 146, 160, 163, 174, 183-184, 186

Mountain of God, 123

mow'ed, 15

Mt. Ararat, 92-93, 121-122, 290

Mt. Moriah, 3, 58, 63

Mt. Sinai, 87, 130, 145

Nazareth, 73-74, 282

new covenant, 19, 3-33, 64, 71-72, 87, 105-106, 171, 175, 178-179, 181, 183-185, 261, 264, 268-270, 280-281

new moon, 15-16, 21-22, 24-26, 139, 203, 232, 238, 273-274, 283

night watch, 226, 228

Nisan, 18-22, 25, 52, 93, 107

Nisan 10th, 44-45, 63, 65, 67, 69, 189-190, 192, 205-206, 235, 239, 246, 253-255

Nisan 14th, 27, 30-32, 42-45, 47-53, 55-58, 63, 67, 69, 77, 79, 84-86, 89, 91, 102-106, 117-121, 132, 136-140, 144, 150, 161-168, 170, 184, 188-190, 193, 195, 197, 199, 201, 203, 211-212, 234-237, 241-245, 261-265, 274, 276-277

Nisan 15th, 27, 39, 42-43, 45, 47-52, 55-57, 83-84, 86, 87, 94-95, 103-105, 117, 119-121, 132-

Nisan 15th (continued) 133, 136-138, 140, 149-150, 160-165, 167, 169, 183, 185, 188-189, 201, 211, 231, 233, 236-237, 241-245, 247-248, 266-267, 274, 276

Nisan 16th, 48-49, 96-97, 104-105, 108, 111, 118-121, 133, 136, 149-153, 190, 193, 195, 197, 199, 201, 207, 211, 233-234, 236-237, 242-243, 245, 247, 267

Nisan 17th, 92-94, 97-99, 101, 150-106, 108-109, 113, 115, 117-120, 125-126, 136, 150, 153, 193, 195, 197, 199, 201, 208-209, 211, 223, 227, 234, 238, 241, 247, 249,250, 268, 270, 277

Nissan, see Nisan

Noah, 93

Noah's Ark, 92-94, 235, 269

Old Covenant, 184-186, 280-281

only son, 4, 58-62

opse, 209-210, 227, 292

paradise, 154, 213, 218-219, 270, 292

Pasch, see Passover

Pascha, see lamb

Passover, 1, 6, 12. 20-21, 27, 29-32,34, 36-38, 40-44, 46-52, 54-58, 61, 63, 65, 73, 77-78, 83, 86, 93-94, ,102-103, 105, 137-

303

Passover (continued), 140, 144, 147, 150, 159-161, 163-165, 168-169, 183-184, 186, 188-190, 193, 195, 197, 199, 201, 203-205, 231-234, 238, 241, 246, 254, 261-265, 274, 276-277, 280, 284-285, 289

Passover bread, see bread

Passover lamb, see lamb

Paul, the Apostle, 32, 37-38, 176, 285

Pentecost, 27, 29, 141, 145-146, 148-149, 151, 157-158, 276-278, 280, 285, 290

Pesach, see Passover

Peter, the Apostle, 32, 89, 134, 146, 168, 217, 264, 268

Pharaoh, Egyptian, 44-45, 48-49, 84, 94-101, 277

Pharisee, 24, 69, 89, 106, 118, 127, 147, 149-151, 160, 163, 186, 190, 208, 233, 247-248

Pilate, 13, 90, 137, 164, 203, 247-248, 262, 266

pilgrimage, 29-30

Pillar of a Cloud, 96, 98-100

Pillar of Fire, 96, 98, 100

plague, 44, 46, 65, 70-71, 83, 277

Polycarp, 30-33

Polycrates, 33

Pope Anicetus, 32-33

Pope Gregory, 39

Pope Pius, 31

Pope Victor, 33

Preparation Day, 43, 137-140, 247

Prince, Joseph, 72

Principle of First Mention, 3, 62, 92, 109, 117, 119, 121, 202, 208, 211, 247, 250

Principle of Progressive Mention, 3, 62, 94, 117, 119, 250

Promise Land, 76, 102, 105-106, 121, 123, 235, 269

Protestant, 38-39

Purim, 22

Quartadecimans, 30-31, 33-34

queber, see grave

Quintus Sept. Flor. Tertulianus, 204

Rabbi Hillel II, 24-25, 27, 139, 145, 232-234, 238, 248, 283

Rahab, 71-72

Red Sea, 84, 94, 96, 99-101, 121, 235, 269

redemption, 34, 36, 65, 67, 91-94, 101, 109, 115-117, 119, 121, 126, 154, 157*158, 174-175, 235, 247, 249, 271, 274, 277

rest, 9-11, 14-15, 22-23, 27-28, 71, 85, 92-93, 122-123, 202, 252

resurrection, 1, 6, 19, 30-35, 38, 42, 62, 81, 93-94, 101, 105-106, 115, 117, 120-122, 124-127, 135-136, 144, 147, 152-156, 189, 193, 195, 197, 199, 201-202, 208-209, 211, 217, 224, resurrection (continued), 226-228, 231, 235, 238-239, 241, 243, 250-251, 268-270, 274, 277-278, 285-286, 295

Roman Catholic, see Catholic Church

Rosh Chodesh, 16

Rosh HaShanah, 27, 276-277

Rounded Number of Days Theory, 243-244

Sabbath, 10-11, 14-15, 22-24, 26-28, 43, 57, 103-105, 117, 129, 135, 137-141, 143, 145, 147-152, 162, 164-165, 189, 193-196, 198-202, 205-211, 226-228, 230-236, 239-241, 246-249, 252, 255, 267, 276, 294-295

Sabbath restrictions, 27, 141, 162, 189, 206, 234-235, 246

sacrifice, 3-4, 42-44, 49-52, 57-58, 60, 62-27, 69, 72, 75-81, 87, 109, 114, 117, 122, 141, 144, 156, 159, 182, 264, 277, 289

morning sacrifice, 144

evening sacrifice, 77

Sadducee, 69, 89, 106, 118, 120, 145, 147-152, 163, 186, 190, 207-208, 233-234, 236, 247, 293

salvation, 1, 5, 37, 65, 80-82, 92, 98, 101, 109, 111-117, 119, 121, 126, 183, 211, 235, 247, 254, 277, 280

Samuel, prophet, 74, 216-217

Sanhedrin, 16, 21-22, 24-25, 28, 69, 151, 160, 163-164, 225-226, 233, 238, 266, 268

Saul, King, 216-217

Septuagint, 149, 209

sepulcher, see tomb

Shabbat, see Sabbath

Shanah Me'uberet, 21

Shavuot, see Pentecost

sheol, 154, 213-220, 227, 237, 266, 269-270, 292

Shevat, 18

silver, 90, 107, 110, 123, 260, 264

Sivan, 18, 27, 145, 149, 151-152

soldiers, 225-226, 228

Solomon, King, 107

Son of God, 69, 91, 101, 273

Spring, 19-22, 25, 102, 275

spring equinox, see vernal equinox

spring festival, see Chag he-Aviv

strong meat, 88, 173, 175, 177, 186

Sukkot, see Feast of Tabernacles

Sunday, 14, 30-33, 35, 40, 119, 128, 135, 145, 148-150, 152-153, 155, 189-190, 192-201, 208, 210-211, 223-224, 227, 230-231, 233-239, 241-245, 247, 249, 253, 295

sunrise, dawn, 12, 45, 48, 51, 99-101, 118-121, 130, 135, 155, 209-210, 223-224, 228, 236-237, 242-243, 268

synod, 32-33, 35, 40

synoptic gospels, 47, 166-170

305

Tammuz, 18

Tartarus, 213

temple, 21-22, 25, 28, 68-69, 74-76, 90, 107-108, 118, 120, 123-124, 139, 144-145, 149-152, 154-155, 159-160, 206, 232-236, 238, 252-253, 256-260, 291

   First Temple, 21, 107-108

   Second Temple, 21-22, 25, 28, 90, 118, 120, 139, 144-145, 149-152, 159-160, 206-208, 232-236, 238, 252-253, 256-260, 291

Tevet, 18

Thayer's Greek Lexicon, 177, 219, 291

third day, see three days,

thirty pieces, see silver

three days, 2, 9, 14, 59, 110, 117-120, 126-137, 144, 189, 192, 194, 196, 198, 211-213, 217, 220-222, 227, 235-238, 242-243, 245, 247, 249, 267, 269

Thursday, 14, 136-137, 152-153, 189-190, 205-206, 211, 229-239, 244, 250

times, 7, 16, 21, 55-56, 72-73, 213-214, 232-233, 284-285, 289

Tishri, Ethanim, 16-20, 27-28, 93, 276, 278-279, 283-284

tomb, sepulcher, 113, 155, 165, 210-213, 216, 218-220, 223, 225-226, 228, 236-238, 244, 247-248, 263, 266-268, 274

Torah, 5, 21, 28, 44, 53-55, 69, 74, 76, 79, 83-85, 141, 155, 160-162, 164-166, 168-170, 184, 190, 206-207, 228, 232, 235, 243, 246, 249-250

Tower of the Flock, see Migdal Eder

Triumphant Entry, 67, 190, 202, 205-207, 235, 239, 246, 249, 253

unleavened bread, see bread

Upper Room, 32, 155, 163, 261

vernal equinox, spring equinox

washing, 162, 261

wave offering, wave-sheaf, 104, 141,-145, 147-148, 153-156, 228

Wednesday, 14, 135, 137, 152-153, 189, 192, 194-199, 201, 213, 218-222, 224, 227-228, 231, 235-236, 238, 244

Yahweh, 44, 81, 107, 144

Yom HaBrikkurim, see Feast of Unleavened Bread

Yom Kippur, see Day of Atonement

zemân, 7

Zonaras Proviso, 39

Are you interested in teaching others,
or hosting a Bible study group
on the topics discussed in this book?

Then check out our other resources.

www.relevantpublishers.com

We have designed books for group study that will empower you to teach a class for your family, friends, and/or congregation to understand God's calendar, the prophetic events surrounding the Lord's Passover, The Feast of Unleavened Bread, The Feast of First Fruits, and uncover how these details encompass Jesus' crucifixion week and His resurrection.

www.ingramcontent.com/pod-product-compliance
Lightning Source LLC
Chambersburg PA
CBHW062242300426
44110CB00034B/1173